Research Methods in Linguistics

Research Methods in Linguistics

Edited by
Lia Litosseliti

continuum

Continuum International Publishing Group

The Tower Building   80 Maiden Lane
11 York Road   Suite 704
London SE1 7NX   New York, NY 10038

www.continuumbooks.com

First published 2010
Reprinted 2011

British Library Cataloguing-in-Publication Data
A catalogue record for this book is available from the British Library.

ISBN: 978-0-8264-8992-0 (hardback)
        978-0-8264-8993-7 (paperback)

Library of Congress Cataloging-in-Publication Data
Research methods in linguistics / edited by Lia Litosseliti.
p. cm. – (Research methods in linguistics)
Includes index.
ISBN: 978-0-8264-8992-0 (hardcover)
ISBN: 978-0-8264-8993-7 (pbk.)
1. Linguistics–Research–Methodology. I. Litosseliti, Lia. II. Title. III. Series.
P126.R465 2010
407.2–dc22

                                       2009048865

Typeset by Newgen Imaging Systems Pvt Ltd, Chennai, India
Printed and bound in Great Britain

For Melina Sofia

Contents

Notes on Contributors

Jo Angouri is a Senior Lecturer at the University of the West of England, UK. She received her first degree and M.Sc. from Aristotle University (Greece) and recently her Ph.D. in Linguistics from the University of Essex (UK). Her research focus is language in the workplace. She has an established record of presentations at major international conferences, both in the fields of Sociolinguistics and Applied Linguistics. She has published work on meeting talk, workplace written discourse and (foreign) language use and language policy in the corporate workplace. Her current work includes a comparative analysis of discourse in business meetings. She has worked on several EU-funded research projects and she is a core network member on the ESRC-funded Discourse Analysis Network.

Paul Baker was awarded a Ph.D. in Linguistics in the Department of Linguistics and English Language at Lancaster University in 2001 and is currently a Senior Lecturer there. His research areas include corpus linguistics, critical discourse analysis and language, gender and sexuality. His five most recent books are *Sexed Texts* (2008), *Using Corpora in Discourse Analysis* (2006), *A Glossary of Corpus Linguistics* (2006, with Tony McEnery and Andrew Hardie), *Public Discourses of Gay Men* (2005) and *Hello Sailor: Seafaring Life for Gay Men* 1945–1990 (2003 with Jo Stanley). He is the commissioning editor for the journal *Corpora*. He has taught corpus linguistics and research methods in corpus linguistics in Lancaster and Hong Kong.

Judith Baxter is a Senior Lecturer in Applied Linguistics at Aston University. She gained her Ph.D. in Language, Gender and Education at the University of Reading in 2000. Her research interests are in the fields of language and gender, discourse analysis, classroom language, leadership language, identity and feminist post-structuralism. She is the author of *Positioning Gender in Discourse: A Feminist Methodology* (Palgrave, 2003) and *The Language of Female Leadership* (Palgrave, 2009), as well as editor of *Speaking Out: The Female Voice in Public Contexts* (Palgrave, 2006). She recently won an ESRC grant to conduct research into gender and the language of business leadership.

Jeff Bezemer is a Research Officer at the Centre for Multimodal Research, Institute of Education, University of London. He received his (post)graduate degrees in Language and Culture from Tilburg University, Netherlands. His research is focused on representation and communication in educational contexts. His latest ESRC-funded project, carried out with Gunther Kress, deals with the social significance of changes in the multimodal design of textbooks published from 1930. In other projects he studied classroom interaction, online interaction and policy papers using a range of different social semiotic and linguistic-ethnographic research methods. He teaches research methods on several training programmes, including the ESRC-funded Researcher Development Initiative on Ethnography, Language and Communication.

Angela Creese is Professor of Educational Linguistics at the School of Education, University of Birmingham, UK. Her research focus is on multilingualism in urban educational settings using linguistic ethnography. Since 2002 she has been researching complementary schools with the support of two ESRC grants. She is associate editor of the journal *Anthropology and Educational Quarterly*. Her books include *Teacher Collaboration and Talk in Multilingual Schools* (Multilingual Matters, 2005), *Ecology of Language: Volume 9 of the Encyclopedia of Language and Education* (Springer Science+Business Media LLC, 2008) edited with Peter Martin and Nancy Hornberger, and *Multilingualism: A Critical Perspective* (Continuum, in press) with Adrian Blackledge.

Nigel Edley is a Senior Lecturer in Social Psychology at Nottingham Trent University. Having completed both a B.Sc. and a Ph.D. in social psychology at Loughborough University, he went on to work for the Open University as a Research Fellow on an ESRC-funded project looking at the discursive construction of men and masculinity. Nigel's research interests are centred around the topics of gender, identity and subjectivity as well as discourse analysis and social constructionism. Co-author (with Margaret Wetherell) of *Men in Perspective: Practice Power and Identity*, he has also published articles in *Discourse & Society*; *Feminism and Psychology*, the *British Journal of Social Psychology* and, more recently, *Sex Roles*.

Julio C. Gimenez holds an MA in TEFL from the University of Reading and a Ph.D. in Linguistics from Queen Mary, University of London. He is a Lecturer at the Centre for English Language Education, University of Nottingham, where he teaches academic literacies to graduate and postgraduate students. His main teaching and research interests are the critical analysis of discourse, academic literacies, research methodologies and language in the workplace. His work has been published in several edited collections and international journals.

Erez Levon is a Lecturer in Linguistics at Queen Mary, University of London. He has conducted sociolinguistic research on language, gender and sexuality in the United States and Israel, among other topics, for the past eight years. He regularly presents his work at such academic venues as the New Ways of Analyzing Variation conference and the meetings of the Linguistics Society of America, the American Anthropological Association and the International Gender and Language Association. His work has also been published in a number of academic journals and edited volumes. His book *Language and the Politics of Sexuality: Lesbians and Gays in Israel* will be published by Palgrave Macmillan in 2010.

Lia Litosseliti is a Senior Lecturer in Linguistics at City University, London, with a Ph.D. in Linguistics from Lancaster University. Her research interests are in the areas of gender and language, discourse analysis, and research methodologies. She is the author of *Using Focus Groups in Research* (2003) and *Gender and Language: Theory and Practice* (2006); and co-editor of *Gender Identity and Discourse Analysis* (2002, with Jane Sunderland) and *Gender and Language Research Methodologies* (2008, with Kate Harrington, Helen Sauntson and Jane Sunderland). Lia is also Educational Development Associate for City University, London, and acts as an external adviser/reviewer, in her areas of interest, for other institutions and organizations.

Carey Jewitt is a Reader in Education and Technology at the London Knowledge Lab, Institute of Education (IoE), University of London. She is Director of Research at the Centre for Multimodal Research (IoE). Carey undertook a degree in Fine Art and Media (Newcastle, UK), an M.Sc. in Sociological Research Theory and Methods (Surrey University), and a Ph.D. at the IoE titled

'A multimodal framework for computer mediated learning'. Her research focuses on representation, technology and pedagogy. Carey is co-editor of the journal *Visual Communication* (published by Sage) and she has edited *The Routledge Handbook of Multimodal Analysis*, London: Routledge (2009).

Sebastian M. Rasinger is a Senior Lecturer in Applied Linguistics at Anglia Ruskin University, Cambridge. He holds a D.Phil. in Linguistics and a CertPG in Social Research Methods, both from the University of Sussex, and he is a Fellow of the Higher Education Academy. His research focuses on sociolinguistic and discourse analytic aspects of second language acquisition and bi- and multilingualism, including such aspects like language and identity, language change and the emergence of 'new' languages in migration contexts.

Jane Sunderland is a Senior Lecturer in the Department of Linguistics and English Language, Lancaster University (from where she gained her Ph.D. in 1996). She teaches Language and Gender to MA and doctoral students, and is Director of Studies of the Ph.D. in Applied Linguistics by Thesis and Coursework programme. Her most recent book publications are *Gendered Discourses* (Palgrave Macmillan, 2004), *Language and Gender: An Advanced Resource Book* (Routledge, 2006) and *Gender and Language Research Methodologies* (co-edited with Kate Harrington, Lia Litosseliti and Helen Sauntson). A recent journal article is 'Contradictions in gendered discourses: feminist readings of sexist jokes?' (*Gender and Language*, 2007).

Introduction
Lia Litosseliti

'I have yet to see any problem, however complicated, which, when you looked at it the right way, did not become still more complicated.' This quote by author and scientist Poul Alderson would seem apt for a book on research methods. My aim in putting together this particular book, however, is to strike an important balance: while aiming to retain and illuminate some of the complexities of research inquiry within linguistics, it tries to do so in an accessible, uncomplicated way.

The ten chapters presented here guide readers through **the key issues, principles, and contributions of core methods in linguistic research**. The ideas presented by these authors are currently spread in the literature across different journals and books, and therefore this collection is aimed as an **essential up-to-date one-stop resource** for researchers and graduate students. The newcomer to the field will appreciate the clear introductions to key concepts, a plethora of illustrative examples, and carefully drawn links between theory and practice. The experienced researcher and teacher of linguistics will find authoritative and critical engagement with current debates in this diverse field (especially in the later chapters). Both types of readers will hopefully find the book a useful resource for the supervision of research projects and theses.

The book does not *purposefully* examine the different stages of project design, data collection and data analysis in linguistics. This is not only because the different chapters are designed to appeal to both experienced and new researchers, but also because there are already excellent guides doing precisely this. However, it will be evident for the reader that issues of design, collection and analysis of data are central to any discussion of methods, and are therefore in the foreground in most of the chapters in this collection (and especially in the earlier chapters). As such, the book could also be used alongside other texts: comprehensive guides (such as 'Projects in Linguistics' by Wray and Bloomer, 2006); more specific introductions (e.g. Dörnyei's 2007 'Research

Methods in Applied Linguistics'); and related textbooks (e.g. existing texts on research methods in education, and research methods in language learning).

The book is organized in three parts:

Issues
Quantitative and Corpus Research Methods
Qualitative Research Methods.

This division is followed here for easy reference purposes; it will be clear to readers not only that some methods cannot be labelled as simply quantitative or qualitative, but also that there are good reasons why they should not be (and a number of contributors in this volume engage with these debates). The larger number of chapters under qualitative methods reflects the considerable prevalence and momentum of such methods currently in the field. However, I absolutely concur with the editors of the new sociolinguistics reader, who state that it is important to resist associating qualitative research with research that is 'new' and 'better informed', and conversely quantitative research with research that is 'old' or 'naïve' (Coupland and Jaworski, 2009: 19).

Each chapter begins with a chapter outline, and then:

- introduces basic concepts and overviews key issues
- features illustrative examples from recent linguistic research studies
- outlines the contribution a method makes to the field, and where appropriate, its potential for combination with other methods
- makes suggestions for further reading in that particular area.

Research methods are inextricably linked with the research questions being asked, as well as with the broader research climate in which they are employed. In this light, the first two chapters (**Part I**) examine some basic principles behind research questions and behind common assumptions about quantitative and qualitative methods. These chapters will be of interest particularly to the newcomer to the field, but will also act as reminders for the more experienced linguists, who are arguably more in danger of becoming entrenched in the research questions and types of methodologies they pursue.

Chapter 1, by Jane Sunderland, looks at research questions: why we need them, where they come from, how they can be categorized and implemented, and what implications they may have for linguistic data and analysis. This chapter offers plenty of examples of types and groupings of research questions from previous sociolinguistic studies.

Jo Angouri, in **Chapter 2**, critically examines the issue of the combination or integration of quantitative and qualitative methods in linguistic research. The chapter includes a discussion of triangulation and mixed methods, and uses research on workplace discourse to illustrate some of the benefits and challenges of combining paradigms.

The next three chapters (**Part II**) deal with *quantitative and corpus research methods* in linguistics. They are intended as detailed overviews of basic quantitative and corpus research designs, with an emphasis on the practical steps needed for researchers to understand and implement such designs. All three chapters offer insights into assumptions surrounding the quantitative/qualitative debate.

Chapter 3, by Sebastian M. Rasinger, introduces the most common principles in quantitative research – forming a hypothesis, and considering the quantifiability, reliability, and validity of data – and the most frequently used quantitative designs in linguistics. It then focuses on the use of questionnaires in quantitative research, offering many practical ideas on how to design, phrase and code questionnaires.

Chapter 4, by Erez Levon, complements the previous chapter by focusing on the nuts and bolts of the quantitative analysis of language, and particularly on how to construct and test hypotheses for such analysis. The chapter then examines in some detail two of the most common statistical tests used in linguistics: chi-square tests and t-tests. Finally, the author discusses the interpretation of quantitative results, and the issue of combining quantitative and qualitative methods in linguistic research.

Paul Baker then introduces corpus linguistics in **Chapter 5**. The chapter examines such issues as the theoretical principles surrounding corpus linguistics techniques, building and annotating a corpus, different types of corpora, and different kinds of research questions that may be addressed through corpus linguistics. Examples of applications of corpora are also given (from previous work in stylistics, discourse analysis, forensic linguistics and language teaching). The chapter finally demonstrates corpus analysis, providing examples of word frequencies, keywords, collocates and concordances.

The five chapters (**Part III**) that follow are concerned with *qualitative methods* in linguistics, representing a selection of current major methods: discourse-analytic approaches, linguistic ethnography, interviews and focus groups, multimodal analysis, and narrative analysis. While some of these can be seen as more general approaches and some as more specific data creation methods, in practice there is considerable overlap between the two, depending on the study. All five chapters adopt critical perspectives on each topic, and make suggestions for new and emerging methodological pathways alongside the more established models. In addition, all chapters in this part of the book engage, to varying degrees, with recent debates about the relationship between the micro and macro levels of linguistic inquiry.

In **Chapter 6**, Judith Baxter reviews four discourse-analytic approaches to text and talk of particular value for current research in linguistics: Conversation Analysis, Discourse Analysis, Critical Discourse Analysis and Feminist Post-structuralist Discourse Analysis. The chapter outlines the background, basic principles, features and contributions of each approach. It also problematizes the relationship between the micro and macro levels of analysis, as this is conceptualized in each approach.

Chapter 7, by Angela Creese, describes linguistic ethnography and its methodological and analytical contribution to the study of language. It covers such issues as interdisciplinarity and theoretical diversity, the benefits of combining different types of data, and the role of fieldnotes and team ethnography in linguistic ethnographic accounts. It also illustrates how linguistic ethnography can be combined with other methods to produce rich data.

In **Chapter 8**, Nigel Edley and Lia Litosseliti critically examine the use of interviews and focus groups within social science and linguistics research. The authors first discuss the criticisms levelled against these methods, and argue that it is problematic to use them as a tool for getting to people's 'true' or 'real' views. Rather, they emphasize the role of interviews and focus groups as collaborative or interactional events that are context-specific and shaped as much by the interviewer as by those being interviewed. The chapter ends with a critical review of the primary strengths and weaknesses of these methods.

Chapter 9, by Jeff Bezemer and Carey Jewitt, deals with multimodal analysis and its relevance for the study of language and communication. It explores the theoretical and methodological implications of the different modes that people use to make meaning beyond language, such as speech, gesture, gaze, image and writing. The authors first discuss the role of multimodality in social linguistic research. They then focus on a social semiotic approach to multimodality, which they illustrate with examples from classroom interaction and textbooks. The chapter ends with a discussion of the potentials and constraints of multimodal analysis.

Finally, in **Chapter 10**, Julio C. Gimenez introduces the key elements of traditional and new emerging sociolinguistic approaches to the analysis of narratives. In terms of the former, he briefly discusses the key features of componential and functional analyses, by drawing on various examples of narratives. In terms of the latter, he presents a *narrative networks* methodology, as developed in the author's own work: its origins and theoretical principles, as well as a step-by-step procedure for designing and analysing narrative networks.

I would like to thank the authors in this volume for their constructive discussions during the different writing, reviewing and editing stages of this book. I truly hope this book will encourage readers to reflect on the relationships between different research paradigms. I also hope it will encourage them to explore new possibilities for interaction and cross-fertilization among them.

References

Coupland, N. and Jaworski, A. (2009), *The New Sociolinguistics Reader*. Houndmills: Macmillan.

Dörnyei, Z. (2007), *Research Methods in Applied Linguistics*. Oxford: Oxford University Press.

Wray, A. and Bloomer, A. (2006), *Projects in Linguistics: A Practical Guide to Researching Language*. London: Hodder Arnold.

Part I
Issues

Research Questions in Linguistics

1

Jane Sunderland

Chapter outline

This chapter takes as given that research questions, appropriately designed and worded, are the key to any good empirical research project. Starting with why we need research questions (as opposed to *topics* or even *hypotheses*), I explore where they might come from, and propose different types of research questions. Research questions of course need to be operationalized, and the chapter explores the implications of different types of research questions for data, data collection and analysis. Equally importantly, research questions need to be explicitly documented, in terms *inter alia* of their origin, rationale and implementation, and the chapter looks at how (and where) this might be done. Research questions are discussed throughout with a specific eye on linguistic studies, exemplified using linguistic research, and there is a focus on linguistic data and analysis.

> [Research questions] are vehicles that you will rely upon to move you from your broad research interest to your specific research focus and project, and therefore their importance cannot be overstated.
>
> (Mason, 2002: 20)

1.1 Why do we need research questions?

Research questions are, I argue, the key to any empirical research project. Without research questions, you will flounder; with them, you will be guided in terms of data needed, data collection methods and data analysis. Ask yourself, 'What data do I need?' The answer is 'That which best enables me to answer my research question(s)'. 'How do I analyse it?' 'In a way which allows me to address my research question(s)'. And so on. This is because a piece of empirical research is normally *designed* to address one or more research questions – the answers to which should constitute a 'contribution to knowledge'.

In the social sciences, empirical research very often employs *explicit* research questions. If you are about to conduct empirical research, first ask yourself, 'What am I trying to find out in my research project?' If you can answer this, you have the basis for a research question.

Many of us go into a research project with our ideas in general, and our research questions in particular, rather broadly formulated. Alternatively, our research questions may be precisely formulated, but, we may discover, erroneous (not amenable to investigation, or otherwise inappropriate). At the start of a project, neither may be too much of a problem, because a research question should not straightjacket you. Rather, you can see it as an initial direction   like a compass point, whose needle is swinging. Further down the line, you may find that issues come up which are interesting and relevant but which do not address your research question(s), that is, which answer questions you have not asked. If these do not require new data, you may wish to consider adding a new research question. At some point, however, your research questions need to stabilize (although there is room for getting their *wording* accurate right up until the end of the research project).

You may be used to the term *hypothesis* rather than *research question*. Hypotheses are more characteristic of the natural than the social sciences. While hypotheses and research questions are related, hypotheses tend to be more precise. A hypothesis is conventionally worded as a statement, which is to be investigated and proved or disproved through empirical study. An example would be 'In terms of school library use, boys in Year 6 of UK Primary Schools borrow (a) more works of non-fiction than fiction, and (b) more works of non-fiction than do girls.' Hypotheses are also perhaps more characteristic of quantitative than qualitative research (see Chapter 3). Research questions, accordingly, are characteristic of *qualitative* research, and are likely to be both broader and more exploratory than hypotheses, for example, 'What are the borrowing practices of UK Primary School Year 6 girls and boys in terms of fiction and non-fiction?'

A set of research questions should be formulated in ways which allow the identification and investigation of further issues that only doing the research can bring to light (i.e. that could *not* have been included in a hypothesis). In her own research questions checklist, Jennifer Mason (2002: 19) includes the following: 'Are they open enough to allow for the degree of exploratory enquiry I require? Will they allow me to generate further questions at a later stage, in the light of my developing data analysis, should I wish?' (see also Andrews, 2003). Of course, a set of research questions should not be too general, vague or multidimensional, and below I show how these pitfalls can be avoided through the use of different *types*, *sequences*, *combinations* and *hierarchies*.

1.2 Where do research questions come from?

One broad answer to this question is 'the literature'. In the process of reading and of writing a literature review around your topic:

- you may come across a suggestion for an (unanswered) research question; however, do check that it has not, in fact, been addressed, and, indeed, that as a question it is both worthy of investigation (is it still interesting and original?) and operationalizable (see below)
- you may decide to replicate someone else's work, perhaps to challenge it, perhaps within a different or particularly interesting context, or perhaps to use a different form of analysis on the same or related data
- you may identify a 'niche' in the research literature, that is, something related to your topic has been asked, but something else has not.

The advantages of arriving at research questions through a literature review are, as Andrews (2003: 17–18) points out, 'that the question(s) will be well-grounded in existing research (assuming the literature review is a good one); there will be a coherence between the literature review and the rest of the thesis (again assuming the rest of the thesis is driven by the questions)'.

A second broad answer is 'a pre-existing topic' (which then drives the literature review). For example:

- you may have identified a recent and unpredictable political, social or natural event, which sheds light on our understanding of a particular social concept; for example, Hurricane Katrina in the United States or the Summer 2007 floods in the United Kingdom might provide 'sites' for studying the sociolinguistic/ethnographic notion of 'Community of Practice', or the 2008 American Presidential elections a site of 'modern political rhetoric'

- you may have identified an interesting linguistic phenomenon or development (e.g. use of the phrase *what's with* . . . to enquire about something unusual; blogs would be another relatively recent example, illustrating the affordances of a particular medium and a new form of communication).

A third possible source of a research question, more controversially, is that it comes out of your own findings. Your data may suggest answers to research questions that you didn't ask; hopefully you will be able to ask them now, of that data – as long as this does not destabilize, divert or unacceptably increase the workload of your entire research project. If it can be addressed *without* dilution or compromise, then there is no reason why a new research question cannot be introduced, and its genesis incorporated into the 'story' of the research project in question.

We can also consider the possibility of some data being 'hypothesis-generating' and some 'hypothesis-testing' (a distinction introduced by Allwright (1983), in which 'hypothesis' can be replaced by 'research question'; see also Salmani-Nodoushan (n.d.)). Diary studies, for example, may be 'hypothesis-generating' (let us imagine a group of students writing about their experience with a new language), in that the preoccupations documented in the diaries may suggest/generate research questions (e.g. 'What is likely to cause anxiety in novice learners of a foreign language?' – see Schumann and Schumann, 1977). These research questions can then be 'tested', or at least empirically addressed (e.g. 'Does reading or listening to words in a new language constitute a greater source of anxiety for novice learners of a foreign language?').

1.3 Research questions, topics and puzzles

When asked what their research question is (e.g. on their Ph.D. proposal form), it's surprising how many novice researchers actually provide a *topic*. In the area of language education, your topic might be, say, 'Teacher beliefs', in particular 'the beliefs of UK primary school teachers about foreign language teaching and acquisition'; or 'Language testing', in particular 'testing foreign language use in genuinely communicative situations'. A research question however is a *question*, and should be worded as an interrogative (see below). It is not a topic, although it grows out of a topic.

Alternatively, some people might consider an *intellectual puzzle* as a basis for their research, for example, 'Why is it that foreign language teachers tend to see girls as almost automatically better language learners than boys?' (see Allwright, 2003; Mason, 2002, for more on intellectual puzzles). Here, you may be drawing on your own experience and (informed) hunches. For example, as a teacher, you might feel that exercises from a certain textbook almost always go down better with the students than exercises from a different textbook, and you are curious to find out why (addressing such puzzles has been conceptualized by Dick Allwright as 'Exploratory Practice' (http://www.prodait.org/approaches/exploratory/)). The answer to this particular research question would have implications for classroom texts and pedagogy beyond the particular teaching situation.

Both topics and puzzles need 'translating' into appropriate research questions, that is, though careful formal expression, including in terms of accurate, appropriate and productive interrogative wording. But to look at wording, we also need to look at *types* of research questions.

1.4 Types of research questions

To illustrate some possible 'types' of research questions, let us take the topic of 'beliefs of UK primary school teachers about foreign language teaching and acquisition'. Within this, your research question(s) might be one (or more) of the following:

- Do French teachers working in UK primary schools agree with the teaching of French to Year 6 primary school children?
- What reasons do French teachers working in UK primary schools give for including the teaching of French to Year 6 children in the curriculum?
- What reasons do French teachers working in UK primary schools give against the teaching of French to Year 6 primary school children?
- How do UK primary school teachers of French believe Year 6 children best learn French?
- What is the range and diversity of beliefs of UK primary school teachers of French in relation to the teaching of French to Year 6 children?
- Why do UK primary school teachers of French hold these beliefs?

Note that these research questions are formulated as *interrogatives*: *Do, What, How, Why*. Other research questions might start with *Is/Are, When,*

Where, Who or *To what extent*? These interrogatives suggest different sorts of research questions: whereas *How, When, Where, What, Is/Are, Do/Does* and *To what extent* may be descriptive,[1] *Why* is clearly explanatory.

You need to consider carefully what you want to ask (often more than one question), and the sequence: it may not be possible to address one research question without having answered a previous one. For example, in many research projects, research question 1 is *descriptive* (*Does . . .?*) and research question 2 *explanatory* (*Why does . . .?*) (I return to the question of 'explanatory' research questions below.)

Novice researchers often wish to address an 'evaluative' research question, such as 'What is the best method of teaching listening in [context X]?' or 'Should EFL teachers be discouraged from using the students' L1 in [context X]?' The difficulty with such research questions, aside from the problem of 'operationalizing' them (see below), is that they tend to entail something like 'According to who/what' or 'If Y is to be achieved . . .', or even a particular desideratum (see Litosseliti, 2003). My feeling is that evaluations, coming out of the findings of descriptive research questions, are best expressed in the form of recommendations (or implications), perhaps in a Discussion section or chapter. For example, the question 'What is the best method of teaching listening in [context X]?' might be addressed not through a research question *per se* but rather through a discussion of findings of research questions such as (a) 'What different methods of teaching listening are employed in [context X]?', (b) 'What are teachers' and students' views?' and (c) 'Is there any correlation between method and test results, here?' Recommendations however still need to be expressed with caution, in part because of the problem of establishing causality (e.g. between use of a new method of listening and improved results in a listening test), and the issue of test validity (i.e. here, of that listening test).

In addition to a categorization of research questions as descriptive, explanatory or evaluative, cutting the research cake in other ways allows still other distinctions to be made, and referred to explicitly in the dissertation or thesis. These include the following:

Primary/secondary   Quite simply, some research questions might be more important than others, in terms of the focus of the study, or simply the quality and/or quantity of data collected, selected or elicited to address a given research question.

Main/contributory   It may not be possible to answer your main research question until an earlier ('contributory') research question has been answered.

For example, a contributory research question such as 'Does X happen . . .?' allows two further (alternative) main research questions to be addressed, for example: 'If X happens, why might this be . . .?' and 'If X does not happen, why might this be . . .?' (see also Andrews, 2003).

Overarching/subordinate Two or more research questions might be grouped hierarchically under a 'higher' one, which together they address; for example,

Overarching research question:	What are some differences in the way [a given political event] is reported in newspaper X and newspaper Y?
Subordinate research question 1:	How are the 'social actors' in each newspaper report nominalized?
Subordinate research question 2:	Which report uses the greatest proportion of agentless passive verb constructions?

The 'overarching' question cannot be 'operationalized' (see below) as it stands, but *can* be operationalized through the two subordinate research questions.

Empirical/methodological/theoretical While your research questions will probably be largely aimed at producing empirical findings (concerning, for example, part of the language system, an aspect of language use, language learning/teaching), you may also be interested in the investigative (methodological) process itself. An example of a methodological research question might be 'Are fieldnotes made by the researcher an effective way to investigate code-switching in workplace talk by migrant hotel workers?', and a second: 'What might effectiveness depend on, here?' Another possibility might be 'Can Critical Discourse Analysis (CDA) be usefully applied to the talk of preschool children?' Don't feel that you *must* have a methodological research question. However, if you are doing something innovative or otherwise interesting methodologically – for example, combining two approaches which are not usually combined – this could constitute an 'intellectual contribution' of your study. If so, it may be worth 'promoting' this aspect of your methodology to the status of a research question.

Theoretical research questions are likely to refer both to theoretical concepts and their deployment in empirical research. Andrews' (2003: 23) illustration of a theoretical research question is: 'What is a theoretical framework within which Hong Kong children's writing [in English] can be analysed and described?', though he does not label this as such.

Researcher-generated/participant-generated Of course, almost all research questions are researcher-generated. But this begs the question of the role of your research participants (assuming you are not doing text-based research). Are you, as Cameron et al. (1992) pointedly ask, doing research on, with or for your participants? Relatedly, Cohen et al. (2007: 88) propose that the researcher asks not only 'What are the research questions?' but also 'Who decides what the questions will be?' and 'Can participants add their own questions?' Someone doing research for their MA dissertation or Ph.D. thesis may have less space to explore the possibility of 'research for' participants than a researcher who has received a grant to do exactly that. However, MA or Ph.D. researchers are often not accountable to a grant-awarding body, and this may be precisely the time when they *can* consider how to work with research participants, and perhaps how to address those participants' own concerns.

Empirical/speculative Some research questions – the *Why* questions above, for example – may need to be speculative, rather than empirical, perhaps informed by the 'answers' to empirical questions (in combination with your own professional or other insights).

As the above set of distinctions suggests, your research questions can and should constitute a coherent whole, that is, be explicitly related to each other. Both sequence and hierarchy are important here. Most obvious, as suggested, might be two research questions, the first (research question 1) being descriptive (e.g. 'To what extent . . .?'), the second (research question 2) explanatory ('Why . . .?'). Alternatively, as shown, an overarching question (research question 1), may not itself be operationalizable, but may be operationalized via two or more subordinate research questions (research question 1a, research question 1b). The relationship between the research questions should be clear, to allow a reader to see what it is you are trying to do in your research project. But this sort of organization is also important for you. Once you have created this coherent structure, you will be able to see if some of your research questions are basically the same (and hence should probably be combined), or if one is in fact a sub-research question of another. Andrews makes the useful suggestion here of writing each research question on a separate strip of paper and organizing them accordingly:

> Experiment with moving the questions so that they seem to make sense in relation to each other. Does one of them seem like the main question? Are some more general or more specific than others? How do they stand in relation to each other? Can some of them be omitted, or fused, or added to?
>
> (Andrews, 2003: 39)

Two final points about the *wording* of research questions. First – every 'content' word in a research question matters. To operationalize your research question, you will need to know *exactly* what each word is to mean as far as your research project is concerned (a 'working definition', that is, 'for the purpose of this dissertation/thesis'). Secondly, and more generally, Mason (2002: 19) reminds us that we should ask of our research questions, 'Would anyone but me understand them?' It is crucial that the answer is 'Yes' – especially if aspects of your study are to be *replicable*. If others cannot understand your research questions, it is worth considering whether they are, in fact, formulated in a way which is clear enough for *you* to address them properly.

1.5 How many research questions?

This question, inevitable after considering the wide range of types of research question, is, however, like asking about the length of the proverbial piece of string. Broadly, most research projects use more than one research question, often of different types. Mason (2002: 21) notes, 'In the early stages, it can be helpful to generate a lot of research questions.' Ultimately, however, the rule of thumb is to ask only as many research questions as can *satisfactorily* be addressed. The issue is not the number of research questions, but what is needed (in terms of data, analysis, time and effort) to answer a given research question, that is, the scale of a given project. Some questions are bigger than others. Andrews (2003: 4) cites 'What is the impact of communication technologies on learning worldwide?' as an unanswerable research question due to its level of generality; other research questions may be unanswerable (especially in postgraduate research) because they require a lengthy longitudinal study (e.g. data collection over five years), or more interviews than the researcher could conduct and analyse. In Mason's (2002: 21) words, 'you will quickly need to focus to ensure that you are designing a manageable project'.

It may be necessary to 'sacrifice' a research question if it cannot be done justice to (see, for example, Sunderland, 1996a). Painful though this may be, it may ensure that you avoid producing a superficial and diluted piece of work – remind yourself that sacrificing a research question and all that goes with it often strengthens the study *and* provides material for a later piece of work (a publication in-the-making). In my own Ph.D. thesis, on classroom interaction, I originally included research questions on wait-time (e.g. the amount of time a teacher gives a student to answer a question before answering it him/herself) and interruption. I abandoned the wait-time question because it would have required special timing equipment, and the interruption question because of its conceptual complexity (which I could not have embraced within the scope of my thesis). These sacrifices entailed a sense of loss but enabled me to address the remaining research questions more fully.

1.6 Research questions and linguistic data

You may have noticed that the research questions in section 1.4 on 'Types of Research Questions', despite being concerned with language education, could largely be addressed through data in which language *itself* was not to be analysed. In much linguistic and applied linguistic study, however, the majority of research questions will include a linguistic component. (Indeed, it is arguable that many research projects outside linguistics would benefit from at least one research question which is concerned with language – something that is actually happening, given the 'discursive turn' across the arts, humanities and social sciences (e.g. Billig, 2001).)

Let us consider a set of research questions from a research project in the field of sociolinguistics:[2]

1. Is the quotative use of *be like* in talk (e.g. *He was like 'I can't stay here'*) on the increase in British English?
2. To what extent (if any) does the quotative use of *be like* in British English vary with age?
3. Is the quotative use of *be like* a greater marker of male or of female adolescent speech in the United Kingdom?

The focus of all three of these research questions is language use. (This clearly guides the data needed, data collection methods, and data analysis – see below.)

However, language can be a focus not only in terms of occurrence, but also perceptions. Other research questions on the topic of the quotative use of *be like* might be

4. Is the quotative use of *be like* in talk in English perceived as gendered by users?
5. If yes, how?
6. If yes, why?

Research questions about language *use* and about *perceptions* of language use are both valid in sociolinguistics, and indeed complimentary in our understanding of particular linguistic phenomena.

A research study can also include linguistically oriented research questions to do with a specific linguistic code or use of that code. When I wrote my own Ph.D. thesis (Sunderland, 1996a) on gender and teacher–student interaction in the foreign language classroom, work had already been done on interaction and gender in classrooms, including a little in second/foreign language classrooms, but there was (to my knowledge, to date) no work on gender and interaction with regard to the foreign language classroom *as such*. This meant that I could ask research questions which had been asked of other classrooms but had not apparently been asked of foreign language classrooms. I could then consider the *special characteristics* of the foreign language classroom: in particular, that two languages (at least) would normally be in use there. This pointed to a need to design a range of research questions focusing on the 'codes' used in this foreign language classroom (the relevant languages were the students' L1, English, and the target language, German).

My empirical research questions asked about teacher talk and student talk. In terms of teacher talk, the *overarching research question* was

- Does the teacher use more or different language to/about boys and to/about girls?

The subordinate research questions were concerned with (a) teacher solicits (i.e. language used with the intention to someone to do or say something), (b) teacher feedback to students' spoken answers to her question, (c) teacher comments and (d) teacher responses to student solicits. The list of subordinate research questions was long, and I include just seven (!) of them here as illustration:

(1) How many male or female students are named (or otherwise identified) in the context of a solicit?
(2) How many words of a solicit are directed to a particular student?
(3) How many solicits are non-academic, how many academic?
(4) Of the academic solicits, does the teacher direct more solicits to girls or to boys in either German, English or both?
(5) As regards the answer to the academic solicits
    (a) does the intended language of response vary with sex of addressee?

⇨

Cont'd

(b) does the intended type of response (predetermined or 'pseudo-open') vary with sex of addressee?

(c) does the intended length of response (one word or potentially longer) vary with sex of addressee?

(6) Does the teacher provide different types of feedback to girls' and boys' broadly 'correct' answers to her academic solicits?

(7) Does the teacher provide different types of feedback to girls' and boys' broadly 'incorrect' responses, or lack of responses, to her academic solicits?

Of the above research questions, though all were concerned with language in the sense of 'teacher talk', research questions 4 and 5a (in bold) were also concerned with use of a particular *linguistic code*: here, German or English.[3] As all the questions were original in that they had not been asked before of the language classroom (most had not been asked of *any* classroom), I saw this particular focus on gendered use of *linguistic code* in the classroom as one of the 'intellectual contributions' of my thesis.[4]

1.7 Operationalizing research questions

For an empirical research question (the sort you can only answer through data) to be *operationalizable* (see also Cohen et al., 2007: 81–3), there must be a way of addressing it, in terms of identifying the appropriate data, collecting and analysing it (see section 1.8). Often there are indications of how to do this in the research question itself. For example, as we have seen, a research question like 'What reasons do French teachers working in UK primary schools give for the teaching of French to Year 6 primary school children?' suggests that the researcher would *elicit* data, for example, might ask teachers a set of interview (or questionnaire) questions which *together*, properly analysed, would address this research question. Note though that the words 'What reasons do [they] give ...?' constitute an important reminder that we cannot get at people's *actual* reasons directly from what they say – at best, these are 'reported beliefs', the beliefs they 'give' (see also Chapter 8). This has implications for the interpretation of findings and the strength of claims that can be made. (Note that interview questions are not the same as research questions. It would be unreasonable to put your research question directly to a respondent.)

Also important in operationalization is defining key terms. For the set of research questions given earlier about the 'quotative use of *be like*', we would need to be clear about what we mean by this. It may seem obvious (as in the example in the research question itself, *He was like 'I can't stay here'*), but there may be cases where it is not clear whether *be like* is quotative or not, and parameters will need to be drawn. Also in need of a working definition (i.e. a definition 'for the purpose of this study') is the concept, in these research questions, of *adolescence* (who counts as an adolescent?). Of course, the terms in your questions will correspond to your theoretical and epistemological focus: this is very evident in words like *ideology* or *discourse*, but even the word *beliefs* in a research question indicates that you consider your research participants' understandings as important, interesting and epistemologically valid in a given research endeavour (see also Mason, 2002).

1.8 Implications of your research questions for data, data collection and analysis

Mason points out that your research questions should be clearly formulated, intellectually worthwhile, and researchable 'because it is through them that you will be connecting what it is that you wish to research with how you are going to go about researching it' (2002: 19). I have already pointed to the role of research questions in identifying appropriate data and accordingly data collection, elicitation (generation), or selection (e.g. when looking at a body of literary or newspaper texts). Of course, you also need to be sure that you can get the relevant data, and can get enough of it.

One example of a research question with clear methodological implications (for data collection, and research design more widely) is Nunan's (1992):

- Are authentic materials more effective in bringing about learning than materials written specifically for the language classroom?

In that this research question is *comparative*, addressing it would entail researcher intervention. The research project would require an experimental set-up, with materials (authentic/written specifically for the language classroom) as the independent variable, and 'effectiveness in bringing about learning' as

the dependent variable. Both 'authentic' and 'effectiveness in bringing about learning' would need to be defined. Of course, the teaching and learning conditions would need to be controlled as far as possible, so that the materials were used by students of similar levels and abilities, who would ideally be taught by the same teacher.

Let us take an example of a research question and work it through: 'How do white female British university students construct their femininity in informal situations in talk with their same-sex peers?' Our *data* might be transcripts of naturally occurring talk of such students in informal situations. (Note that if we elicited data, for example, through interviews, we would be answering a question about how these students *understand* or *report* their construction of femininity.) To *collect* this data, we would need to identify an 'informal situation' and then do some audio and/or video recording, either including participant observation (which might distort the data, and would indeed make the event less 'naturally occurring'), or recording without the researcher present, perhaps asking the students to wear radio-microphones and giving them control of the recording equipment. Alternatively, we might identify and use a corpus of spoken British English which included conversations between white female British university students. In terms of *preparing the data for analysis*, we would need to carefully consider how to transcribe the recorded data. This is not a mechanical procedure: on the contrary, again, it depends on the research questions. Let us say, for example, that we were interested in the role of overlapping speech in the construction of femininity, perhaps as a measure of articulated empathy and/or support (see Coates, 1996). In this case we would have to make an active decision to indicate overlapping speech on the transcript, and further to decide (and document) *how* to do this.

As regards analysis, your research questions and data are likely to suggest a particular approach or framework related to the theoretical underpinnings of your work. For this example, we would probably decide on some form of discourse analysis (see Chapter 6), say, Conversation Analysis (CA) (Hutchby and Wooffitt, 2001), Critical Discourse Analysis (CDA) (Fairclough, 2001), Feminist Post-structuralist Discourse Analysis (FPDA) (Baxter, 2003), or perhaps a combination. Analysis is not however a self-evident or straightforward procedure based on, say, a decision to do with efficiency, but more to do with what we might call 'ontological alignment'. For example, not all researchers self-identify as feminist; and opposition to both CDA and CA can be ideological, based on views about the appropriate stance and role of the analyst. What is likely is that your idea of your theoretical/analytical approach will in fact inform your topic and indeed your research questions, so that when you come to analyse your data, your analytical framework is, if not exactly 'waiting for you', a 'rational' decision which is theoretically consistent with your entire research project. If you are interested in language, power and ideology – and accordingly in CDA – your topic and research question(s) are likely to reflect this (you might be investigating the 'legitimation' of racism in talk, for example, or verbal dominance of one group over another in a public meeting), and you are likely to wish to analyse your data through one of the several versions of CDA (see Wodak and Chilton, 2005).

Let us now return to two of the language education research questions referred to earlier in this chapter:

- Do French teachers working in UK primary schools agree with the teaching of French to Year 6 primary school children?
- What reasons do French teachers working in UK primary schools give for including the teaching of French to Year 6 children in the curriculum?

and research questions 4 and 5 (above) about *be like*:

4. Is the quotative use of *be like* in talk in English *perceived* as gendered by users?
5. If yes, how?

For these research questions, you would need to *elicit* data, since you are dealing with (reported) attitudes, reasons, beliefs and perceptions. You could record people's naturally occurring talk, hoping that they would express their understandings of these very topics – but you might wait for a very long time. You would therefore probably consider using questionnaires or individual or group interviews (see Chapter 8).

In contrast, for research question 1 about the quotative *be like*

1. Is the quotative use of *be like* in talk (e.g. *He was like 'I can't stay here'*) on the increase in British English?

you would need a corpus of spoken English (with talk collected more and less recently), as this research question is about change, in actual language use, over time. And for the second *be like* research question:

2. To what extent (if any) does the quotative use of *be like* in British English vary with age?

you might, in addition to corpus data, use naturally occurring data, that is, samples from speakers of different ages.

Some research questions can be answered from existing data. Look again at the fifth language education research question (p. 13)

- What is the range and diversity of beliefs of UK primary school teachers of French in relation to the teaching of French to Year 6 children?

Here, the researcher needs to identify the range and diversity of beliefs from the total set of those s/he has already identified. This is important: a research question does not *necessarily* require its own specific dataset.

Finally, let's revisit the last 'language education' research question, and research question 6 about quotative *be like*.

- Why do UK primary school teachers of French hold these beliefs?
- If yes, why [is the quotative use of *be like* in talk perceived as gendered by users]?

These research questions are more difficult to address. In the social sciences, it is almost impossible to answer a 'Why' question in a way which is completely satisfactory. I have already mentioned the problem of establishing causality (as opposed to association). Of course, even without any data from the questions preceding each of these two research questions, it is possible (and may be instructive) to speculate about many possible answers. But even *with* data, a variety of explanations (answers to 'Why?') will suggest themselves, constituting what can be called 'competing hypotheses' (Dick Allwright, personal communication). And even if we ask teachers 'Why do you hold these beliefs about teaching French to Year 6 primary school children?', we cannot see the teachers' answers as 'truth' or 'facts'. While interview respondents may not be deliberately deceiving the researcher, or deceiving themselves, their responses are nevertheless 'co-constructions': jointly co-constructed with the interviewer, within the interview process itself (see Chapter 8). Put simply, a respondent might pick up on the words of the interviewer, might tell the interviewer what s/he thinks the interviewer wants to hear, or might construct an answer newly suggested to her/him by the interview prompt (see Litosseliti, 2003, for a discussion of types of prompts and questions typically used in focus groups). 'Why' questions thus have to be handled with a great deal of caution, and 'answers' expressed in a way which is neither overstated nor reductionist. For this reason, the (very important) question of 'why' is often addressed in the discussion of findings, rather than asked through a research question 'at the outset'.

1.9 Documenting your decisions in your article, dissertation or thesis

The many decisions described above are not a 'private' or implicit matter. When writing an MA dissertation or Ph.D. thesis, it is most important to document *all* your decisions, and reasons for them. Helpful here is to start by summarizing your methodology in a table such as this:

	Research Question	Data needed	Data collection	Data analysis
1				
2				
3				

Such a table will help you organize your thinking and documenting of decisions; it will also help those all-important readers of your thesis or dissertation. Things are, however, rarely quite so cut and dried. For example, one research question might require two sources of data; conversely, as suggested above, one source of data might address more than one research question – and therefore your table will need adapting. But if you find that you have an empirical research question lacking data with which to address it, or data with no corresponding research question, then you have a useful alert to the fact that you need to reconsider your research design.

Documenting your decisions around your research questions however goes beyond justifying their operationalization through associated data, data collection methods and analytical framework. You also need to show that the research questions *themselves* have not 'fallen from the sky'; each needs a rationale (see section 1.2 'Where do research questions come from?'). This is related to originality and your own 'contribution to knowledge'. It is worth indicating in what sense each of your research questions is original – for example, has it ever been asked? or has it perhaps been asked before, but of a different context? For example, while most of my own Ph.D. research questions had not, to my knowledge, been asked before, others had – but of a classroom other than a foreign language classroom.

Equally importantly, research questions can (indeed, *should*) be referred to throughout the work – especially if different parts of the study address different research questions. In terms of data collection, different data will probably be collected with different research questions in mind. And all the research questions should almost certainly be referred to in the discussion: not so much in terms of you having 'answered' each research question, but, having addressed it, discussing it, and identifying the implications of what has been found. Continuous reference to your research questions (e.g. in each analytical chapter, to those research questions you are addressing there) will not only help you stay on track and organize your thesis as a whole; it will also help the reader appreciate the reasons for what you are writing at all times.

Notes

1. Note also that these particular *Is/Are/Do/Does* questions 'expect' more than a Yes/No answer!
2. I am grateful to Kate Harrington (2008) for this example of a research topic.
3. I would not now necessarily employ (or recommend) a long list of subordinate research questions. Proper operationalization of an overarching research question should not result in what Cohen et al. call 'an unwieldy list of sub-questions' (2007: 89).
4. In many cases the differences were non-existent or statistically insignificant (by no means disappointing). In particular, girls and boys had an approximately equal chance of being asked a solicit by the teacher in either German or English. Findings of *gender differential* tendencies related to linguistic code included that (a) girls were asked a greater proportion of academic solicits to which they were expected to respond in German than were boys (near statistical significance at 5% level), and (b) girls volunteered more answers than boys in German (statistically significant at 5% level) and English (non-significant).

Further reading

Andrews (2003) – A useful book for different levels of students in Higher Education whose research has a social or (language) education focus. Using several actual case studies, Andrews looks at the genesis and types of research questions and methodological implications, as well as problems researchers may encounter.

Cameron, Frazer, Harvey, Rampton and Richardson (1992) – A thought-provoking book, which looks at the questions of research 'on', 'for' or 'with' participants, and, implicitly, at where the research questions for a given study come from.

Cohen, Manion and Morrison (2007) – An extremely substantial and comprehensive 'classic' work, which is relevant to research both within and outside education. Make sure you get the latest edition (currently sixth)! 'Research questions' are covered in chapter 3.

Mason (2002) – A very thoughtful book encouraging reflection throughout. Mason has always been something of a pioneer in the qualitative research field. Research questions are referred to explicitly in relation to different stages of research.

Nunan (1992) – Despite its relatively narrow research focus, a methodologically very useful book which includes a section on 'developing a research question'.

Sunderland (1996b) – This paper looks at the 'paring down' of chapters and words – a frequent characteristic of thesis-writing. Research questions are dealt with in the 'refining' section.

References

Allwright, R. L. (1983), 'Classroom-centered research on language teaching and learning: a brief historical overview', *TESOL Quarterly*, 17, 191–204.

Allwright, R. L. (2003), 'Exploratory practice: rethinking practitioner research in language teaching', *Language Teaching Research*, 7/2, 113–41.

Andrews, R. (2003), *Research Questions*. London: Continuum.

Baxter, J. (2003), *Positioning Gender in Discourse: A Feminist Methodology*. Basingstoke: Palgrave Macmillan.

Billig, M. (2001), 'Humour and hatred: the racist jokes of the Ku Klux Klan', *Discourse & Society*, 12, 291–313.

Cameron, D., Frazer, E., Harvey, P., Rampton, B. and Richardson, K. (1992), *Researching Language: Issues of Power and Method*. London: Routledge.

Coates, J. (1996), *Women Talk*. Oxford: Blackwell.

Cohen, L., Manion, L. and Morrison, K. (2007), *Research Methods in Education* (6th edn). London: Routledge.

Fairclough, N. (2001), 'The discourse of New Labour: critical discourse analysis', in M. Wetherell, S. Taylor and S. Yates (eds), *Discourse as Data: A Guide for Analysis*. London: Sage/Open University, pp. 229–66.

Harrington, K. (2008), 'Perpetuating difference? Corpus linguistics and the gendering of reported dialogue', in K. Harrington, L. Litosseliti, H. Sauntson and J. Sunderland (eds), *Gender and Language Research Methodologies*. London: Palgrave Macmillan, pp. 85–102.

Hutchby, I. and Wooffitt, R. (2001), *Conversation Analysis: Principles, Practices and Applications*. Cambridge/Oxford: Polity/Blackwell.

Litosseliti, L. (2003), *Using Focus Groups in Research*. London: Continuum.

Mason, J. (2002), *Qualitative Researching* (2nd edn). London: Sage.

Nunan, D. (1992), *Research Methods in Language Learning*. Cambridge: Cambridge University Press.

Salmani-Nodoushan, M. A. (n.d.), 'Research in the language classroom: State of the Art', http://www.translationdirectory.com/article894.htm

Schumann, F. E. and Schumann, J. H. (1977), 'Diary of a language learner: an introspective study of second language learning', in H. D. Brown, C. A. Yorio and R. H. Crymes (eds), *On TESOL '77, Teaching and Learning English as a Second Language: Trends in Research and Practice*. Washington, DC: TESOL.

Sunderland, J. (1996a), *Gendered Discourse in the Foreign Language Classroom: Teacher-Student and Student-Teacher Talk, and the Construction of Children's Femininities and Masculinities*. Ph.D. thesis, Department of Linguistics and English Language, Lancaster University.

Sunderland, J. (1996b), 'Focusing, sacrificing, refining', in Kyratzis, Sakis and Tzanne, Angeliki (eds), *Muddy Fields: Doing Research in Applied Linguistics*. Department of Linguistics and English Language, Lancaster University.

Wodak, R. and Chilton, P. (eds) (2005), *A New Research Agenda in (Critical) Discourse Analysis: Theory and Interdisciplinarity*. Amsterdam: John Benjamins.

Quantitative, Qualitative or Both? Combining Methods in Linguistic Research

2

Jo Angouri

Chapter outline

The twofold purpose of this chapter is to problematize the widely held *quantitative versus qualitative* research dichotomy, and to address the issue of integrating the two paradigms in research projects in linguistics. While there is an increasing body of research placing value in mixed methodologies, recent work has also indicated potential barriers and limitations in viewing the 'third paradigm' as a *necessary* alternative. Following Tashakkori and Creswell's (2007) recent overview of the conceptual and epistemological challenges in mixed methods research, one of the key issues I focus on here is the ongoing discussion on the amount of integration of the quantitative and qualitative elements in research designs. The chapter draws on studies that have used a wide range of methodologies and discusses the merits as well as the challenges in combining paradigms but also methodologies and methods. By way of illustration, attention is paid to research in the broadly defined area of workplace discourse. I discuss the ways in which mixed methods designs can contribute to the dissemination of findings and the applicability of such research, as well as help overcome specific challenges involved in conducting research in this area.

2.1 Introduction

Projects in the field of linguistics often subscribe to either the quantitative or qualitative paradigm even though a closer examination would indicate that a large number of these studies fall somewhere between the two ends of the continuum (Miles and Huberman, 1994). The benefits of combining the two paradigms have been repeatedly discussed in the social sciences/humanities research methodology literature (e.g. Creswell, 1994). In fact, there is a lot of work in the (applied and socio) linguistic field on the value of combining either direct or indirect data gathering methods (e.g. Harrington et al., 2008; Litosseliti, 2003) or applying diverse techniques for data analysis. In a seminal early work, Greene et al. (1989) reviewed studies taking a mixed methods approach and argued that combining the two paradigms is beneficial for constructing comprehensive accounts and providing answers to a wider range of research questions. In the same vein, Tashakkori and Teddlie (2003) in their recent work suggest that mixed methods, often operationalized as almost a synonym for collecting different datasets or applying more than one method for the data analysis, provide 'ways to answer research questions that could not be answered in any other way' (2003: x). And research in sociolinguistics has shown that combined methodologies can shed light on 'different layers of meaning' (Holmes, 2007: 5). For example, Stubbe et al.'s (2003) work has shown the benefits of applying a wide range of analytic approaches, traditionally with methodologically distinct boundaries, to workplace discourse. At the same time there has been a shift towards multidisciplinary research (e.g. Brannen, 2005) as more and more researchers undertake joint projects bringing together fields of study and subsequently the methodologies that are often associated with these fields.

It is still quite commonplace, however, for the two paradigms to be directly contrasted. As Green and Preston recently suggested in the editorial of a special issue devoted to mixed methods research, 'the image of the introverted statistician . . . or the hang-loose ethnographer are by no means eliminated' (2005: 167). They also referred to the *paradigm war* of the 1970s and 1980s (Tashakkori and Teddlie, 2003), where the ontological and epistemological differences of the quantitative and qualitative approaches to research were foregrounded and sharply contrasted. Following a strong and long held tradition of paradigm incompatibility, this quote also nicely encapsulates the stereotypes that have been associated with researchers aligning their work with the quantitative and qualitative paradigm respectively.

Against this backdrop, and in line with Dörnyei (2007), the stance I take here is that this juxtaposition of the paradigms may point to the researchers' (diverse styles and) world-views rather than the mutual exclusiveness of the two approaches. Further, I adopt a *pragmatist*'s stance, according to which methodologies represent a collection of techniques (Bryman, 2001; Rossman and Wilson, 1985) as opposed to a *purist*'s stance, which would see qualitative and quantitative methods as being incompatible. I do not aspire to exhaust the discussion on the merits and challenges of mixed methods here. My aim however is to problematize both a range of issues relevant to aligning a research project to a specific paradigm, and the practicalities that may affect research designs, the collection and interpretation of data and dissemination of findings. I discuss the notions of 'integrating' and 'mixing' both at the level of overarching paradigms (namely mixed methods, qualitative and quantitative) but also at the level of specific methodologies associated with fields of study. In order to illustrate these issues I draw on studies in the field of business discourse.

This chapter is organized into four parts. In order to place the discussion in context, a brief overview of current issues in mixed methodologies is provided. I next move on to the thorny issue of triangulation and the way it is frequently used by researchers. I then discuss studies in the broadly defined field of workplace discourse, paying special attention to the relationship between mixed methodologies and applicability of research. I finally turn to the implications and conclusions that can be drawn.

2.2 Qualitative, quantitative, mixed and multimethod designs[1]

As Seliger and Shohamy (1989; DeVaus, 2002), among many others, suggest, the research methods and techniques adopted in any research project depend upon the questions and the focus of the researcher. However, this may suggest a rather 'instrumental' stance which does not always capture the philosophical and conceptual underpinning as well as theoretical debates and complexities of the 'approach' researchers choose, thus reducing it to 'what works' (Sunderland and Litosseliti, 2008; Tashakkori and Teddlie, 2003). Even though the uneasiness deriving from a 'what works' position is rather straightforward, the extent to which it is relevant to the mixed methods paradigm is debatable. In fact, over the last few years an increasing volume of work has appeared (e.g. Bryman, 2006; Johnson and Onwuegbuzie, 2004) which illustrates (a) the conceptual decisions researchers make in choosing a particular design within this paradigm, and (b) the robustness of the paradigm itself. In addition, there is great variety in mixed methods designs; Tashakkori and Teddlie (2003) have identified over 40 types of designs within their recent handbook. Hence mixed methods 'is not to be mistaken for an "anything goes disposition", (Dörnyei, 2007: 166) and should not be seen as an unstructured 'fusion' of quantitative and qualitative research or as just the additive 'sum' of both paradigms.

Another important issue that is often discussed in association with mixed method research is the compatibility and transferability of various paradigms and methodologies, within and across different disciplinary and epistemological communities. While there is a growing consensus that combining approaches is not only feasible but also beneficial in revealing different aspects of 'reality' (Lazaraton, 2005: 219), there is an open question as to whether many methods and types of research would comfortably sit under the same design. 'The question, then, is not whether the two sorts of data and associated methods can be linked during study design, but whether it should be done, how it will be done, and for what purposes' (Miles and Huberman, 1994: 41).

Within the linguistic field, Sunderland and Litosseliti (2008) provide clear examples of how 'affiliation' to certain epistemological approaches may influence the approach taken and methodologies selected. In the case of discourse analysis, for instance, there are widely recognized approaches (including Conversation Analysis (CA), Interactional Sociolinguistics, Critical Discourse Analysis (CDA), Discursive Psychology, Interpretative Discourse Analysis, and Post-structuralist Discourse Analysis (PDA)), each with a recognizable associated set of methodological tools. These different approaches often stay somewhat insulated within specific disciplinary boundaries, each working with distinctive conceptions of discourse, as well as distinctive tools and processes (e.g. regarding the operationalization of the context of interactions for the interpretation of discourse data). A discussion of how approaches (and researchers taking a certain stance) do not always sit comfortably under one design can be found in Harrington et al. (2008); also many a reader will be familiar with the debate that was published in *Discourse & Society* (e.g. Schegloff, 1997) around the different theoretical assumptions made by CA and CDA researchers. It is beyond the scope of this chapter to consider potential barriers in reconciling different theoretical assumptions, however, the question on the extent to which quantitative and qualitative methodologies are compatible is relevant. A growing number of researchers

> have consistently argued for, and indeed, adopted approaches which attempt to *integrate* [emphasis mine] quantitative and qualitative methods of analysis, using the patterns identified by the quantitative analysis as essential background to assist in the detailed qualitative interpretation of the discourse.
>
> (Holmes and Meyerhoff, 2003: 15)

In the editorial of the *Journal of Mixed Methods Research*, Tashakkori and Creswell (2007) provide a useful overview of the conceptual and epistemological challenges in 'bridging' quantitative and qualitative research designs. While recently the mixed methods paradigm was defined as 'the class of research where the researcher mixes or combines' (Johnson and Onwuegbuzie, 2004: 17) quantitative and qualitative elements, according to Bryman (2007) the key issue to be considered is the amount of 'integration' of the two paradigms; for instance, Geluykens (2008) suggests that most studies in his subfield of cross-cultural pragmatics *combine* rather than *integrate* research methods. A growing number of works distinguish between combination/integration. I follow here Tashakkori and Creswell's (2007) approach and the studies I discuss later combine *or* integrate the qualitative/quantitative element in one of the following ways:

- two types of research questions (with qualitative and quantitative approaches)
- the manner in which the research questions are developed (participatory vs. preplanned)
- two types of sampling procedures (e.g., probability and purposive)
- two types of data collection procedures (e.g., focus groups and surveys)
- two types of data (e.g., numerical and textual)
- two types of data analysis (statistical and thematic), and
- two types of conclusions (emic and etic[2] representations, 'objective' and 'subjective', etc.).

(Tashakkori and Creswell, 2007: 4)

Typically the discussion on integration refers to the sequence and importance (or dominance) of the qualitative/quantitative component. Brannen (2005) usefully provides exemplar studies showing how the second (either qualitative or quantitative) component can be introduced at (a) the design, (b) the fieldwork and/or (c) the interpretation and contextualization phase of any research project.[3]

Whether combining or integrating quantitative/qualitative elements, mixed methods designs arguably contribute to a better understanding of the various phenomena under investigation; while quantitative research is useful towards generalizing research findings (see Chapter 3), qualitative approaches are particularly valuable in providing in-depth, rich data. However, mixed methods research designs do not indicate 'necessarily better research' (Brannen, 2005: 183) nor should they be seen as *deus ex machina*. The data (as in all paradigms) need to be analysed and interpreted systematically and following rigorous theoretical grounding. It is however the case that, when consistent, mixed methods research allows for 'diversity of views' and 'stronger inferences'

(Tashakkori and Teddlie, 2003: 674), and as such it is often associated with the concept of *triangulation*, the focus of the next section.

2.3 Triangulation: An overused term?

Triangulation as a central methodological concept comes high on the list of key features of good research designs (Cohen and Manion, 1994: 233). The way the term is conceptualized by scholars is however epistemologically varied. Denzin's (1970: 472) early work indicated that there is more than one type of triangulation:

- *Data triangulation* (the application of more than one sampling method for data collection)
- *Investigator triangulation* (the involvement of more than one researcher)
- *Theoretical triangulation* (the use of more than one theoretical stance)
- *Methodological triangulation* (the use of more than one methodology).

Data triangulation and methodological triangulation are arguably the most common operationalizations of the term; the former refers to data gathering methods, while the latter is broader and refers to the use of more that one methodology in a research design. Denzin also drew an interesting distinction between inter-method and intra-method triangulation – the former referring to the use of facets of the same method and the latter referring to the use of two (often contrasting) methods (see Schryer, 1993, for an example).

Triangulation is often one of the key reasons for undertaking mixed methods research. The question, however, is what triangulation means in this context, as the use of the term is not consistent among researchers. According to the typology of mixed methods designs suggested by Greene et al. (1989) – but also more recently by (Bryman, 2006) – the *term* stands for *convergence* of findings and *corroboration* of research results. According to this view, the expectation is that different datasets or different methodologies will lead to similar results and hence allow for 'confident interpretation' (e.g. Lyons, 2000: 280) of the findings and strengthen the researcher's conclusions. As such the term is also widely associated with the concept of credibility of research findings. A problem associated with this approach is the assumption that data collected using different methods can necessarily be compared and/or contrasted in order to answer the same set of research questions. This view assumes that there is one single objective 'reality' or 'truth' – not only a problematic assumption (as seen in various chapters of this book), but also, as argued by Harden and Thomas (2005) one that ignores that data from different sources often reveal conflicting realities.

At the same time it is important to stress that *triangulation* (as defined above) is not the *only* purpose of mixed methods research. In their early work, Greene et al. (1989) suggested an influential typology of mixed methods designs including four mixed methods purposes (apart from triangulation): *initiation* – aiming at discovering meaningful contradictions and 'the paradox'; *complementarity* – aiming at shedding light on different aspects of the same phenomenon; *development* – aiming at using findings elicited by the use of one method for the design of the second or subsequent one; and *expansion* – aiming at broadening the scope and objective of the research (see Tashakkori and Teddlie, 2003, for further discussions of the model, and Bryman, 2006). Bryman (2006) further showed that a large number of scholars undertake mixed methods research in order to further *elaborate* their findings.

I focus on *triangulation* here as it is the term most commonly used, and also often used in a generic way to refer to *all* purposes of mixed methods research. As Tashakkori and Teddlie argue, over the years triangulation has become a 'veritable "magical" word' (2003: 674), with the concept being criticized for being so broad that it is debatable whether it has any analytical value. Triangulation is so commonly associated with mixed methods research that Tashakkori and Teddlie encourage 'mixed methodologists to refrain from using it unless they specify how it was specifically defined in their research context' (2003: 674).

Having said that, we need not question the value of triangulation *per se* but we need to differentiate between the *technical term* and the *concept* of mixed methods designs as a whole. Even though neither is a *panacea* for any research design, when applied in relation to a robust conceptual framework (see Creswell et al., 2003) triangulation (in either sense) does lead to a better understanding of complex research questions and environments. For example, Dörnyei (2007) suggests that a better understanding of phenomena can emerge from triangulated findings (whether convergent *or* divergent), and also reports on the value of mixed methods designs for classroom research where challenges (such as the diversity of student/teacher body) may be addressed through versatile designs (I return to the issue of versatility in relation to mixed methods later in this chapter).

A final point about triangulation emerges from Bryman's analysis (2006) of 232 articles in the social sciences, suggesting that it is often an outcome of mixed methods research despite the fact that the desire to triangulate was *not* the original motivation for opting for this type of research. As put by Holmes and Meyerhoff (2003: 12), 'researchers fruitfully combine aspects of different methodologies to answer the questions that arise in the course of their research', and often they are not concerned with the surrounding epistemological debates (or they take what Teddlie and Tashakkori (2003) describe as the *a-paradigmatic* stance). In other words, researchers undertake mixed methods research in order to answer their specific research questions without positioning themselves to either qualitative, quantitative or mixed methods paradigms (Harden and Thomas, 2005). Bryman (2006) further usefully distinguishes between rationale (where explicitly stated) and practice: in 27% of all articles he analysed, the researchers did not explicitly state the purpose for undertaking mixed methods research, and out of the 80 articles that applied a triangulation design, only 19 set this as an explicit rationale. Interestingly surveys (quantitative) and interviews (qualitative) seem to be the most dominant methods used by researchers.

Whether explicitly mentioned or not, it remains the case that, multilayered designs are often preferred to one-dimensional ones for eliciting rich findings (e.g. Northey, 1990). To further illustrate this, I now turn to studies that have used a wide range of methodologies in the field of workplace discourse.

2.4 Applying mixed methodologies in research on workplace discourse[4]

Given the multifaceted nature of research on discourse, it has been argued that collecting data from different sources in an iterative way is an appropriate way to address research questions in this area (Beaufort, 2000). While discourse studies are often seen as 'by nature' qualitative, being largely based on naturally occurring 'real-life' data, recent work (e.g. Holmes and Marra, 2002) has shown how quantitative and qualitative paradigms can be combined for a better understanding of the interactants' norms and practices in discourse.

To illustrate the issues addressed in the chapter so far, I now discuss examples of (socio and applied) linguistic studies of spoken and written discourse in the workplace. The objective of this section is not to provide a review of research in the area but to showcase some of the issues involved in bringing together quantitative/qualitative methodologies. As suggested by Bargiela-Chiappini et al., 'one of the defining features of business discourse research is that it has not relied on any one approach or methodology' (2007: 15). As such, it is a particularly apt area on which to focus for the purposes of our discussion here.

Researchers from a number of disciplines (not only linguistics but also management, sociology and psychology) have focused on the workplace as a research site. Moreover, this work operates from different perspectives and with different foci. Within linguistics, the overarching foci of workplace-related research are (a) the identification of patterns of language use and/or development of the skills employees need in order to be competent users of the language(s) for work-related purposes and (b) the study and/or description of the spoken/written language – or rather the discourse – workplace participants engage in. Hence the former often has a pedagogic concern, while the latter is focused on understanding and describing how people communicate, say, in a business/corporate context, and often aspires to make the findings relevant to real-life concerns of employees or practitioners. Put simply, the two areas currently correspond to two broad fields of linguistic research, namely, Language for Specific Purposes (LSP) and (applied) sociolinguistics (see Bargiela-Chiappini et al. (2007) for a succinct overview of the development of the field).

Even though we find work that draws on both of these fields (e.g. in genre analysis, corpus-based studies) and studies that show how research findings on workplace discourse can feedback into teaching practice, these two overarching areas often have different aims and adopt different techniques for data collection and analysis (with the latter often being qualitative rather than quantitative in its aims and objectives). It is not unusual for researchers from one field to be sceptical towards the outputs of the other. Often LSP is criticized for not capturing the diversity and complexity of workplace interactions, by taking a static view of language and by separating the study of spoken and written professional language (Gunnarsson, 1995: 115; see also Holmes and Stubbe, 2003, and Sarangi and Roberts, 1999). Bargiela-Chiappini and Nickerson (2002: 276) go as far as to argue that any static skills-based approach, or indeed any quantitative method, cannot *by itself* meet the needs of business communication'. In fact, any studies (quantitative or qualitative) which rely *only* on indirect sources, such as interviews with personnel, observations and questionnaires, can and have been criticized for failing to capture the dynamic nature of interactions (Bargiela-Chiappini and Harris, 1997; Holmes and Stubbe, 2003; Stubbe, 2001). This has prompted a large number of studies in workplace discourse which incorporate or are based on naturally occurring discourse data (e.g. Holmes and Marra, 2002; Sarangi and Roberts, 1999). In the light of such debates, in a recent project on intra-company variation in written processes and products (Angouri and Harwood, 2008), a case was made for more multifaceted, multimethod research on workplace discourse. Questionnaires, face-to-face interviews and participant observations were used and a corpus of real-life data was collected. In this particular study (which is part of a large project on language use in multinational companies), quantitative and qualitative methods were integrated at different stages of the research (in line with Brannen's 2005 work, discussed earlier in this chapter) in the *design, fieldwork* and *analysis* phases. These methods yielded different types of results. The analysis of the naturally occurring data indicated markedly different practices in the various communities of practice[5] studied, while the quantitative data revealed a pattern as to the genres (such as business letters, faxes and emails) the employees had to handle more frequently. The authors argue that variation in practices could not be understood without a closer analysis of ethnographic data and a discourse corpus. At the same time, the analysis of the quantitative data showed inter- and intra-company macrovariation according to the informants' posts.[6] Hence it was through the use of mixed methods that conclusions were drawn on discourse practices in the communities of practice studied. The dialectic relationship between the quantitative and qualitative elements is clear here, as the instruments used to collect quantitative data were designed on the basis of ethnographic observations, and the patterns revealed were studied further through a corpus of discourse data.

There are many other examples of mixed methods designs in workplace discourse studies. Jorgensen's 2008 work on governmental discourse, makes a strong case for combining methodologies in genre analysis, by using interviews, questionnaires and an extensive corpus of written documents. A case for integrating the two paradigms is also made by Holmes and Marra (2002) in a study on the functions of humour in communities of practice within different New Zealand workplaces. I consider this study to be a clear example of how quantitative and qualitative components can be combined to address a research topic that many would associate solely with qualitative research. The quantitative data in this study reveal different frequencies of humour instances as well as humour types. The researchers distinguish between supportive and contestive humour and also classify humour instances according to style (collaborative or competitive). At the same time the closer qualitative analysis of discourse data shows how 'humour is used' in the workplaces they study and the way the employees 'do humour' (Holmes and Marra, 2002: 1702) to achieve their interactional goals.

The work briefly discussed above has shown how data from indirect sources and quantitative analysis can complement the findings of work focused on the microlevel of naturally occurring interactions, and that there are 'insights to be gained by applying a range of different theoretical and methodological approaches to the same piece of discourse' (Stubbe et al., 2003: 380).

However apart from contributing to more in-depth analyses of research questions, mixed methods research also has an important part to play in reaching diverse audiences and overcoming challenges associated with certain research settings. For example, Mullany (2008) shows how mixing methods (in this case recordings, interviews, observations and written documents) contributed to a wider dissemination of the findings in the form of written reports for the companies involved. Similarly, in my research with seven multinational companies (Angouri, 2007), by using quantitative methods, I was able to identify patterns of foreign language use and the viability of existing language policies, which were major concerns for HR managers. By also drawing on my ethnographic observations and interviews, I produced written reports which turned out to be useful for the companies to assess current strengths and potential areas for further development. Even though my main focus was to examine the role of discourse in 'how people do things', particularly in the context of meeting talk in multilingual settings, I soon found out that adding another dimension to my design, namely analysing, from a macroperspective/ quantitatively (foreign) language use in different departments of the companies, was not only informative but also the best (and possibly the only) way for me to gain access to this very particular workplace setting. Adding this dimension, which was relevant and important for the HR managers themselves, meant that they in turn were willing to further collaborate and in effect I was able to carry out the rest of the study.

It would then appear that mixed methods have a role to play in overcoming some of the challenges of the workplace as a site of research that is notoriously difficult in terms of gaining access and collecting data. The 'setting ... shap[es] the methods that a researcher is able to employ' (Mullany, 2008: 46; see also Stubbe, 2001), especially when HR managers are to be convinced of the value of a research project, and research designs need to be adapted to accommodate the exigencies of specific research settings (see Angouri, 2007 for concrete examples). This can be achieved more easily through mixed methods designs that can address issues that are of immediate concern to the people involved in the projects. While mono-dimensional studies can and do also result in rich datasets, mixed methods designs are *versatile* and can arguably address, from a more holistic perspective, issues the participants themselves relate to. As such they provide a powerful tool for research findings to feed back into research settings 'in order to draw attention to and challenge unquestioned practices' (Holmes and Meyerhoff, 2003: 14) such as gender and power hierarchies in workplace settings. If research is to produce findings that will be relevant and useful to those being studied, this then needs to be reflected in research designs and methodologies and mono-dimensional studies do not necessarily provide the means to meet this need. This is important, in the light of voices urging linguists and practitioners to work closely together in researching workplace discourse from different angles (see Roberts and Sarangi, 2003), and to draw on the real-life concerns or the 'habitus' (Bourdieu, 1993) of both research participants and practitioners. Making linguistic research applicable and relevant to real-world issues is certainly not a new concern for academics (e.g. Sarangi and Candlin, 2003). It is however becoming part of a growing trend in academia, and the emphasis placed on Knowledge Exchange by the Research Councils in the United Kingdom is a clear indication of this.

Before closing this chapter, I would like to consider some of the implications of the issues discussed. First, we should consider scholars' expected uneasiness and scepticism towards 'what works' research designs, given that these designs are constrained in a number of ways. However, factors outside each research project, such as the disposition of academic departments, journals, graduate programmes, funding agencies, policy making bodies (Brannen, 2005), peer pressure (Denscombe, 2008), and the preference and background training of researchers (Bryman, 2007) affect research designs – most obviously, in the choice of research topics, but also methodologies and methods and in the presentation of research findings. Tashakkori and Teddlie (2003) also discuss what they call the 'residue of the paradigm wars' (2003: 699), arguing that it has an impact on both research designs and students, whereby young researchers often find themselves in programmes or organizations that align their work with either the qualitative or quantitative paradigm and 'proclaim the inferiority of the other group's orientation and methods' (2003: 699). As *mixed methods* are gaining momentum, there is a need for this 'third' paradigm to find its place in graduate programmes and research methods curricula. This would involve not only creating the context where issues of researchers' inclinations, affiliations and accountability are discussed, but also equipping novice researchers with the necessary knowledge and skills for undertaking mixed methods research (and which requires competences in both quantitative and qualitative research). At the same time, mixed methods is not and should not be seen as a *necessary* alternative and the 'natural inclination', individual preferences and research strengths of researchers should not be overlooked (Dörnyei, 2007: 174). In this vein Green and Preston (2005: 171) suggest caution towards the 'omni-competent professional research, the generic paragon of knowledge production'.

Overall, mixed methods research can and does cross-disciplinary boundaries and overcome limitations that have been associated with mono-dimensional approaches to the study of complex phenomena and research sites (such as the workplace). As we have seen, mixed methods research also helps in making the research relevant to wider audiences, but also in avoiding orthodoxies such as those imposed by mono-dimensional, purist approaches to research that 'are potentially damaging to the spirit of enquiry' (Holmes and Meyerhoff, 2003: 15). Accordingly this chapter argues that using a wide range of tools for data collection, and combining quantitative and qualitative paradigms, can provide rich datasets and enhance our understanding of complexities in most research areas in linguistics in general (and workplace talk in particular).

Notes

1. The definition by Creswell et al. (2003: 210) is adopted here according to which the term design refers to 'a procedure for collecting, analysing and reporting research'.
2. The terms emic and etic are widely used in social sciences to refer to accounts that are either particular to a certain group or system (emic) or observations about a group or system from the standpoint of an outsider (etic).
3. See also Creswell et al. (2003) for a discussion on generic types of concurrent and sequential designs (referring to the quantitative/qualitative components).
4. Capturing the dynamics of 'workplace discourse' as a field of study is not one of the aims of this paper. I will not distinguish between professional/organizational/institutional discourse and organizational discourse studies. The reader is referred to Grant and Iedema (2005) for a discussion and Bargiela-Chiappini (2009).
5. The concept of communities of practice is frequently adopted in research on workplace discourse. Eckert and McConnell-Ginet (1992: 464) define a community of practice as 'an aggregate of people who come together around mutual engagement in an endeavor. Ways of doing things, ways of talking, beliefs, values, power relations – in short, practices – emerge in the course of this mutual

endeavor. As a social construct, a community of practice is different from the traditional community, primarily because it is defined simultaneously by its membership and by the practice in which that membership engages'.

6. The sample in the study is stratified according to their post and level of responsibility. Three strata are identified, namely, post holders, line managers and senior managers. The line managers are responsible for a subsection of a department or groups of employees within a department, and the postholders are responsible for no one but themselves. Senior Managers are responsible for either a subsection or a department or even a cluster of the company, depending on the company's size and structure.

Further reading

Dörnyei (2007) – This book provides an up-to-date and very useful overview of research methods in applied linguistics. It discusses qualitative, mixed methods and quantitative projects. It takes a step-by-step approach and examines all stages of research from collecting the data to presenting the findings and writing up academic research. It tackles ontological and epistemological issues and it will be helpful for all students conducting research in applied linguistics.

Tashakkori and Teddlie (eds) (2003) – This edited volume presents a thorough discussion of mixed methods or 'the third paradigm'. Even though it is not aimed specifically at linguists, students and researchers will find it very useful for its overview of recent developments in this area. It also constitutes a comprehensive collection of sampling techniques for mixed methods designs.

References

Angouri, J. (2007), 'Language in the workplace. A multimethod study of communicative activity in seven multinational companies situated in Europe'. Ph.D. thesis, University of Essex, UK.

Angouri, J. and Harwood, N. (2008), *This is Too Formal for Us . . . A case study of variation in the written products of a multinational consortium. Journal of Business and Technical Communication*, 22, 38–64.

Bargiela-Chiappini, F. (ed.) (2009), *The Handbook of Business Discourse*. Edinburgh: Edinburgh University Press.

Bargiela-Chiappini, F. and Harris, S. J. (1997), *Managing Language: The Discourse of Corporate Meetings*. Amsterdam: John Benjamins.

Bargiela-Chiappini, F. and Nickerson, C. (2002), 'Business discourse: old debates, New Horizons', *IRAL*, 40 (4), 273–86.

Bargiela-Chiappini, F., Nickerson, C. and Planken, B. (2007), *Business Discourse*. New York: Palgrave Macmillan.

Beaufort, A. (2000), 'Learning the trade: a social apprenticeship model for gaining writing expertise', *Written Communication*, 17 (2), 185–224.

Bourdieu P. (1993), *The Field of Cultural Production: Essays on Art and Literature*. Cambridge: Polity Press.

Brannen, J. (2005), 'Mixing methods: the entry of qualitative and quantitative approaches into the research process', *International Journal of Social Research Methodology*, 8 (3), 173–84.

Bryman, A. (2001), *Social Research Methods*. Oxford: Oxford University Press.

—. (2006), 'Integrating quantitative and qualitative research: how is it done?', *Qualitative Research*, 6 (1), 97–113.

—. *(2007)*, 'Barriers to integrating quantitative and qualitative research', *Journal of Mixed Methods Research*, 1 (1), 8–22.

Cohen, L. and Manion, L. (1994), *Research Methods in Education*. London and New York: Routledge.

Creswell, J. W. (1994), *Research Design: Qualitative and Quantitative Approaches*. Thousand Oaks, CA: Sage.

Creswell, J. W., Clark, V. L., Gutmann, M. and Hanson, W. (2003), 'Advanced mixed methods research designs', in A. Tashakkori and C. Teddlie (eds), *Handbook of Mixed Methods in Social and Behavioral Research*. Thousand Oaks, CA: Sage, pp. 619–37.

Denscombe, M. (2008), 'Communities of practice: a research paradigm for the mixed methods approach', *Journal of Mixed Methods Research*, 2, 270–83.

Denzin, N. K. (1970), *The Research Act in Sociology*. Chicago: Aldine.

DeVaus, D. A. (2002), *Research Design in Social Research*. Thousand Oaks, CA: Sage.

Dörnyei, Z. (2007), *Research Methods in Applied Linguistics*. Oxford: Oxford University Press.

Eckert, P. and McConnell-Ginet, S. (1992), 'Think practically and look locally: language and gender as community-based practice', *Annual Review of Anthropology*, 21, 461–90. Reprinted in C. Roman, S. Juhasz and C. Miller (eds) (1994), *The Women and Language Debate*. New Brunswick: Rutgers University Press, pp. 432–60.

Geluykens, R. (2008), 'Cross-cultural pragmatics: definition and methodology', in R. Geluykens and B. Kraft (eds), *Institutional Discourse in Cross-Cultural Contexts*. München: Lincom, pp. 49–84.

Grant, D. and Iedema, R. (2005), 'Discourse analysis and the study of organizations', *Text,* 25 (1), 37–66.

Green, T. and Preston, J. (2005), 'Speaking in tongues: encouraging diversity in mixed methods research', *International Journal of Social Research Methodology*, 8 (3), 167–71.

Greene, J. C., Caracelli, V. J. and Graham, W. F. (1989), 'Toward a conceptual framework for mixed-method evaluation designs', *Educational Evaluation and Policy Analysis*, 11, 255–74.

Gunnarsson, B. L. (1995), 'Studies of language for specific purposes – a biased view of a rich reality', *International Journal of Applied Linguistics*, 5 (1), 111–34.

Harden, A. and Thomas, J. (2005), 'Methodological issues in combining diverse study types in systematic reviews', *International Journal of Social Research Methodology: Theory and Practice*, 8, 257–71.

Harrington, K., Litosseliti, L., Sauntson, H. and Sunderland, J. (eds) (2008), *Gender and Language Research Methodologies*. Basingstoke: Palgrave.

Holmes, J. (2007), 'Humour and the construction of Māori leadership at work', *Leadership*, 3 (1), 5–27.

Holmes, J. and Marra, M. (2002), 'Having a laugh at work: how humour contributes to workplace culture', *Journal of Pragmatics*, 34, 1683–710.

Holmes, J. and Meyerhoff, M. (2003), 'Different voices, different views: an introduction to current research in language and gender', in J. Holmes and M. Meyerhoff (eds), *Handbook of Language and Gender*. Oxford: Blackwell.

Holmes, J. and Stubbe, M. (2003), *Power and Politeness in the Workplace*. London: Pearson Education.

Johnson, R. B. and Onwuegbuzie, A. J. (2004), 'Mixed methods research: a research paradigm whose time has come', *Educational Researcher*, 33 (7), 14–26.

Jorgensen, P. E. F. (2008), 'Taking a multiple analysis approach to discourse', in R. Geluykens and B. Kraft (eds), *Institutional Discourse in Cross-Cultural Contexts*. München: Lincom, pp. 29–47.

Lazaraton, A. (2005), 'Quantitative research methods', in E. Hinkel (ed.), *Handbook of Research in Second Language Teaching and Learning*. New Jersey: Lawrence Erlbaum.

Litosseliti, L. (2003), *Using Focus Groups in Research*. London: Continuum.

Lyons, E. (2000), 'Qualitative data analysis: data display model', in G. Breakwell, S. Hammond and C. Fife-Shaw (eds), *Research Methods in Psychology*. London: Sage, pp. 269–80.

Miles, M. B. and Huberman, A. M. (1994), *Qualitative Data Analysis* (2nd edn). Thousand Oaks, CA: Sage.

Mullany, L. (2008), 'Negotiating methodologies: making language and gender relevant in the professional workplace', in K. Harrington, L. Litosseliti, H. Sauntson and J. Sunderland (eds), *Gender and Language Research Methodologies*. Basingstoke: Palgrave, pp. 43–56.

Northey, M. (1990), 'The need for writing skill in accounting firms', *Management Communication Quarterly*, 3, 474–95.

Roberts, C. and Sarangi, S. (2003), Uptake of discourse research in interprofessional settings: reporting from medical consultancy. *Special Issue of Applied Linguistics*, 24 (3), 338–59.

Rossman, G. B. and Wilson, B. C. (1985), 'Numbers and words: combining qualitative and quantitative methods in a single large-scale evaluation study', *Evaluation Review*, 9 (5), 627–43.

Sarangi, S. and Candlin, C. N. (2003), 'Trading between reflexivity and relevance: new challenges for applied linguistics', *Applied Linguistics*, 24 (3), 271–85.

Sarangi, S. and Roberts, C. (eds) (1999), *Talk, Work and Institutional Order. Discourse in Medical, Mediation and Management Settings*. Berlin: Mouton de Gruyter.

Schegloff, E. A. (1997), 'Whose text? Whose context?', *Discourse & Society*, 8 (2), 165–87.

Schryer, C. (1993), 'Records as genre', *Written Communication*, 10, 200–34.

Seliger, H. and Shohamy, E. (1989), *Second Language Research Methods*. Oxford: Oxford University Press.

Stubbe, M. (2001), 'From office to production line: collecting data for the Wellington language in the workplace project', *Language in the Workplace Occasional Papers 2*. Retrieved April 2005 from http://www.vuw.ac.nz/lals/research/lwp/docs/ops/op2.htm

Stubbe, M., Lane, C., Hilder, J., Vine, E., Vine, B. and Marra, M. (2003), 'Multiple discourse analyses of a workplace interaction', *Discourse Studies*, 5 (3), 351–88.

Sunderland, J. and Litosseliti, L. (2008), 'Current research methodologies in gender and language study: key issues', in K. Harrington, L. Litosseliti, H. Sauntson and J. Sunderland (eds), *Language and Gender Research Methodologies*. London: Palgrave Macmillan.

Tashakkori, A. and Creswell, J. (2007), 'The new era of mixed methods', *Journal of Mixed Methods Research*, 1 (1), 3–8.

Tashakkori, A. and Teddlie, C. (2003), 'The past and the future of mixed model research: from "Methodological Triangulation" to "Mixed Model Designs"', in A. Tashakkori and C. Teddlie, *Handbook of Mixed Methods in Social and Behavioral Research*. Thousand Oaks, CA: Sage.

—. (eds) (2003), *Handbook of Mixed Methods in Social and Behavioural Research*. Thousand Oaks, CA: Sage.

Part II
Quantitative and Corpus Research Methods

Quantitative Methods: Concepts, Frameworks and Issues

3

Sebastian M. Rasinger

Chapter outline

This chapter will introduce readers to the most common concepts and issues of quantitative research. It starts off with a discussion of the general characteristics of quantitative research, based on an exploration of the key differences between quantitative and qualitative methodology, with a clear focus on the former. Based on real-linguistic examples, we will discuss the concept of 'quantifiabil-ity' of data – the quality of being measurable – and compare it to qualitative approaches, such as many discourse-analytic frameworks. Section 3.2 also intro-duces and defines the concepts of quantitative linguistic variables, hypotheses, theories and laws, as well as reliability and validity. Section 3.3 consists of a critical evaluation of the most frequently used research designs in quantitative research, such as longitudinal, cross-sectional or experimental designs. Section 3.4 looks in some detail at the issues surrounding the use of questionnaires in quantitative research, highlighting general design features, as well as aspects such as question phrasing, sequencing and the various tools available to measure different variables usually of interest in linguistic studies. This section also includes a short discussion of questionnaire coding.

3.1 Introduction

This book introduces some of the various different approaches to collecting and analysing linguistic data, in order to provide readers with a thorough overview of the tools and methods available. At the very end, however, we can distinguish between two basic types of methodological frameworks under which all other methods and approaches – in linguistics or any other discipline – can be subsumed: qualitative methods on the one side, and quantitative methods on the other. Yet, over the last decade or so, in social science research this dichotomy has become less rigid, and the use of mixed methods methodologies and triangulation approaches (the use of several methods to support each other) has increasingly led to the simultaneous use of quantitative and qualitative methods (for a concise summary, see Flick 2006, *inter alia*; also see Chapter 2), whereby '[s]tructural features are analyzed with quantitative methods and processual aspects with qualitative approaches' (Flick, 2006: 33).

For the sake of clarity and due to the limited scope of this chapter, I will have a closer look at quantitative methods in a rather isolated way only, with specific reference to their application in linguistics and other language-related subjects. This chapter starts with a comparison between quantitative and qualitative methods in general (section 3.2), followed by a discussion of various research designs that can be used under a quantitative framework (section 3.3). In the last part (section 3.4), we take a closer look at the design and use of questionnaires. Questionnaires come with the reputation of being a quick and easy way to amass vast amounts of data and are hence a tool frequently used in quantitative studies. Yet, as we will see, questionnaires, like any other methodological tool, need thorough planning in order to provide valid and reliable data.

3.2 Quantitative versus qualitative methods

There are probably only few issues in research that are as fundamentally misunderstood as the difference between qualitative and quantitative approaches to data analysis. This misconception comes from the use of the terms in daily discourse, where 'quality' usually refers to 'good' (unless something is of 'bad quality'), whereas 'quantity' frequently refers to 'much'. When we use the terms qualitative and quantitative in the context of a methodological framework, however, we have to modify these definitions. The following is an extract from a conversation between a mother (M) and a 2.5-year-old child (C) (Peccei, 1999: 95).

> C: daddy is coming down too
> M: who's coming down too?

C: daddy
M: daddy? No. where's daddy?
C: me want – daddy come down
M: working sweetie
C: no, no. Find her cheque book
M: finding her cheque book

There is a multitude of ways to analyse these eight lines. We could, for example, look at the transcript with a focus on the conversational exchange between mother and child, with reference to theories of first language acquisition, such as child directed speech. In this case, we would mainly be interested in what is going on between the two interlocutors during the conversation: there is a clear question and answer sequence, and we could argue that the mother, as the linguistically more competent, is guiding the exchange – not to say she is controlling it. She is also, to a certain extent, adjusting her language, for example syntactic complexity, towards a linguistically less competent child. In general terms, we could look for certain *patterns* or *sequences* in the text in order to come to a result. In yet other words, we could analyse the text with regard to its main *characteristics* or *qualities* – and hence carry out a *qualitative analysis*.

However, we can also take an entirely different approach. Language acquisition research is, ultimately, always concerned with the development of linguistic proficiency, and in first language acquisition, the Mean Length of Utterance (MLU) has been around for a long time as a frequent – albeit somewhat unreliable – way of measuring children's first language proficiency and development (see, *inter alia*, Bates et al., 1995; Whong-Barr and Schwartz, 2002). The MLU is an index which tells us, as the name implies, the average length of children's utterances in words or morphemes. To calculate the MLU for our example, we count all of C's words and divide it by the number of utterances:[1]

C: daddy is coming down too	5 words
C: daddy	1 word
C: me want – daddy come down	5 words
C: no, no. Find her cheque book	6 words
Total number of words:	17
Number of utterances:	4

$$MLU = \frac{17}{4} = 4.25$$

For our example, the MLU is 4.25, that is, on average the child produces utterances of 4.25 words length. So, the MLU allows us to put a numeric value onto something that originally is nothing else but text; in other words, it allows us to *quantify* proficiency by giving us a – more or less meaningful – number. Unsurprisingly, then, the MLU is a *quantitative* measure.

Put briefly, *qualitative* research is concerned with structures and patterns, and *how* something is; *quantitative* research, however, focuses on *how much* or *how many* there is/are of a particular characteristic or item. The great advantage of quantitative research is that it enables us to compare relatively large numbers of things/people by using a comparatively easy index. For example, when marking student essays, a lecturer will first look at the content, the structure and coherence of the argument, and the presentation, that is, analyse it qualitatively, but will ultimately translate this into a mark (i.e. a number), which allows us to compare two or more students with each other: a student gaining a 61% did better than a student achieving a 57%, because 61 is larger than 57 – we do not need to look at the essays *per se* once we have the numerical, quantitative value indicating their quality. Quantitative data can be analysed using statistical methods, that is, particular mathematics tools which allow us to work with numerical data.

There is another fundamental difference between qualitative and quantitative studies. Qualitative studies are, by their very nature, *inductive*: theory is derived from the results of our research. A concrete example: Rampton (1995) in his study on linguistic 'crossing' was interested in how South Asian adolescents growing up in the United Kingdom use code-switching between English and Punjabi to indicate their social and ethnic identity. Using interview data from interaction between teenagers of South Asian descent, he identified particular patterns behind code-switches, and was able to infer what the underlying 'rules' with regard to use of a particular language and construction of identity were; as such, he used an *inductive qualitative* approach: theory was derived from (textual) data.[2]

Quantitative research, however, is *deductive*: based on already known theory we develop hypotheses, which we then try to prove (or disprove) in the course of our empirical investigation. *Hypotheses* are statements about the potential and/or suggested relationship between at least two variables, such as 'the older a learner, the less swear words they use' (two variables) or 'age and gender influence language use' (three variables). A hypothesis *must* be proven right or wrong, and hence, it is important for it to be well defined. In particular, hypotheses must be *falsifiable* and not be *tautological*: the hypothesis 'age can either influence a person's language use or not' is tautological – independent from our findings, it will always be true. A good hypothesis, however, *must* have the potential of being wrong. For a detailed discussion of hypotheses (and laws, and how they can be combined to form theories), see Scott and Marshall (2005).

A typical example is the age of acquisition onset debate in second language acquisition research. Based on a now substantial body of previous research (see, for example, Birdsong and Molis, 2001; Johnson and Newport, 1991), we can develop a particular hypothesis, such as 'second language learning becomes more difficult the older a learner is'. In a quantitative approach, we use these hypotheses and develop a methodology which enables us to support – ideally to prove – their correctness or incorrectness. In the example, this is usually done by finding adequate numerical measures for language proficiency, whereby a high value indicates high proficiency. Age, by its very nature, is already a numerical value, so, using appropriate statistical methods we can compare how the two sets of values – proficiency and age – are related, allowing us to draw a conclusion about the relationship between these two factors and to prove our hypothesis right or wrong: if the age values go up while the proficiency values decrease, there is some evidence that our hypothesis 'the older the learner the more difficult it is to learn a second language' is true.

Talking about quantitative methods inevitably means talking about *variables*, and it is worth defining what exactly variables and other crucial concepts in quantitative research really are – particularly since misconceptions of these terms may lead to serious problems during any quantitative study. The *Oxford English Dictionary* (*OED*) defines *variable* (noun) as

> Something which is liable to vary or change; a changeable factor, feature, or element.

In slightly different words, a variable is a feature of a particular *case*, and a particular case can take one of a set of possible features. An example: a frequent variable in linguistics (and other social and psychological sciences) is gender. Gender is a variable which, with human beings, can have two possible values: male or female. Now imagine we are standing in front of a class with 20 students and we are trying to find out how many women and how many men we have in the class: in this example, we have 20 *cases*, that is, 20 'items' for which we have to assign a particular value for the variable 'gender'. Now comes the important part: every case can only take *one* value (or 'outcome') for the particular variable, that is, any one student in our class can only be *either* male *or* female, but cannot be both at the same time.[3]

The attribution of a particular variable outcome – male or female – to a particular case is made by means of *measurement*: we assign a variable value to a particular case using *predefined criteria*. And here is the crux of the matter: how exactly do we define these criteria? Let's assume that, when assigning gender, we only take into account certain physical features of a person, and based on our experience and preconceptions, we come up with the following three criteria for our two gender categories:

Female	Male
Long hair	Short hair
No facial hair	Facial hair
Wears make-up	Does not wear make-up

Two problems should immediately strike us: First, how exactly do we define 'long hair' and 'short hair'? In other words, we again need certain predefined criteria for our defining criteria. Second, what about men who have long hair, are clean shaven and wear make-up? Or women with short hair who do not wear make-up? Inevitably, our criteria will fail to assign the correct gender value; that is, by using our three criteria we cannot accurately measure gender. We would probably have to use other, more biologically founded ones (admittedly rather difficult in a classroom setting).

This rather daft example illustrates one of the most important aspects of quantitative research (and indeed all research): whenever we want to quantitatively measure something, that is, assign a variable value to a particular case, we need to thoroughly think about a reliable way to make this decision. We need a set of clear and objective definitions for each category or outcome. Moreover, our measure should be designed in such a way that it comprises as many cases as possible. For example, for human beings it is usually sufficient to define two values for the variable 'gender', however, in the animal kingdom, and especially with some invertebrates, 'male' and 'female' might be categories which are just not up to the job, as organisms such as worms or sponges are hermaphrodites, that is, have *both* male and female characteristics. So which category to put them into, bearing in mind that any one variable can only have one outcome for any one case?

Let's think about a more linguistic example. Traditionally, dialectology, and later sociolinguistics, has looked at the presence, absence, or different realization of certain linguistic features, often in the area of phonetics and phonology, but also in morphosyntax. Milroy in her well-known Belfast study (1987), for example, has looked at, among many other things, how the realization of the vowel /e/ in different linguistic environments, particularly the merge of the /e/ as in *peck* with /æ/ as in *pack* into homophones, relates to the degree of a speaker's inclusion into the social network, with a high frequency of non-standard /æ/ in both contexts indicating a higher degree of inclusion (1987). To cut a long story short, at the very end it comes down to *measuring* (in this case, count) the number of different realizations of the vowels: how often does /e/ occur in words such as *peck*, and how often is /e/ replaced by /æ/ making it homophone to *pack*. Anyone vaguely familiar with phonology will know that this can be difficult at times, and it is important to establish a clear set of rules as to what constitutes an /e/ and what counts as an /æ/. Depending on the level of detail needed, we may have to go as far as a proper acoustic analysis using specialist equipment and software to find out the exact physical properties of a sound and base our decision on this. We may say, anything up to x Hertz counts as an /e/ and everything below as an /æ/. This procedure that leads to the 'translation' of (physical) properties of a case into a numerical value is known as *operationalization*.[4]

Once we have established our measure and have operationalized it, we must not ever change it in the course of our study, as this will distort the results. For example, most of us have a rather good idea of how long an inch is, so if someone tells us that an object is about 2 inches wide, we implicitly know its width. However, this only works because an inch *always* refers to the same amount of length (namely around 25 millimetres). Imagine someone would arbitrarily change 1 inch to 45 millimetres – how could we possibly make any reliable statements about an object whose width is 2 inches if we do not exactly know what an inch refers to?

Closely related to the issue of measurement are the concepts of *reliability* and *validity*. *Reliability* refers to our measure repeatedly delivering the same (or near same) results. Ideally, if we use the same measure with the same people under the same conditions, our measure should give us the same result. In basic chemistry, this works well: if we add exactly the same amount of chemical A to exactly the same amount of chemical B, with external conditions such as temperature being identical, we should reliably get chemical C. Working with human beings is more difficult. For a start, external factors are notoriously difficult to keep constant. Also, people learn from experience, so if we run the same test with the same people again and again, they will – eventually – improve just through experience. A common way of checking reliability, the *test-retest method*, is hence problematic. A quick and easy solution to check a measure's reliability is the *'split-half' method* (see, for example, Schnell et al., 2005: 152): we take a group of people, measure whatever we like to measure, then randomly split the group into two smaller groups and compare the results. If the measure is reliable, we should get very similar results for both subgroups. If we get substantially different results, we should become very cautious and investigate the reliability a bit further, through re-tests (with other people!) or by adjusting the measure.

   Validity, however, can be more problematic. It refers to our measure actually measuring what it is supposed to measure. Hence it is also known as *measurement validity* or *instrument validity* (Bernard, 2006: 38).[5] Validity is often an important issue when using questionnaires – as discussed in section 3 of this chapter – and in particular when we measure abstract concepts such as attitudes. There are several sophisticated mathematical procedures for checking a measure's validity, all of which go beyond the scope of this chapter; Bryman (2004) and Scott and Marshall (2005) provide good overviews on these issues, while authors such as Allen and Yen (1979/2001) or Kaplan (2004) discuss the mathematical intricacies of measures such as 'Cronbach's Alpha' – a mathematical approach to determining reliability. The easiest, but only to a certain extent reliable, way to insure validity is to use common sense: if we get significantly different results from previous research, under very similar circumstances, we should carefully look at our method before we get too enthusiastic about our results. We will return to the issue of validity in section 3.

3.3 Research designs

In the previous section we have looked in some detail at variables and measurement, and have outlined some basic definitions. Assume we would like to investigate the impact of corrective feedback given by a caregiver on 2-year-old children's first language acquisition. Based on previous research, we have a clear hypothesis in mind: 'The more corrective feedback children receive, the quicker they progress' – bear in mind we are working deductively, so we already have the theory. Let's also assume we have a set of well-working methods to measure both the amount of feedback and language development; both are quantitative measures so we can later process our results statistically, trying to prove or disprove our hypothesis. What we need to do now is to think about the actual *structure* of how we go about our study, in other words, we have to consider the *research design*.

The research design is best understood as a framework or scaffold around which we organize our study, but it does not refer to the actual tools we use to carry out our research (questionnaires, recordings, etc.). In other words, not only do we need a set of tools to get our data, we also need to think about a coherent and solid framework around which we organize our data collection. For example, we might have a well-working questionnaire (which we have used before, and which we know is reliable and valid) and a brand-new digital recording device. However, we need to think carefully about how, when, in which order, and who with (in terms of sample) we deploy them. If we just randomly record people and ask them to complete the questionnaire, what we will get is a pile of data (good!) but certainly not the kind of data we want and need in order to answer our research questions (bad!).

It should not take too long to see that research design, theoretical background and actual methods used are inseparably linked and form the overall framework for our study, hence it is crucial that these three parts work well together. We can imagine research designs to be designed either along the dimension 'time' or the dimension 'cases', and we will discuss the different types in each dimension in what follows.

Research designs frequently used in linguistics, psychology and other social sciences are *cross-sectional designs*: we collect a comparatively large amount of data at one point in time, hence obtaining a snapshot of the status quo. In our example, in order to establish the impact of feedback on 2-year-old children, we would measure both proficiency and feedback for a group of, for example, a hundred 2-year-old children, and, using statistical methods, look at how the two variables are related. This would provide us with a cross-sectional view or 'snapshot' of the relationship between proficiency and feedback.

Longitudinal studies, however, are based on the *repeated collection* of data over a longer period of time, hence enabling us to observe any changes in variables which may occur over time. We may, for example, take a 12-month-old child and, over a period of two years, that is until age 3, assess both its proficiency and the extent of feedback in regular intervals by testing it every six months. In this example, we get data at five points in the child's life: at 12, 18, 24, 30 and 36 months of age, which will enable us to trace the child's development – something we cannot do using a cross-sectional design with only one data collection.

Longitudinal designs come in two types: *panel designs* use a sample randomly drawn from the population, and data is taken repeatedly from the members of the panel. *Cohort designs* are slightly different, in that the members of the cohort share certain – often temporal – characteristics. For example, we may be interested in the change of attitude towards the use of taboo words over time (hypothesis: older people are more critical towards taboo words than younger ones). In a panel design, we randomly select 100 people from the population, both male and female, from all socioeconomic backgrounds and all age groups. In a cohort design, we may select a particular cohort, such as 100 ethnically white adolescents between the age of 15 and 17, and we observe them for let's say five years. According to Bryman (2004), the crucial difference between panel and cohort designs is that while panel designs allow us to observe both cohort and aging effects, cohort studies can only identify aging effects, hence allowing us to control for third variables. In our taboo word example, we may only be able to observe that with increasing age, tolerance towards taboo terms decreases, but with a heterogeneous group we cannot account for exactly what is responsible for this change. With a cohort design as outlined, we can more accurately pin down age as a major factor contributing to the change in attitudes.

The biggest advantage of longitudinal designs – the ability to observe change in real time – is also its biggest disadvantage: if we want to observe a group of people over a prolonged period, we must make sure that these people are available for observation over the entire period; in other words, we have to consider the difficulty of *sample retention*. Another problem is resources: repeated observations and/or testing cost time and money, both of which are increasingly unavailable in research. An elegant way to circumvent problems related to longitudinal designs is to simulate them. In particular, in Labovian sociolinguistics, this is known as *real time* and *apparent time studies*. Bayley (2004) explains that we can design a cross-sectional (or synchronic) study in such a way that we can infer, to some extent, diachronic, that is longitudinal, development. For example, Woods (2000) in her study on sound changes in New Zealand, collected data from three generations of one family at (more or less) the same time (the 'real time'), and was able to use generational differences to 'simulate' time and make inferences about longitudinal change (the 'apparent time').

An entirely different approach to research design is to look at it not from a temporal point of view (like the designs discussed above), but to consider *how* data is collected. In particular in sociolinguistic research – longitudinal or cross-sectional – language is observed in its natural environment, that is, when it is used by its speakers, and the data we obtain is 'natural', spontaneous speech. In technical terms, this way of collecting data does not allow us to manipulate the variables we are interested in: we might be interested in whether a particular speech community shows a particular linguistic feature, but through observation we can only observe – not manipulate how frequently members of this community actually use this feature. This is where *experimental designs* come into play. In experimental designs, we as researchers deliberately and explicitly manipulate the variables in order to prove/disprove our hypothesis. In addition, experiments usually comprise two groups of participants: the *experimental group* (EG), that is, the group that is undergoing the 'treatment' or stimulus, and the *control group* (CG), which is unaffected by the stimulus. Li (1988) analysed the impact of interaction on second language learners' comprehension using a pre-/post-test set-up based on three groups: an EG 1, receiving premodified input, but no interaction; an EG 2, receiving interaction but no premodified input, and a CG receiving neither. A pretest showed that there were no significant differences between the three groups. After the introduction of the different stimuli, though, Li observed changes in comprehension in the two EGs, but less so in the CG, as illustrated in Table 3.1.

Li's study is interesting as it combines two types of experimental set-ups in one: it is a *within-subject design*, as it compares members of a group (e.g. EG 1) in two situations, namely pre- and post-stimulus, but is also a *between-subject design* as he compares several groups with each other. A 'pure' within-subject design tests only one group of people twice (pre-/post-stimulus), while a pure between-subject design compares EG and CG once. Both within- and between-subject designs have advantages and disadvantages. Probably the most problematic issue about within-subject designs is the fact that repeated testing of the same group can lead to participants' performance changing through

Table 3.1 Experimental pre-/post-test set-up with three groups

Step 1	Step 2	Step 3	Step 4	Step 5	Step 6
EG 1	P	EG 1 =	Stimulus 1	P	EG 1 ≠
	R			O	
	E			S	
EG 2	T	EG 2 =	Stimulus 2	I	EG 2 ≠
	E			-	
	S			T	
	T			E	
CG		CG	No Stimulus	S	CG
				T	

experience with the task, boredom or fatigue. Between-subject designs are arguably more difficult to control for other factors, as they only produce reliable results when both groups are very equal in terms of their characteristics (e.g. age, gender, linguistic proficiency). A careful consideration of the research question and other factors (resources being increasingly one of them) is hence essential for the choice of experiment type.

3.4 Panacea questionnaires: Design, use and abuse

There are probably as many different methodological tools for collecting quantitative data as there are research projects. We test, record and measure, trying to come to meaningful answers for our research questions; and as every undergraduate student is told in their first year at university, these methods need to be carefully adapted to provide us with the data we require. One method (or rather type of method) which is frequently used for collecting data across most linguistic subdisciplines are questionnaires. Questionnaires are frequently used to measure people's attitudes to and perception of languages (or variations of particular languages, such as dialects and accents) or groups of speakers. Prominent examples for the effective (and extensive!) use of questionnaires include studies surrounding the concept of 'ethnolinguistic vitality' (see, *inter alia*, Bourhis et al., 1981; Giles et al., 1977), or investigations into language use and choice (e.g. Extra and Yagmur, 2004; Rasinger, 2007).

In this final section, we will have a closer look at the issues surrounding the use of questionnaires in quantitative research, highlighting design, advantages and pitfalls. This section is best read in conjunction with Chapter 4 (following in this volume), which discusses the processing and analysing of data generated by questionnaires.

Let's start with having a look at one of the major benefits of questionnaires: they can, potentially, generate a large amount of data which is comparatively simple to process. While interviews are time-consuming to conduct and transcribe, and the coding of qualitative data is sometimes difficult, questionnaires, with their neat tick-boxes, seem like a blessing. Unfortunately, it is not that easy. Questionnaires must be perfect *before* we distribute them: we must be confident that they work well and that they reliably generate valid data. A questionnaire that is in the hand of respondents cannot be changed – it either works, or it does not. Questionnaire design is a complex area and a detailed discussion goes far beyond the scope of this chapter (or even this book), so we will focus on some of the core aspects.

A common problem, especially for student researchers, is the number of questions a questionnaire should include. As a general guideline, a questionnaire should include exactly the number of question it needs to investigate a particular issue validly and reliably – no more, no less. Before we start writing our questionnaire, then, we should therefore ask ourselves the following two questions:

1. What data do I want my questionnaire to give me, that is, which of my research questions should it answer?
2. Which questions do aim at answering my research questions?

Less experienced researchers will stumble across the first question – very often, research questions are too vague and need to be defined more clearly (see also Chapter 1). But even for the most experienced of us, the second question can pose a major problem. How do I phrase my questions so they address *exactly* the issues I want to investigate? Here, we will focus on a few guidelines that can help us to solve this problem.

Ask what you need to know A common problem is questions that have been, quite simply, badly phrased and do not address the actual issue. For example, a student of mine is looking at the impact of learners' motivation on their L2 English development. As one of the key questions in a questionnaire, she planned to ask a group of teachers:

'Do you think the students are interested in learning English?'

On the surface, this might do the job. It allows for a yes/no answer, and she could eventually count the instances of 'yes' and 'no' answers to draw whatever conclusions she wants to draw. However, on second sight, the question does not actually give us any useful information, just because all we get is either a 'yes' or a 'no'. Even worse, the respondents might be unable to answer the question as such because the available answer options are too general. What we would *really* like to know is not only *whether* students are interested in a subject or not, but to what *extent* they are interested in it. And hence, the question needs to be rephrased accordingly:

'To what extent do you think your students are interested in learning English?'

With questions like this one, questionnaires usually give their participants a range of available answer options, usually in the form of a *scale* or a *semantic differential*: respondents can indicate their answer on a numerical scale (where a higher number signals higher agreement) or on a scale between two opposing terms:

> 'On a scale from 1 to 5, whereby 5 indicates "very interested" and 1 indicates "not interested at all", to what extent do you think your students are interested in learning English? Please circle your answer'
>   1   2   3   4   5

This time, the question includes two types of information: whether teachers think students are interested or not – replacing the former 'yes'/'no' option – but also the extent to which their teachers think they are interested.

A related concept is *Likert scales*, where respondents indicate their agreement or disagreement to a particular statement on a scale. For example, we may want to measure how satisfied first year linguistic students are with their choice of academic discipline. We produce a set of three questions, based on 5-point Likert scales.

> 'Please indicate how strongly you agree or disagree with the following statements on a scale from 1 to 5, with 1 meaning "strongly disagree" and 5 meaning "strongly agree". Please circle your answer'
> (1) I could not live without linguistics.   [1] [2] [3] [4] [5]
> (2) Linguistics is the only passion in my life.   [1] [2] [3] [4] [5]
> (3) Linguistics has changed the way I see the world.   [1] [2] [3] [4] [5]

It may take some time to getting used to phrasing questions in such a way that they give you exactly the kind of information you need, and this presupposes that you yourself are absolutely certain what kind of information you actually want – is the question you want to ask worth asking, and how can you phrase it to get the most information out of it? All too often we do not think about this thoroughly enough.

Ask comprehensive and 'objective' questions Related to this issue is the fact that we as researchers are 'experts' in the field we are investigating,[6] however most of our respondents are usually not. Hence, we should avoid using any technical terminology or jargon as there is a substantial risk that respondents do not understand them.

A common misconception is that a questionnaire should be designed is such a way that it gives you the answers that fit your hypothesis and argument best. Sometimes questions are phrased in such a way that they imply a particular answer; other questionnaires avoid questions which bear the potential of eliciting an 'unwanted' response altogether. However, questionnaires are nothing but scientific tools that help us to measure different aspects of 'reality' – very similar to a voltmeter measuring an electric potential. And as such, it must measure *neutrally* and *objectively*. That means that questions should avoid as much as possible being biased or leading; in other words, they should not be phrased in such a way that they imply the 'correct' answer – quite simply because there is no 'correct' answer *per se*. Typical (and rather extreme) examples of leading questions take the form of 'Don't you think that . . .?', or include semantically strongly loaded terms which are best avoided, for example, 'good'/'bad' and their synonyms, 'ugly', 'stupid' or 'unnecessary' (see also Litosseliti, 2003). Try this: Compile a list of adjectives and adverbs and test how different people react to them – you will be surprised by the differences in reaction you receive.

Open versus closed questions and multiple item responses We could have an endless debate about what is better: open questions, which allow respondents to write down their answers in their own words, or closed questions which provide respondents with a set of possible answers to tick from. From a quantitative point of view, the latter is preferable as they are just easier to process. Similar to the phrasing of questions, we have to take great care in designing our answer options. Since respondents cannot give an answer in their own words, we must provide them with a set of *all* possible (and/or relevant) answers in order to get an accurate picture. Hence, especially with large-scale studies, researchers often conduct prestudies with interviews or focus groups (see, for example, Litosseliti, 2003 for an overview; and Harris, 2006, and Spotti, 2008, for examples) to see what potential issues/answers a particular topic raises.

When designing answer options, especially scales or semantic differentials of the 'agree/disagree' type, we also have to be aware of what is known as *response sets* and *acquiescence responses* (see Johnson et al., 2005, or Ping, 2005). The former refers to some people's tendency to go for a particular direction of the scale, for example, 'agree', *independent* from what they might actually think. The latter is the phenomenon whereby respondents give the answer which they *think* is the 'correct' one – it is particularly frequent with questionnaires dealing with socially delicate issues where political correctness or constructing a particular version of self may override true thoughts or genuine beliefs. Too many response set and acquiescence responders may have a negative impact on your questionnaires' validity. Thus, it is important to phrase both questions and answer options carefully. In Rasinger (2008) I discuss question and answer designs which avoid response sets in more detail.

Before we can move on and analyse our data – Erez Levon will guide you through this in the next chapter – we need to go through a final step: the coding of the questionnaire. So far, our questionnaire consists of nothing more than ticked (and unticked) boxes and a few numbers (for respondents' age, for example) or possibly individual words or short phrases (in open-ended questions where respondents are asked to write down their answer). The use of computer software for coding will be extremely useful at this stage. I discuss the coding of questionnaires with specific reference to analysing data using the Microsoft Excel software[7] in detail in Rasinger (2008), so will limit the explanations here to the basics.

Essentially, in order to enable a computer-assisted analysis, we need to 'translate' all variable outcomes in our questionnaire into a neat set of numbers. If the variable is already a number, we do not need to do anything but can transfer this straight into our programme. For example, if a respondent's age is 25 (years), then we can input 25 without any 'translation'. It becomes slightly trickier when we have a question regarding gender (or sex) and provide respondents with two tick-boxes: one for male, and one for female. Because some statistical software is unable to deal with text, we may need to translate our answer options into numbers. A common way of coding sex is to assign the number '1' to 'male' and the number '2' to 'female' (or vice versa). Depending on whether a respondent is a woman or a man, we can then input '2' or '1' respectively, into our software. In theory, for this type of categorical data (see Chapter 4), we can allocate any two different numbers (such as '23' for 'female' and '88' for 'male'), but it makes sense to keep it simple and logical.

Imagine the respondent whose questionnaire we are inputting right now is John, who was born in 1980 and is 28 years old. The data matrix for John would hence look like Table 3.2; apart from the respondent identifier (first column), all data is in numbers. Note that we have coded 'male' as '1'.

Table 3.2 Fictive data matrix

Respondent	Sex	DOB	Age
John*	1	1980	28

*In real life it is good practice, if not a legal requirement, to use pseudonyms or abbreviations so as to ensure respondents' anonymity.

The coding of all other variables works analogically: every potential variable value is assigned a particular numerical value (i.e. a number). If, for example, we have a Likert scale with the options strongly agree, agree, neutral, disagree, strongly disagree, we would assign numbers from 1 to 5 (or any other sequence of numbers that logically reflects the hierarchical order of answers) to each value (although we may want to inverse the order):

Strongly agree	Agree	'Neutral'	Disagree	Strongly disagree
5	4	3	2	1

A final example, based on our discussions of Likert scales (see above) and questionnaire coding: Susan is a 19-year-old linguistics student, who could hardly live without linguistics (variable NOLIFE), which is her one and only passion in life (PASSION); the respondent has, in fact, dramatically changed the way she sees the world (VIEW). Her data matrix would look like Table 3.3.

3.5 Summary

In this chapter, I have tried to outline some of the very basic concepts and ideas of quantitative research. You as a reader should now have an overview of the differences between qualitative and quantitative research (and be aware of the problems and overlaps this dichotomy may bear), and should be familiar with the key terms and frameworks and general approaches to doing quantitative research. The second part of this chapter has focused on questionnaires, a method widely used (and possibly overused) in many linguistic subdisciplines, trying to highlight the advantages and disadvantages of using questionnaires as tools for data collection and giving advice on the design and processing of questionnaire-based data. If you had been following this chapter in parallel to carrying out an actual quantitative study, you would now be sitting in front of your PC, with coded questionnaire data waiting to be analysed. This is where I stop. In the following chapter, Erez Levon will explain how to make

Table 3.3 Data matrix

Respondent	Sex	DOB	Age	NOLIFE	PASSION	VIEW
Susan	2	1989	19	4	5	5

our data 'talk', that is, how to perform a quantitative analysis that enables us to answer our research questions and prove our hypotheses.

Notes

1. This example is obviously greatly simplified.
2. Nowadays it is difficult to argue that there is no theory whatsoever on any one research topic. However, qualitative research is not aimed at *proving* theories.
3. For the sake of illustration, I refrain from discussing biological borderline cases.
4. Bernard (2006) provides a good overview of operationalization and operational definitions.
5. There are other, even more complicated forms of validity which we shall ignore here.
6. I deliberately put the terms 'experts', 'objective/ly', 'reality' and 'neutral/ly' in inverted commas, as all of them are inherently problematic: can anything involving a human mind ever be fully unbiased? Cameron et al. (1992) provide an interesting discussion of this issue.
7. Field (2005) provides an excellent introduction into analysing data using SPSS.

Further reading

Bayley (2004) – This chapter thoroughly discusses real- and apparent time research designs in the context of language change and linguistic development.

Bryman (2004) – An introductory textbook geared towards the social sciences, which provides a comprehensible starting-point for all aspects related to quantitative and qualitative research.

Fowler (2002) – A comprehensible introduction to survey-based research with a discussion of various techniques available.

Rasinger (2008) – This book focuses explicitly on quantitative analysis in linguistics.

References

Allen, M. J. and Yen, W. M. (1979/2001), *Introduction to Measurement Theory*. Long Grove: Waveland.

Bates, E., Dale, P. S. and Thal, D. J. (1995), 'Individual differences and their implications for theories of language development', in B. M. Whinney (ed.), *The Handbook of Child Language*. Oxford: Blackwell, pp. 96–151.

Bayley, G. (2004), 'Real time and apparent time', in J. K. Chambers, P. Trudgill and N. Schilling-Estes (eds), *Handbook of Language Variation and Change*. Oxford: Blackwell, pp. 312–22.

Bernard, H. R. (2006), *Research Methods in Anthropology: Qualitative and Quantitative approaches*, Walnut Creek: AltaMira.

Birdsong, D. and Molis, M. (2001), 'On the evidence for maturational constraints in second-language acquisition', *Journal of Memory and Language*, 44, 235–49.

Bourhis, R. Y., Giles, H. and Rosenthal, D. (1981), 'Notes on the construction of a subjective ethnolinguistic vitality questionnaire', *Journal of Multilingual and Multicultural Development*, 2, 145–55.

Bryman, A. (2004), *Social Research Methods*. Oxford: Oxford University Press.

Cameron, D., Frazer, E., Harvey, P., Rampton, M. B. H. and Richardson, K. (1992), *Researching Language: Issues of Power and Method*. London: Routledge.

Extra, G. and Yagmur, K. (2004), *Urban Multilingualism in Europe: Immigrant Minority Languages at Home and School*. Clevedon: Multilingual Matters.

Field, A. (2005), *Discovering Statistics Using SPSS*. London: Sage.

Flick, U. (2006), *An Introduction to Qualitative Research*. London: Sage.

Fowler, F. J. (2002), *Survey Research Methods*. London: Sage.

Giles, H., Bourhis, R. Y. and Taylor, D. M. (1977), 'Towards a theory of language in ethnic group relations', in H. Giles (ed.), *Language, Ethnicity and Intergroup Relations*. London: Academic Press, pp. 307–48.

Harris, R. (2006), *New Ethnicities and Language Use*. Basingstoke: Palgrave Macmillan.

Johnson, J. and Newport, E. L. (1991), 'Critical period effects on universal properties of language: the status of subjacency in the acquisition of a second language', *Cognition*, 39, 215–58.

Johnson, T., Kulesa, P., Cho, Y. I. and Shavitt, S. (2005), 'The relation between culture and response styles. Evidence from 19 countries', *Journal of Cross-Cultural Psychology*, 36 (2), 264–77.

Kaplan, D. (2004), *The SAGE Handbook of Quantitative Methodology for the Social Sciences*. London: Sage.

Li, X. (1988), 'Effects of contextual cues on inferring and remembering meanings of New Words', *Applied Linguistics*, 9 (4), 402–13.

Litosseliti, L. (2003), *Using Focus Groups in Research*. London: Continuum.

Milroy, L. (1987), *Language and Social Networks*. Oxford: Blackwell.

Oxford English Dictionary (1989), Second Edition. Online.

Peccei, J. S. (1999), *Child Language* (2nd edn). London: Routledge.

Ping, T. L. (2005), 'Does the survey response scale format matter?', *IMTA – International Military Testing Association*. Singapore.

Rampton, B. (1995), *Crossing: Language and Ethnicity among Adolescents*. London: Longman.

Rasinger, S. M. (2007), *Bengali-English in East London: A Study in Urban Multilingualism*. Oxford: Peter Lang.

—. (2008), *Quantitative Methods in Linguistics: An Introduction*. London: Continuum.

Schnell, R., Hill, P. and Esser, E. (2005), *Methoden der Empirischen Sozialforschung*. Munich: Oldenbourg.

Scott, J. and Marshall, G. (2005). *A Dictionary of Sociology*. Oxford: University Press.

Spotti, M. (2008), 'Ethnolinguistic identity in a Dutch Islamic primary classroom', in T. Omoniyi and G. White (eds), *The Sociolinguistics of Identity*. London: Continuum, pp. 188–200.

Whong-Barr, M. and Schwartz, B. D. (2002), 'Morphological and syntactic transfer in child L2 acquisition of the English dative alternation', *Studies in Second Language Acquisition*, 24, pp. 579–616.

Woods, N. (2000), 'New Zealand English across generations: an analysis of selected vowel and consonant variables', in A. Bell and K. Kuiper (eds), *New Zealand English*. Wellington: Victoria University Press, pp. 84–110.

4 Organizing and Processing Your Data: The Nuts and Bolts of Quantitative Analyses

Erez Levon

Chapter outline

In the previous chapter, you were introduced to the basic principles underlying quantitative research methods. You learned, for example, that quantitative tests employ *deductive* reasoning to examine predetermined *hypotheses*, and that these tests are subject to certain constraints, such as *reliability* and *validity*. In this chapter, we build upon this theoretical base, and discuss some of the concrete issues involved in the quantitative analysis of language. We begin in the first section (section 4.1) with an extended discussion of how to construct hypotheses for quantitative investigation. We also examine the basic concepts required for testing these hypotheses. We then turn, in sections 4.2 and 4.3, to a detailed exposition of two of the most common statistical tests used in linguistics, *chi-square tests* and *t-tests*. You will learn what these tests are, how to use them and what they can (and cannot) tell you. Finally, in section 4.4, we look at how to go about interpreting quantitative results, and discuss some of the ways in which quantitative and qualitative methods can be brought together in linguistic research.

4.1 What quantitative analyses do

Quantitative analyses are all about *counting* something. In the first section of this chapter, we discuss what we mean when we talk about *counting* in an analytical or scientific sense. We then turn, in the remaining sections, to a detailed explanation of how we actually *do* that counting in linguistics research.

In order for something to be counted, two conditions are normally considered to be necessary: (a) what you want to count must itself be 'countable' (i.e. *quantifiable*), and (b) what you want to count must have the potential to be *variable* (i.e. be able to change). Imagine, for example, that you were conducting a poll on which issues most affected voters' choice of candidate in recent parliamentary elections. The condition of quantifiability requires that you *operationalize* the possible set of responses so that they can be counted in a clear and coherent way (see section 3.2). You may, for instance, decide that you will group responses into categories, such as 'environment', 'economy' and 'education', such that you a give a certain structure to the diversity of responses you receive (this is typically called coding). It is this structure that will then allow you to quantitatively analyse the results, by, for example, counting how many responses fall into each of your predetermined categories.

The condition of variability, however, is a more abstract and basic one. It requires, simply, that the possibility of variation exist in your response set. In your poll of voter motivations, this condition is met, since all voters are presumably not motivated by the same things. Now, you may find in conducting your poll that in fact all voters do claim to be motivated by the same issue, the 'environment', for example. This result, however, does not mean that the condition of variability is violated since they *could* have been motivated by other things, and it just so happens that they are all motivated by the same thing. The condition of variability is therefore a requirement about the *possible* existence of variation, and does not mean that variation will actually be found.

Because of this variability requirement, the things that we count in quantitative analyses are called *variables*. Let's take another example. Say we are interested in the colour of shoes people buy in a certain shop. The first thing we need to ask ourselves is whether this variable (shoe colour) is quantifiable. The answer is straightforwardly 'yes'. The second thing we need to ask ourselves is whether this variable is in fact variable. Once again, the answer is straightforwardly 'yes' (i.e. the possibility exists that not everyone will buy shoes of the same colour). With these two conditions met, we can proceed to quantitative analysis. Obviously, the first step is actually conducting the research. So, let's say that we spend a week in the shop noting down what colour shoes every customer buys. There are three shoe colour options: black, brown and red. We therefore have three options for the shoe colour variable. In addition, imagine we are also interested in gathering additional information about the customers, for example, whether or not they are wearing earrings. We can create two categories of customers, those with earrings and those without, and note the different colour shoes that each category of customers purchases.

After seven days of collecting data, we turn to the quantitative analyses. In terms of these analyses, we have several options. We may decide that we want to simply *describe* the situation in the shoe shop. To do so, we use what are called *descriptive statistics* (e.g. Sternstein, 1994). Descriptive statistics are indices that give information about the general shape or quality of the data, and include such things as the *mean* (i.e. average) and the *median* (i.e. middle) of the data. Using descriptive statistics, we could, for example, calculate the median number of black shoes purchased per day in the shop. Or, we could decide to analyse the data in more detail and calculate the mean number(s) of red shoes purchased per day by customers with and without earrings, respectively. What these calculations allow us to do is identify *potential* patterns in our data set. Say in calculating the mean number of red shoes purchased per day, we find that customers without earrings bought on average three times more pairs of red shoes per day (24 pairs) than customers with earrings did (8 pairs). We therefore seem to have identified a pattern in which customers without earrings buy more red shoes than customers with earrings do. However, we are *unable* to make this kind of claim based solely on the descriptive statistics. In other words, we cannot know at this point whether what appears to be a pattern really is one, or is just a product of chance. In order to try and determine whether there really is some meaningful correlation between red shoe buying and wearing earrings, we must turn to a different kind of statistical analysis, what is called *inferential statistics*.

Inferential statistics are designed to determine whether apparent patterns in a data set really are patterns – whether they are what we call *statistically significant*. It might be the case, for example, that the apparent pattern of people without earrings buying more red shoes than people with earrings is the result of the simple fact that there are more customers overall without earrings than customer with earrings. This would mean that the correlation between not wearing earrings and buying red shoes could simply be an artefact of the subject population of our study. Inferential statistics can test this possibility, and make predictions about the validity of the patterns observed. In other words, descriptive statistics allow us to define patterns in the data. Inferential statistics then allow us to determine whether those patterns truly exist in some kind of meaningful way.

In order to conduct inferential statistical analysis, we must first come up with a *hypothesis* (i.e. an educated guess) to be tested. This hypothesis is called the *experimental hypothesis*, and is normally derived from the patterns identified by the descriptive statistics. An experimental hypothesis always takes the form of a statement that a certain variable (e.g. number of red shoes purchased) is affected in a predictable and systematic way by some other variable (e.g. wearing earrings). In this scenario, the variable that gets affected is called the *dependent* variable, that is, it *depends* on something else. The thing (or things) that the dependent variable depends on is (are) called the *independent* variable(s). As a general rule, experimental hypotheses make the claim that a relationship exists between a dependent variable and one or more independent variables, such that the independent variable(s) affect the dependent variable in some predictable way. In the current example, then, the experimental hypothesis would be that buying red shoes (dependent variable) is in some predictable way affected by whether or not the buyer wears earrings (independent variable).

Experimental hypotheses never exist alone, but are instead always paired up with their polar opposite, what we call the *null hypothesis*. Null hypotheses are in a sense the counter-claim of experimental hypotheses; null hypothesis predict that *no* relationship exists between the dependent and independent variables. For our example, then, the null hypothesis would be that there is no relationship between red shoe buying and wearing earrings. Interestingly, in quantitative analyses, we always test the *null* hypothesis, not the experimental one. In other words, we examine whether there seems to be *no* relationship at all between our dependent and independent variables. If through our analyses of the null hypothesis, we determine that there is *not no* relationship (note the double negative), then we can claim that a relationship between the dependent and independent variable(s) does seem to exist (i.e. that the experimental hypothesis may be true).

You will notice that I state that the best our analyses can do is tell us that the experimental hypothesis *may* be true, not that it necessarily *is* true. This is because inferential statistics provide a *probabilistic* measure – that is, they measure the *likelihood* that the null hypothesis is true. This 'likelihood' is expressed by a probability figure (abbreviated as 'p = X', where 'X' is some percentage). The easiest way to think about this p-value is as a measure of 'percent-sure'. So, for example, a statistical test can be 99% sure that the null hypothesis is true and that no relationship exists between the dependent and independent variable(s); we would write this 'percent-sure' figure as 'p = 0.99'. Or, a statistical test can be only 1% sure that the null hypothesis is true; this time, our 'p-value' would be 'p = 0.01'. As a convention in the humanities and social sciences, we take 5% sure that the null hypothesis is true ($p = 0.05$) as a cut-off point. Greater than 5% sure ($p > 0.05$), we cannot reject the null hypothesis; less than or equal to 5% sure ($p \leq 0.05$), we reject the null hypothesis. Since the null and experimental hypotheses are two sides of the same coin, when we *reject* the null hypothesis, we conversely are able to *support* the experimental hypothesis. In this situation, we claim that the quantitative analysis was statistically significant. What this significance means is that we are less than 5% sure that the null hypothesis is true, and thus at least 95% sure that a relationship does in fact exist between our dependent and independent variable(s).

Up until now, we have been discussing the theoretical concepts underlying quantitative analysis in somewhat abstract terms. In the next two sections, we will illustrate these concepts with concrete linguistic examples, and see how experimental and null hypotheses work in action. Before we get to that, however, make sure that you have a good grasp of the basic schematic structure of quantitative analyses, summarized as follows:

- We identify the variable of interest (dependent variable)
- We use descriptive statistics to get ideas about potential patterns in the data
- These patterns then help us to devise experimental and null hypotheses
- We then use inferential statistics to test the null hypothesis
- If these inferential statistics return a p-value less than or equal to 0.05, then we have statistical significance and can reject the null hypothesis
- If the p-value is greater than 0.05, then the null hypothesis cannot be rejected and we are unable to support the claims made by the experimental hypothesis.

4.2 What quantitative method to use

There are hundreds of different inferential statistical tests than can be used in quantitative analyses. The choice of which test to use depends primarily on the kind and number of variables in your data set, and the sorts of relationships that exist between the variables you consider. In this section, we briefly go over some of the basic concepts involved in choosing an appropriate statistical test, before turning to a more detailed examination of two of the more commonly used tests.

In general, we distinguish between two basic kinds of variables: *categorical* variables and *continuous* variables. Categorical variables are those variables whose values can be easily separated into discrete categories. In our example from above, shoe colour purchased is a categorical variable since we can group the choices available (black *or* brown *or* red) into distinct, non-overlapping groups. Similarly, whether or not a customer is wearing earrings is also a categorical variable. Categorical variables are common in linguistics, especially when studying phenomena such as allophony (e.g. alveolar *or* dental realization of /t/) and allomorphy (e.g. presence *or* absence of third-person singular verb marking in English). Continuous variables, however, cannot be easily classified into categories this way. Rather, they are variables whose values exist on a mathematical scale. A canonical example of a continuous variable is age, where one variable value (e.g. 36) is straightforwardly larger than another (e.g. 24) and smaller than a third (e.g. 45). The difference between these values is also mathematically meaningful. We can say, for example, that someone who is 36 years old is closer in age to someone who is 45 (e.g. 9 years difference) than she is to someone who is 24 (e.g. 12 years difference). Now, we obviously can create categories for continuous variables like age, deciding, for example, to label 0–24 years old as 'young', 25–60 years old as 'middle' and 60+ years old as 'old'. Yet, these categories are in a certain sense arbitrary, and are not a part of the age measurement itself. Rather, what we are doing in creating age categories is transforming a continuous variable into a categorical one (see Rasinger's discussion in section 3.2). In linguistic research, we also often analyse continuous variables, whether in terms of various social aspects (e.g. income) or linguistic ones (e.g. vowel formants, utterance length).

Different statistical tests are used depending on whether the variables you are examining (both independent and dependent) are continuous or categorical. For the sake of simplicity, in this chapter we will only consider cases where the independent variables are categorical. Statistical tests exist for examining continuous independent variables (e.g. correlation analyses) or for examining a combination of continuous and categorical independent variables (e.g. Generalized Linear Models, Linear Mixed Models); these tests, however, go beyond the scope of what we are able to do here (see, for example, McCullagh and Nelder, 1989). In addition, we will also only consider cases that involve *one* dependent variable and *one* independent variable. Again, tests exist for examining multiple independent and dependent variables (e.g. ANOVAs, MANOVAs, Linear Regressions – see Bryman and Cramer, 2008), but these tests require a more advanced explanation than we can provide here. We will therefore restrict our discussion to situations in which there is *one* independent variable and *one* dependent variable and the independent variable is *categorical*. In situations of this kind, two possibilities arise: (a) the dependent variable can be categorical or (b) the dependent variable can be continuous. When the dependent variable is categorical, the statistical test we use is called a *chi-square test* (sometimes abbreviated as χ^2). When the dependent variable is continuous, the statistical test we use is called a *t-test*.

Chi-square tests examine the distribution of data across the categories of our analysis. The goal of chi-squares is to determine whether the proportional distribution we observe in our sample population (e.g. X% of values in one category, Y% of values in another) is significantly different from the distribution we would expect to find in any population of the same size and shape. In other words, chi-square tests calculate what the distribution of variable values would be if the null hypothesis were true for our sample. They then compare this 'null' distribution to the distribution that we actually found in collecting our data, and determine whether the two are significantly different from one another. So recall our fictitious example from above, where people without earrings bought three times as many red shoes per day as people with earrings. A chi-square test would be able to tell us whether this descriptive difference is in fact a significant one (i.e. the experimental hypothesis) or is instead just a result of the fact, for example, that three times as many people came into the shop without earrings than did with earrings (i.e. the null hypothesis). In the next section, we will go through linguistic examples of chi-square tests in detail and you will learn how to perform the mathematical calculations required for these tests.

Because they compare proportional distributions across *categories*, chi-square tests cannot be used to examine data from continuous variables where no *a priori* categories exist. Instead, when dependent variables are continuous we examine them through the use of t-tests. In order to understand what t-tests actually do, we must first think about what the distributions of continuous variables look like. Take any continuous variable, height for example. We can measure the height of a sample population of 10 people, and come up with the following data set (in centimetres): 154, 163, 166, 166, 174, 176, 179, 181, 182, 186. There are many ways in which we can *describe* this data set. We can look at the *range* of values (32 cm). We can also determine the *median* height in our sample (175 cm). Yet one of the most common measures for describing a series of continuous data is the *mean* (i.e. average) and *standard deviation*. The mean refers to an imagined central point of the data set; it is a figure that can be used to represent the overall character of the data. In our current example, the mean height of the sample population is 172.7 cm. The standard deviation is then a measure of how much the data varies around that mean, that is, how well the mean represents the actual variation found in the data. Here, the standard deviation is 10.1 cm. For the mean to be a good representative index of a sample population, we want the majority of the data to be clustered within ±1 standard deviation from the mean. This is the case in our example above, where 8 out of the 10 values are within 1 standard deviation of the mean (i.e. 172.7 ± 10.1).[1]

What t-tests do is examine the means and standard deviations of two sample populations in order to determine whether the populations are significantly different from one another. At first glance, this could seem like a relatively easy task. We could, for example, compare our sample population above and its mean height of 172.7 cm with another sample population of 10 people who have a mean height of 165.4 cm. Just by looking at these raw descriptive statistics, it would seem that the two populations have significantly different means. Imagine, though, that the population whose mean height is 165.4 cm

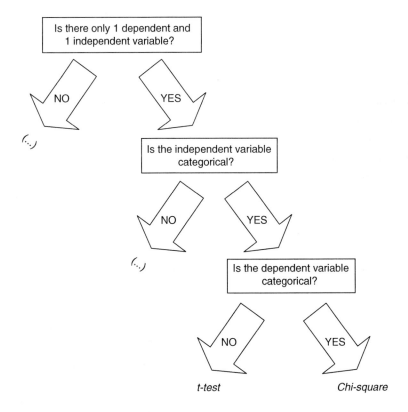

Figure 4.1 Decision tree for statistical tests

has a standard deviation of 21.6 cm. This could mean that the mean value of 165.4 may not be very representative of the actual height distribution across the population (i.e. the standard deviation is relatively large). There may in fact be many people who are much taller than the mean of 165.4 cm, meaning that the actual distribution of this second population may not be as different from the distribution of the first population as it initially seems. T-tests examine this possibility, and determine whether the means of two sample populations are in fact significantly different from one another (i.e. the experimental hypothesis) or not (i.e. the null hypothesis).

Before moving on to the next section, remember that the most important considerations to take into account when deciding which statistical test to use are the *number* and *kind* of variables you are examining. As illustrated schematically in Figure 4.1, you should first ask yourself how many dependent and independent variables you have. If you have more than one of either, you cannot use t-tests or chi-squares and would instead need a more sophisticated test (such as an ANOVA or a linear regression). If, however, you only have one of each, you should then ask yourself whether your independent variable is categorical. If not, you also cannot use chi-squares or t-tests and would again need a more sophisticated statistical test (such as a Linear Mixed Model). Finally, if you have only one dependent and one independent variable, and your independent variable is categorical, you then ask yourself whether your dependent variable is categorical or continuous. If continuous, you would use a t-test to analyse your data; if categorical, you would use a chi-square. With this decision tree in mind, let us now turn to a detailed illustration of how chi-squares and t-tests are used in linguistic research.

4.3 Processing the data

In this section, we will apply the ideas and concepts introduced above to the analysis of actual linguistic data. In the interest of demonstrating the range of applicability of chi-square tests and t-tests, we will see how to apply these two methods to linguistic research based on both natural language data (i.e. recordings) and questionnaire-based data. Note that the discussion below assumes that the collected data is ready to be processed. In other words, we will not go through the steps required for collecting and coding the raw data (but see Chapter 3), and instead only describe the methods to follow once the data is ready to be examined.

4.3.1 Chi-square tests

We begin with an illustration of chi-square tests as they can be applied to natural language data. For the purpose of this illustration, we use data drawn from Sharma's (2005) examination of definite and indefinite article use among speakers of Indian English. In the data we consider, Sharma investigates speakers' article use in sentences like the following (adapted from Platt et al., 1984, cited in Sharma 2005: 539):

> 1) I want to spend some time in *a* village, definitely if I get *a* chance.

The article of interest to us is the indefinite *a*, as in 'a village' and 'a chance'. In Hindi, the L1 of the speakers Sharma considers, noun phrases (NPs) like 'a village' and 'a chance' (what we call *non-specific indefinites*) take no article. Among Indian English speakers, then, what is often found is an apparent L1 transfer pattern, where the indefinite article system of Hindi is calqued into English. The sentence in (1) thus becomes as in (2):

> 2) I want to spend some time in Ø village, definitely if I get Ø chance.

This calquing of the Hindi article system into English is a variable process, and it is the variability that is the focus of Sharma's analysis. In her research, Sharma hypothesizes that variation in the use of Hindi-derived articles in English is related to speakers' levels of education and functional use of English (where lower levels of education in English and experience speaking in English would be correlated with an increased use of Hindi-derived articles). To test her experimental hypothesis (i.e. that educational and functional use of English influences the use of Hindi-derived articles), Sharma examines data drawn from 12 Indian English speakers. She divides these speakers into 3 groups based on their functional and educational mastery of English, where group 1 consists of those with the lowest levels of mastery and group 3 of those with the highest. In this scenario, the dependent variable is *use of Hindi-derived articles* and the independent variable is *speakers' educational and functional level in English* (i.e. group 1, 2 or 3). Since both the dependent and the independent variables are categorical, a chi-square test is appropriate.

Table 4.1 presents the results found in Sharma (2005). Note that the numbers in Table 4.1 refer to *actual* (also called *raw*) numbers of tokens (or examples of the target variable), not to proportions or percentages. This is important

Table 4.1 Null article use with non-specific indefinite NPs (adapted from Sharma, 2005: 551)

Observed	Null article	Overt article	Total
Group 1	34	8	42
Group 2	117	89	206
Group 3	26	106	132
Total	177	203	380

since chi-square tests must always be performed on raw numbers like these, and never on percentages. Another thing to keep in mind when first considering your data is the amount of data necessary. Students often ask 'how many tokens do I need to collect?' While the answer in quantitative research is usually 'the more the better', for chi-square tests, a good benchmark is at least 5 tokens per cell, or a total of five times the total number of cells. In Table 4.1, there are 6 total data cells (excluding the Total row and column). That means that in order for the chi-square test to be robust, we need at least 30 tokens. We have a total of 380 tokens and no cells with less than 5 tokens, so we have no problems in terms of amount of data. So to recap, the first thing you do when conducting a chi-square test is to create your table of *observed* data (i.e. the data that you actually found). Make sure that you make that table using raw data (not percentages), and also make sure to include row and column totals. Finally, verify that you have at least 5 tokens in each cell and/or a total number of tokens that is greater than 5 times the total number of cells.

The next thing to do is to construct your table of *expected* values. Recall that chi-square tests examine the extent to which the distribution of your observed data varies from the distribution that would be expected if the independent variable had no effect on the dependent variable (i.e. the null hypothesis). Constructing a table of expected values is relatively straightforward (if a bit tedious). What you do is for every cell, you multiply that cell's *column total* by that cell's *row total* and then divide that number by the *grand total* of values. This process is illustrated in Table 4.2.

You will notice in Table 4.2 that the row and column totals for the expected values remain the same. This is because what you have done is construct the expected distribution of data for a population of the same size and shape. This is what allows us to compare this expected distribution in Table 4.2 to the

Table 4.2 Expected values for null article use of non-specific indefinite NPs

Expected	Null article	Overt article	Total
Group 1	(42 × 117) / 380 = 19.6	(42 × 203) / 380 = 22.4	42
Group 2	(206 × 177) / 380 = 96	(206 × 203) / 380 = 110	206
Group 3	(132 × 177) / 380 = 61.5	(132 × 203) / 380 = 70.5	132
Total	177	203	380

observed distribution in Table 4.1. In order to actually make this comparison, what we need to do is compute the chi-square statistic. Once again, the computation of a chi-square statistic is rather straightforward (if again a bit tedious). Basically, for every cell, we compute the *difference* between the observed value and the expected value (i.e. observed – expected). We then *square* this difference (i.e. raise the difference to the second power). Finally, we *divide* this squared difference by the *expected value*. After we have done this for each cell, we simply *add* up all the resulting figures for each cell. This new total figure is our chi-square statistic. This entire calculation can be expressed mathematically as in (3):

3) $\sum \dfrac{(\text{Observed} - \text{Expected})^2}{\text{Expected}}$

Doing the calculations with our current example, we get the following:

4)

a) $\chi^2 = \dfrac{(34-19.6)^2}{19.6} + \dfrac{(8-22.4)^2}{22.4} + \dfrac{(117-96)^2}{96} + \dfrac{(89-110)^2}{110} + \dfrac{(26-61.5)^2}{61.5} + \dfrac{(106-70.5)^2}{70.5}$

b) $\chi^2 = \dfrac{14.4^2}{19.6} + \dfrac{-14.4^2}{22.4} + \dfrac{21^2}{96} + \dfrac{-21^2}{110} + \dfrac{-35.5^2}{61.5} + \dfrac{35.5^2}{70.5}$

c) $\chi^2 = \dfrac{207.4}{19.6} + \dfrac{207.4}{22.4} + \dfrac{441}{96} + \dfrac{441}{110} + \dfrac{1260.3}{61.5} + \dfrac{1260.3}{70.5}$

d) $\chi^2 = 10.6 + 9.3 + 4.6 + 4.0 + 20.5 + 17.9$

e) $\chi^2 = 66.9$

We see from the calculations in (4a–e) above that the chi-square statistic associated with Tables 4.1 and 4.2 is 66.9. Now the last thing we need to do is to determine the *p-value* that corresponds to this chi-square. In order to determine the p-value, we need to know one last thing about the distributions we are examining, and that is what is called the distribution's *degrees of freedom* (abbreviated as *df*). It is not necessary for us to get into a definition of what degrees of freedom represent in a mathematical sense. You can just think of them as the general parameters under which the statistical test holds true. All you need to know to finish the chi-square calculations is the *number* of degrees of freedom present. We calculate this number by using the following simple formula: df = (# of chart rows – 1) × (# chart columns – 1). For our current example, this translates to: df = (3 – 1) × (2 – 1) = 2.

Now armed with our chi-square statistic (66.9) and our df (2), what we do is turn to a chi-square *significance chart*.[2] These charts, which can be found in the back of all statistics textbooks and on the internet, provide the critical p-values for chi-square statistics with x degrees of freedom. This may sound complex, but all it means is that the chart can tell us what p-value is associated with a chi-square statistic of 66.9 with 2 degrees of freedom. In Table 4.3, I reproduce the first five lines of this kind of chart. In Table 4.3, the numbers across the top row (0.10, 0.05, etc.) represent p-values (i.e. the chance that the null hypothesis is true). The numbers down the left-hand column (1, 2, etc.) represent degrees of freedom. What we do with this chart is locate the row that corresponds to how ever many degrees of freedom we have in our analysis. In our case, that is two. When we look at the first entry in this row, we see the number 4.605. This means that in order for an analysis with two degrees of freedom to have a p-value of 0.10, the chi-square statistic must be *at least* 4.605. Recall that the standard p-value required in the humanities and social sciences is 0.05. When we look at the relevant requirement for this p-value, we see that we need to have a chi-square statistic that is at least 5.991. With our chi-square value of 66.9, we go above and beyond this requirement, and thus can claim statistically significant findings.[3]

What does this statistical significance mean? It means that there is at least a 95% chance that the null hypothesis is *incorrect*. That indicates that we have *quantitative* support for our experimental hypothesis that educational and functional level in English affects speakers' use of null non-specific indefinite articles. If we were writing up this result in an essay or presenting it in an academic setting, we would therefore be able to talk about the *descriptive* facts (that the group least functionally proficient in English, for example, uses more

Table 4.3 Chi-square significance values

df	0.10	0.05	0.025	0.01	0.001
1	2.706	3.841	5.024	6.635	10.828
2	4.605	5.991	7.378	9.210	13.816
3	6.251	7.815	9.348	11.345	16.266
4	7.779	9.488	11.143	13.277	18.467
5	9.236	11.070	12.833	15.086	20.515

than four times as many null articles than overt articles) and state that these facts are *significant* at the $p < 0.05$ level. In essence, then, what the chi-square test does (like all inferential statistical tests) is provide a *predictive* power to the descriptive facts, and tell you that there is at least a 95% chance that the independent variable does in fact have an effect on the dependent variable.

Let's go through another example of chi-square analysis, this time with data drawn from language questionnaires. Note that even though the data comes from a different source, the procedure for conducting the chi-square test is exactly the same. The data that we will use this time is drawn from Blake and Cutler's (2003) analysis of New York City high school teachers' attitudes to African American Vernacular English (AAVE). In this study, Blake and Cutler surveyed 88 teachers from 5 different New York City high schools: what they call Bilingualism High (BH), Inner City High (ICH), Self-Choice High (SCH), Upperside High (UH) and West Indian High (WIH). Their goal in the study was to examine whether the different demographic compositions and educational offerings of the schools had an effect on teachers' affective evaluations of AAVE as a linguistic system. The experimental hypothesis is therefore that *school has an effect on teachers' affective reactions to AAVE* (the null hypothesis is that *there is no such effect*). Data was collected from a questionnaire that contained 19 statements, to which respondents indicated their relative agreement or disagreement on a 5-point Likert scale (see Chapter 3). For ease of quantitative comparison, Blake and Cutler re-coded the Likert results into a binary system of 'agree' and 'disagree' responses. We will only concern ourselves here with the results to the statement 'African American English (Ebonics) is a form of English.' These results are presented in Table 4.4.

You will notice that Table 4.4 is similar to Table 4.1, above, in that it lists the dependent variable across the columns and the independent variable down the rows. Totals are also given for all columns and rows. The first thing to do

Table 4.4 Responses to the question 'AAVE is a form of English' (adapted from Blake and Cutler, 2003: 176)

Observed	Agree	Disagree	Total
BH	20	3	23
ICH	13	4	17
SCH	5	6	11
UH	13	10	23
WIH	11	3	14
Total	62	26	88

with the table is check that raw data is listed (not percentages) and that there is enough data to satisfy the requirement of five times the total number of cells. Both of these conditions are met. The next step is then the calculation of the expected frequencies, given the size and shape of the subject population. Remember that we do this by multiplying the row total and the column total for each cell, and dividing that number by the grand total. In the interest of space, I will not produce those calculations here. If, however, you are unsure of where the values in Table 4.5 come from, have another look at the relevant discussion of Tables 4.1 and 4.2 above.

With the expected values as given in Table 4.5, we can proceed directly to the calculation of the chi-square statistic. Recall that we do so by taking the difference between the observed and expected values for each cell and squaring it. We then divide this number by the expected value for that cell. Once we have repeated this process for all of the cells, we add up each of the numbers obtained. Doing this for the values in Tables 4.4 and 4.5 yields a chi-square statistic of 9.19. Now, the last thing we need to do is calculate the number of degrees of freedom so that we can see whether this value of 9.19 is large

Table 4.5 Expected values for the question 'AAVE is a form of English'

Expected	Agree	Disagree	Total
BH	16.2	6.8	23
ICH	11.99	5.01	17
SCH	7.75	3.25	11
UH	16.2	6.8	23
WIH	9.86	4.14	14
Total	62	26	88

enough to be statistically significant. In Tables 4.4 and 4.5, we have 5 rows and 2 columns. We therefore have 4 degrees of freedom in our analysis (df = (5–1) × (2–1)). If we refer back to the chi-square significance chart given in Table 4.3, we see that in order to be significant at the p = 0.05 level, a chi-square value with 4 degrees of freedom must be at least 9.488. Our result is, therefore, technically non-statistically significant.[4] What this means is that it is impossible for us to reject the null hypothesis. We are therefore unable to support the experimental hypothesis that a relationship exists between high school and teachers' attitudes on the question of whether AAVE is a form of English. In order to continue investigating this question, we would be forced to conduct further research.

Before moving on to the next subsection, make sure that you understand how to proceed through each of the steps of a chi-square analysis, as listed in the checklist below:

- Create table of observed frequencies (be sure to include row and column totals)
- Make sure that the numbers in the Observed table represent raw data and not percentages; Verify that there is enough data for the chi-square to be robust
- Compute the relevant values for the Expected table
- Using the formula given in (3) on page 79, calculate the chi-square statistic
- Calculate the number of degrees of freedom (df)
- Consult a chi-square significance chart to determine whether the chi-square statistic obtained is significant at the $p \leq 0.05$ level.

4.3.2 T-tests

We now turn to the application of t-tests. Recall that t-tests are what we use to examine *continuous* dependent variables (i.e. those whose values are not inherently categorized). We take our first example from Fought's (1999) analysis of vowel fronting among Latino speakers in Los Angeles. Fought's interest is in whether Latino speakers are taking part in the widely studied California Vowel Shift, or whether this shift is arguably a property of Anglo speakers only. The most salient aspect of the California Vowel Shift, and the feature upon which Fought focuses, is the movement of the high back rounded vowel /u/ forward in the vowel space, to the point where it can almost begin to crowd the high front vowel /i/. To test this, Fought calculated a ratio that compared each of 26 speakers' second formant frequencies (F2) for /u/ with their F2s for /i/. Doing so allowed her to gauge the position of each speaker's /u/ vowel in relation to the rest of their vowel space.

Table 4.6 Ratio of /u/ to /i/ F2s
(adapted from Fought, 1999: 14)

Middle class	Working class
0.77	0.71
0.76	0.71
0.72	0.7
0.71	0.66
0.69	0.64
0.67	0.63
0.67	0.61
0.66	0.59
0.65	0.59
0.64	0.52
0.62	0.51
0.6	0.46
0.48	0.46

Fought hypothesizes that /u/ fronting may not in fact be linked to ethnicity (i.e. Anglo versus Latino), but may instead be related to a speaker's social class. The experimental hypothesis she proposes is that speakers of a higher social class will show more /u/ fronting than those of a lower social class (with the null hypothesis that there will be no difference). Fought divides her speaker sample into two basic categories: Middle Class and Working Class (see Table 4.6).[5] These class categories represent the *independent* variable, the one that she hypothesizes has an effect on the *dependent* variable, which is /u/ fronting. (It should be clear that the independent variable is categorical and that the dependent variable is continuous; if not, see the discussion in section 4.2.)

The first thing to do when conducting a t-test is to calculate the *mean* and *standard deviation* for each of the two groups. Recall from section 4.2 that what a t-test does is examine whether two sets of continuous data have significantly different distributions. It does this by comparing the mean and standard deviation of one group with the mean and standard deviation of the other. To calculate the mean of each group, we simply find the average (i.e. add up each of the values and divide by the total number of values). In our example, the mean of the Middle Class group is 0.665 and the mean of the Working Class group is 0.599. Calculating the standard deviations is somewhat more involved, and I do not have the space to describe the process in detail here (many calculators and all spreadsheet and statistical software can do it for you). Let me just therefore tell you that the Middle Class group has a standard deviation of 0.075 and the Working Class group has a standard deviation of 0.089. With these descriptive statistics in hand, we can turn to the computation of the t-test statistic. There are multiple computational formulas that can be used for t-tests, and your choice of which one to use depends on two things. First, you need to decide if you have *paired* or *unpaired* data. Paired data refer to experiments where there is some natural relationship between subjects in each of the two groups before the data is even collected. The most common example of paired data is what is called a *repeated measures* experiment, where you measure a variable value on the same person twice (usually before and after some experimental treatment). We will not deal with paired measures t-tests here (but see Urdan, 2005). If you have unpaired data (as we do here), you need to determine whether the two groups in your analysis are equal or unequal in size. In Table 4.6, we see that both the Middle Class and Working Class groups have 13 members, and so are equal in size. We will therefore use the formula for computing the t-test statistic for independent (i.e. unpaired) equal samples. This formula is presented in (5).

$$5) \quad t = \frac{\bar{x}_1 - \bar{x}_2}{S_{\bar{x}_1 \bar{x}_2}} \quad \text{where} \quad S_{\bar{x}_1 \bar{x}_2} = \sqrt{\frac{s_1^2 + s_2^2}{n}}$$

In this formula, $\bar{x}$ refers to the mean of each of the groups, with the subscripts 1 and 2 referring to the groups themselves. The t-test statistic is calculated by taking the difference of these two means (i.e. group 2 mean subtracted from the group 1 mean) and then dividing that difference by what is called the *pooled standard deviation* (s stands for standard deviation). This pooled standard deviation is calculated by adding the squares of the standard deviations of each of the groups (i.e. s_1 and s_2), dividing that sum by the number in each group, and then taking the square root of that quotient. This all sounds much more complicated than it actually is. To see how this formula works in action, let's go through our example from above and calculate the t-statistic for the data in Table 4.6.

$$6)$$
$$a) \quad t = \frac{0.665 - 0.599}{\sqrt{\dfrac{0.075^2 + 0.089^2}{13}}}$$

$$b) \quad t = \frac{0.665 - 0.599}{\sqrt{\dfrac{0.0056 + 0.0079}{13}}}$$

c) $t = \dfrac{0.665-0.599}{\sqrt{\dfrac{0.0135}{13}}}$

d) $t = \dfrac{0.665-0.599}{\sqrt{0.001}}$

e) $t = \dfrac{0.665-0.599}{0.032}$

f) $t = \dfrac{0.066}{0.032}$

g) $t = 2.063$

In (6a), we substitute the values for the mean and standard deviation for each group into the formula given in (5). In the numerator of (6a), we subtract the mean value of the Working Class group (0.599) from the mean value of the Middle Class group (0.665). In the denominator, we take the square root of a fraction composed of, in the numerator, the sum of the squares of the standard deviations for the Middle Class group (0.075) and the Working Class group (0.089) and, in the denominator, the number of people in each group (13). In (6b–6f), we perform the arithmetic calculations, which result in the t-value of 2.063 (6g).

Now that we have this t-value, we once again need to calculate the degrees of freedom for our analysis. Just as with the chi-square tests above, the degrees of freedom are what allow us to determine whether the t-value obtained reaches a level of statistical significance. For t-tests of independent samples with equal sample size, we calculate the degrees of freedom by taking the *total* number of subjects in both groups and subtracting 2. In our case, then, df = 26 – 2 = 24. Knowing now the t-statistic and the degrees of freedom, we consult a t-test significance chart. This chart is just like the one described above for chi-square statistics, except that it is used for evaluating the results of t-tests (note: you *cannot* use a chi-square significance chart for evaluating t-tests and vice versa). I have reproduced the relevant row from a t-test significance chart in (7).

7)

df	0.1	0.05	0.01	0.001
24	1.71	2.06	2.80	3.75

We see in (7) the row from the t-test significance table for 24 degrees of freedom. Going across the row to the 0.05 column, we see that our calculated t-value of 2.063 is greater (if only slightly) than the required 2.06. This means that our result *is* statistically significant, and that our analysis is at least 95% sure that the null hypothesis can be rejected. In other words, Fought's experimental hypothesis that Middle Class speakers show higher levels of /u/-fronting than Working Class speakers appears to be borne out.

Let's have a look at another example of t-tests, this time from questionnaire-based data. For this example, I take inspiration from Lambert et al.'s (1960) germinal study of language attitudes towards French and English in Montreal.[6] In this study, Lambert et al. were interested in examining the affective reactions that residents of Montreal (both French-speaking and English-speaking) have to speakers of the two languages. To hone in on attitudes towards language itself, Lambert et al. conducted what is called a *matched-guise experiment*. Listeners were told that they were going to hear ten recorded male voices, five speaking French and five speaking English. What they were not told was that eight of these voices belonged to only four bilingual speakers. In other words, four French-English bilinguals were recorded once reading a passage in English and once reading a passage in French (the other two recordings, one in French and one in English, were decoys and were not considered in the analysis). So, in reality, what listeners heard was two recordings from each of four different speakers, where the only difference between the two recordings for each speaker was the language spoken (i.e. French or English). By examining whether listeners' reactions to the speakers changed depending on whether the speaker was speaking in French or in English, Lambert et al. were able to tease out listeners' affective judgements of the *languages* under consideration, not the *speakers*.

The subject population comprised 130 listeners, 66 of whom were English-speaking and 64 of whom were French-speaking. After hearing each recording, the listeners were asked to rate the voice of each speaker on a variety of personality traits (e.g. height, good looks, intelligence, sense of humour). These rating were done on a 6-point Likert scale that ranged from '1/very little' to '6/very much'. Lambert et al. then tallied up the listeners' ratings of each recording. A hypothetical result of these tallies for the trait 'intelligence' for one of the English-speaking recordings is presented in Table 4.7.

In Table 4.7, we see that the English-speaking listeners gave the English recording an average score of 2.39 (which would translate to something like

Table 4.7 Hypothetical result for listeners' ratings of 'Intelligence' in Lambert et al. (1960)

	Mean score	Standard deviation	N =
English-speaking listeners	2.39	1.08	66
French-speaking listeners	4.52	1.18	64

'not very intelligent'). The French-speaking listeners, however, gave the English recording an average score of 4.52 (or something like 'relatively intelligent'). On the face of it, we would seem to have a difference between how French- and English-speaking listeners judged the intelligence of the speaker for this English recording. To test, however, whether that difference is a significant one, we need to conduct a t-test.

The first thing we do is decide whether the two groups in our analysis (French- and English-speaking listeners) are *paired*. We can decide that they are not (i.e. there is no inherent relationship between the groups). Next, we need to determine whether the two groups are of equal size. In this example, they are not equal in size: the English-listener group has 66 people, while the French-listener group has 64 people. What this means is that we do not use the formula for calculating the t-statistic as in (5), but instead use the one given in (8) below.[7]

$$8)\ t = \frac{\bar{x}_1 - \bar{x}_2}{(S\bar{x}_1\bar{x}_2)\left(\sqrt{\frac{1}{n_1} + \frac{1}{n_2}}\right)} \quad \text{where}\ S\bar{x}_1\bar{x}_2 = \sqrt{\frac{(n_1-1)s_1^2 + (n_2-1)s_2^2}{(n_1 + n_2)-2}}$$

The equation in (8) is slightly more complicated than the equation we saw in (5), above. This is because the sample sizes are unequal, and so the t-test needs to take the size of each sample into account. You should, however, be familiar with all of the mathematical symbols in the equation. The means for each group are still represented by $\bar{x}_1$ and $\bar{x}_2$; the standard deviations by s_1 and s_2. In (8), we also see n_1 and n_2, which refer to the size of groups 1 and 2, respectively. Plugging the values from Table 4.7 into the equation in (8), we get the following:

$$9)\ t = \frac{2.39 - 4.52}{\left(\sqrt{\frac{(66-1)\,(1.08)^2 + (64-1)\,(1.18)^2}{(66+64)-2}}\right)\left(\sqrt{\frac{1}{66} + \frac{1}{64}}\right)}$$

Before moving on, make sure that you understand where each of the values in (9) comes from (note: all of the information you need is in Table 4.7). We will not take the time to go through all of the arithmetic steps of the calculation. If we were to do so, however, the result we would get is t = –10.7. With the t-statistic computed, we now need to determine the number of degrees of freedom. We do so here in exactly the same way as we did above, by taking the total number of subjects in both groups and subtracting 2: df = (66 + 64) – 2 = 128. If we were then to look at a t-test significance chart, we would find that a t-statistic of 10.7 (note that we ignore the negative sign, and treat the t-value as if the result were positive) with 128 degrees of freedom is significant at the p < 0.001 level. This means that for the current data set, there is at least a 99.9% chance that the null hypothesis is not true, and that English-speaking listeners and French-speaking listeners do in fact rate the intelligence levels of this English recording differently.

Having now gone through two examples of t-tests, one with natural language data and the other with questionnaire-based data, make sure that you understand how to proceed through each of the steps of a t-test, as listed in the checklist below:

- Identify the two groups to be compared (this should correspond to the two possible values of your independent variable)
- Calculate the mean and standard deviation for both groups
- Determine whether the data in your two groups are paired or unpaired (recall that we have only gone over the procedure for *unpaired* data)
- Determine whether your two groups are equal in size; choose the correct formula for calculating the t-test based on whether the sample size are equal (as in 5) or unequal (as in 8)
- Calculate the t-statistic using the appropriate formula
- Calculate the number of degrees of freedom
- Consult a t-test significance chart to determine whether your finding is statistically significant at the $p \leq 0.05$ level.

4.3.3 Resources for quantitative analyses

Even though we have just spent quite a bit of time going through the detailed calculations involved in t-tests and chi-square analyses, most researchers do not work these calculations out on their own by hand. This is both because of the time it can take, and because of the likelihood of human error in all of the arithmetic computations. There are hundreds of electronic resources for running t-tests and chi-square tests, including both spreadsheet and statistical analysis software and various internet-based calculators (a search for 't-test calculator' on an internet search engine, for example, will turn up hundreds of responses). Though you will likely make use of these resources in your future work, it is important that you understand where the chi-square statistic or the p-value that a computer programme may provide you with comes from. Many students end up relying too heavily on the results of statistical tests without considering the explanatory limits of those tests. This can cause them to make false or overgeneralized claims that are not substantiated by their analyses. Knowing what steps the computer is taking to calculate a given number gives you better insight into what that number actually means and what it can (and cannot) tell you. By having learned how to calculate both t-tests and chi-squares by hand, you are now better prepared to *interpret* the results of quantitative analyses, which is the subject of the next and final section.

4.4 You're not done yet: Interpreting your results

Determining statistical significance is an important, if not crucial, step in quantitative research. It is, however, only the first step in your analysis. Once all the calculations are done and you have found that your analysis is in fact significant at the $p \leq 0.05$ level, what you then need to do is decide what that result means, if it means anything at all. This is what we mean when we talk about interpreting results.

Let's reconsider Fought's data with respect to /u/-fronting among Latinos in Los Angeles. Recall that our t-test showed that speakers in the Middle Class group have more fronted /u/ vowels (with an average /u/ to /i/ F2 ratio of 0.665) than speakers in the Working Class group (with an average /u/ to /i/ F2 ratio of 0.559). The first thing we want to ask ourselves in interpreting this result is whether it really represents a difference that is large enough to be salient in the real world. While the quantitative analysis can tell us that mathematically an average of 0.665 is significantly larger than an average of 0.559, the question remains as to whether somebody just walking down the street would be able to hear that difference. In other words, *statistical* significance and *real-world* significance are not always the same thing. Whenever interpreting a statistically significant result, it is important to question whether that finding really corresponds to something meaningful in the world. Sometimes, we can do this just by looking at the quantitative results where, roughly, a large difference (and corresponding small p-value) is more likely to be salient than a small one. More often, however, we need to do further research to help us understand what our significant results may indicate.

This further research can take a variety of forms. In the case of Fought's data, for example, we could conduct perceptual salience testing on groups of Los Angeles residents to examine whether listeners can hear the difference between a ratio of 0.665 and 0.559, and whether that difference has any meaning to them. A more common method, however, is to introduce *qualitative* evidence into our analysis. As you learned in the previous chapter, qualitative research methods can focus on pinpointing the qualities or characteristics of a given group. Qualitative research methods may therefore allow us to determine that speakers in Los Angeles are in fact highly attuned to variation in the pronunciation of /u/; that, for example, they comment on it (even if indirectly) regularly, or that they make use of it when impersonating different kinds of speakers. This finding would support the quantitative result, and perhaps indicate that the statistical significance does in fact correspond to something in the real world.

The basic point is that quantitative methods can only take you so far. They can act as a crucial first step in mapping out the sociolinguistic terrain and in telling you *what* people are doing with language. To understand, however, *why* people may be doing what they are doing, you normally need to bring in qualitative considerations. Qualitative research methods are explored later in this volume, while Chapter 2 (earlier in the volume) looks specifically at issues around combining quantitative and qualitative methods in linguistics.

Notes

1. This is a very brief and simplified overview of concepts such as *mean* and *standard deviation*. While sufficient for our current purposes, rest assured that a great deal more mathematical complexity is involved in defining and interpreting these terms.

2. This kind of chart is also often called a Table of Chi-Square Critical Values.

3. In fact, if we look all across the chart we see that our value of 66.9 is even greater than what is necessary to have a p-value of 0.001. This means that we can claim that our analysis is at least 99.9% sure that the null hypothesis is incorrect.

4. The actual p-value for this analysis is $p = 0.51$. This is so close to the significance border that we might be able to argue that the result does in fact meet the quantitative requirement. How we might go about doing so, however, is beyond the scope of our discussion here.

5. Fought's original analysis makes a four-way distinction that I have simplified here for the purposes of illustration. Note also that I have artificially adapted the data (from 32 to 26 speakers) for ease of explanation.

6. Lambert et al. (1960) provide no raw data, only tables listing significant values. The data presented above is therefore hypothetical, and constructed to reflect the original study's significant findings.

7. I am ignoring a detail here, which is the distinction between groups that can be assumed to have equal variance and those that cannot. For our present purposes, I am assuming equal variance.

Further reading

Baker (1992)   This book on language attitudes offers a comprehensive introduction to the field of attitude testing and the various methods involved in using language questionnaires.

Bryman and Cramer (2008); Miller (2002) – Both texts give detailed and accessible instructions on the use of the popular statistical software package SPSS.

Milroy and Gordon (2003) – This book provides an excellent introduction to variationist (i.e. Labovian) sociolinguistics, including an exposition of both theory and research methods.

Weinberg and Schumaker (1981) – A classic introductory text in statistics for the social sciences (both inferential and descriptive), written in a simple and engaging style.

References

Baker, C. (1992), *Attitudes and Language*. Clevedon: Multilingual Matters.

Blake, R. and Cutler, C. (2003), 'AAE and variation in teachers' attitudes: a question of school philosophy?', *Linguistics and Education*, 14, 163–94.

Bryman, A. and Cramer, D. (2008), *Quantitative Data Analysis with SPSS 14, 15, and 16: A Guide for Social Scientists*. London: Routledge.

Fought, C. (1999), 'A majority sound change in a minority community: /u/-fronting in Chicano English', *Journal of Sociolinguistics*, 3, 5–23.

Lambert, W. E., Hodgson, R. C., Gardner, R. C. and Fillenbaum, S. (1960), 'Evaluational reactions to spoken language', *Journal of Abnormal Psychology*, 60, 44–51.

McCullagh, P. and Nelder, J. (1989), *Generalized Linear Models*. Boca Raton, FL: CRC Press.

Miller, R. (2002), *SPSS for Social Scientists*. Basingstoke: Palgrave Macmillan.

Milroy, L. and Gordon, M. (2003), *Sociolinguistics: Methods and Interpretation*. Oxford: Blackwell.

Platt, J., Weber, H. and Ho, M. L. (1984), *The New Englishes*. London: Routledge.

Sharma, D. (2005), 'Language transfer and discourse universals in Indian English article use', *Studies in Second Language Acquisition*, 27, 535–66.

Sternstein, M. (1994), *Statistics*. Hauppauge, NY: Barron's Educational.

Urdan, T. (2005), *Statistics in Plain English*. London: Routledge.

Weinberg, G. H. and Schumaker, J. A. (1981), *Statistics: An Intuitive Approach*. Belmont: Brook's/Cole.

Corpus Methods in Linguistics

5

Paul Baker

Chapter outline

This chapter examines how corpus linguistics techniques can be used to aid a range of linguistic analyses. The chapter begins by defining corpus linguistics and describes some of the theoretical concepts surrounding the field (such as the importance of using large bodies of naturalistic data in order to investigate language usage, and the distinction between corpus-based and corpus-driven approaches). I then discuss various principles that are useful to take into account when building and annotating a corpus, as well as the different types of corpora that can be built, their relationship to the various fields of linguistics that corpus research has contributed to, and the sorts of research questions that corpus linguistics can enable us to ask. Then, a number of techniques of analysis are demonstrated on general corpora of British English. These include comparisons of word frequencies, a keyword analysis, and examinations of collocates and concordances. The chapter ends with a critical discussion of issues that need to be considered when carrying out corpus analysis, noting that corpus methods should not be considered as only quantitative, but rather an approach which can combine both qualitative and quantitative processes.

5.1 Introduction

Corpus linguistics is an increasingly popular field of linguistics which involves the analysis of (usually) very large collections of electronically stored texts, aided by computer software. The word *corpus* is Latin for *body* – a corpus is therefore a 'body' of texts. McEnery and Wilson (1996: 1) characterize corpus linguistics as a 'methodology' rather than a traditional branch of linguistics like semantics, grammar, phonetics or sociolinguistics.

This chapter examines some of the most important ways in which corpus linguistics can be used for linguistic research, focusing on theoretical concepts (section 5.2), building, obtaining and annotating corpora (section 5.3), types and applications of corpora (section 5.4), analytical procedures (section 5.5) and critical considerations (section 5.6). As with other chapters in this book, it is only possible to give a broad overview of the field, so I end with a short list of books which provide more detailed coverage of some of the issues that are addressed.

5.2 Theoretical concepts

Corpus linguistics is firmly rooted in empirical, inductive forms of analysis, relying on real-world instances of language use in order to derive rules or explore trends about the ways in which people actually produce language (as opposed to models of language that rely on made-up examples or introspection). There are sound theoretical justifications for this approach: humans do not always make accurate introspective judgements regarding language, instead relying on cognitive and social biases (see, for example, Kahneman and Tversky (1973), Mynatt et al. (1977), Vallone et al. (1985)). In addition, computers can calculate frequencies and carry out statistical tests quickly and accurately, giving researchers access to linguistic patterns and trends – such as collocational information (e.g. instances where two words tend to co-occur such as *tell* and *story*) – that were previously inaccessible. Corpus analysis can therefore enable researchers to confirm or refute hypotheses about language use, as well as allowing them to raise new questions and theories about language that otherwise would not have been possible.

A further advantage of the corpus linguistics approach is that it can enable researchers to quantify linguistic patterns, providing more solid conclusions to be reached – for example, rather than making a claim such as 'men swear more than women', a corpus analysis would not only allow us to support or reject this hypothesis, but also show proportionally how often men swear than women, the range of swear words that they use, along with their relative frequencies, as well as affording evidence regarding differences and similarities of particular contexts or functions of swearing. One aspect of corpus linguistics research that has come to light is that patterns are rarely absolute, but are instead based on gradients. In addition, large corpora allow researchers to find evidence of rare or unusual cases of language, as well as shedding light on very frequent phenomena.

Within corpus linguistics a distinction has been made between corpus-driven and corpus-based approaches. Corpus-driven linguists tend to use a corpus in an inductive way in order to form hypotheses about language, not making reference to existing linguistic frameworks. However, corpus-based linguists tend to use corpora in order to test or refine existing hypotheses taken from other sources. Some corpus-based linguists have been accused of discarding inconvenient evidence that does not fit the precorpus theory, while corpus-driven linguists have been said to be committed to 'integrity of the data as a whole' (Tognini-Bonelli, 2001: 84). However, McEnery et al. (2006: 8) argue that the distinction is somewhat 'over-stated' and these positions should be viewed as extremes.

5.3 Building and annotating corpora

At the centre of corpus linguistics is the concept of the corpus. Any text or collection of texts could be theoretically conceived of being a corpus (and it is possible to carry out corpus analysis on very small texts (cf. Stubbs' (1996: 81–100) analysis of two letters consisting of a few hundred words each). However, McEnery and Wilson (1996) note that a corpus normally consists of a sample that is 'maximally representative of the variety under examination' (p. 22), is 'of a finite size' (p. 22), exists in 'machine readable' form (p. 23), and 'constitutes a standard reference for the language variety which it represents' (p. 24). This means that it will be large enough to reveal something about frequencies of certain linguistic phenomena, enabling researchers to examine what is typical, as well as what is rare in language.

There are no hard rules regarding how large a corpus ought to be, instead size is dictated by a number of criteria. One of these criteria concerns the aspects of language that the corpus is used to investigate. Kennedy (1998: 68) suggests that 'for the study of prosody' (i.e. the rhythm, stress and intonation of speech), 'a corpus of 100,000 words will usually be big enough to make generalizations for most descriptive purposes'. However, Kennedy goes on to say that an analysis of verb-form morphology (i.e. the use of endings such as -*ed*, -*ing* and -*s* to express verb tenses) would require half a million words. For lexicography (i.e. the analysis of words and their uses, often for dictionary building), a million words is unlikely to be large enough, as up to half the words will only occur once (and many of these may be polysemous, that is, have a number of different meanings). However, Biber (1993) suggests that a million words would be enough for grammatical studies. In addition, the type of language being investigated needs to be taken into account – a rule of thumb is that the more varied the language, the larger the corpus required. So the British National Corpus, which covers a very wide range of written and spoken language genres and is intended to act as a standard reference for British English, is 100 million words in size. A corpus of a restricted language variety such as weather forecasts could be much smaller. Finally, there may be more pragmatic reasons for building a corpus of a particular size – depending on what texts are available, how much money or time we have to devote to a project or whether we can obtain permission from copyright holders to include a text in a corpus (essential if the corpus is to be made public or kept for a long period of time).

Sampling, balance and representativeness are key theoretical concepts in corpus linguistics. Because a corpus ought to be representative of a particular language, language variety, or topic, the texts within it must be chosen and balanced carefully in order to ensure that some texts do not skew the corpus as a whole. So corpora may not contain whole texts, instead utilizing parts of texts. For example, if we wanted to build a corpus of Victorian fiction, we may select 30 authors of that period and take, say, 3 of each of their novels for inclusion in the corpus. However, some authors may write longer novels than others, resulting in their style of writing being overrepresented in the corpus. As a result, we may decide to only take equal-sized samples from each novel (say, 30,000 words). However, we would also need to ensure that we balanced these samples by taking them from different places in the novels – if we only took the first 30,000 words from each novel, we would have a corpus of the beginnings of novels. Therefore, we would need to ensure that text was equally sampled from beginnings, middles and ends of different novels. In other cases, sampling does not need to be so carefully considered – if we were only collecting text from one author, or if we wanted to consider whole texts, or if the texts were very short, then this might mean we would include whole texts rather than samples.

Corpora are often annotated (or tagged) with additional information, allowing more complex calculations to be performed on them. Such information can take several forms, for example, individual texts within a corpus are often stored as separate files and each one can contain a 'header' which gives information about the text such as its author, date of publication, genre, etc. This information can be useful in allowing researchers to focus on particular types of texts (e.g. just newspaper articles) or carry out comparisons between different types (e.g. male vs female authors). Such annotation sometimes employs standard generalized mark-up language (SGML), whereby tags take the form of codes (known as *elements*) inside matching angle brackets < >. In addition, certain characters such as letters with accents are represented with codes known as *entities*. These always begin with an ampersand character and end in a semi-colon. For example, the accented letter é can be represented as the SGML entity é.

Tagging the text in a corpus with SGML codes can also be a useful way of representing information like quotes, headings, accented characters, paragraph breaks, etc., which can change form depending on which computer software is used with the corpus. For example, the SGML element <p> is often used to represent a paragraph break. The example below is taken from the start of a text in the FLOB (Freiberg Lancaster-Oslo/Bergen) corpus of early 1990s British English. As well as <p>, there are the SGML codes <head> (to show headings) and <hi> (to show highlighted text), while the word Thérèse is represented as Thérèse.

<text><text id=FLOBE01><head> Basic Techniques: Knotted Balls
 Pamela Watts </head>
 One of the many delights of embroidery is piecing together the history of a technique, and the insight this gives into the lifestyle of the women who practised it. An understanding of our heritage of embroidery can enrich the creative interpretations we all seek in our own embroidery today.
 The only mention I have been able to find of knotted balls is in the <hi>Encyclopedia of Needlework</hi> by Thérèse de Dillmont.

As well as tagging stylistic features of the text, words, phrases or sentences can be tagged with additional linguistic information. The most common way of doing this is to add part of speech information to each word in the form of tags. The following is an example of a grammatically tagged sentence (using the C5 tagset[1]) taken from the British National Corpus.

405 <w PNI>Nobody <w VVZ>seems <w TO0>to <w VHI>have <w VVN>explained <w DT0>this <w PRP>to <w PNP>her <c PUN>, <w CJC>but <w AV0>finally <w PNP>she <w VVZ>understands <c PUN>. 406 <w DPS>Her <w NN2>daughters <w VHB>have <w AV0>however <w VBN>been <w VVN>contacted <w CJS>so <w PNP>I <w VVB>agree <w TO0>to <w VVI>keep <w DPS>her <w NN1>company <w CJS>until <w PNP>they <w VVB>arrive <c PUN>.

The tag <w PN1> means 'word' (the w part), followed by the code PNI (meaning indefinite pronoun). Tagging can be carried out automatically by computer programs, although hand-checking is usually required as tagging software tends to be close to but not always 100% accurate, and normally works best on texts that contain grammatically predictable sentences and relatively well-known words. Texts containing spoken conversations with lots of interruptions and false starts, jokes which contain wordplay, or technical documentation which may contain a lot of unusual lexis, do not always have high tagging accuracies.[2]

Fortunately, most corpus analysis software allows the tags to be hidden if required, so they do not interfere too much when humans try to read the text. Part of speech tagging is useful because it allows us to distinguish between different grammatical uses of the same word; in the example above, compare the two uses of *to*:

Nobody seems *to* (infinitive marker) have explained this *to* (preposition) her.

It is also possible to tag a corpus for other types of linguistic information. For example, a popular semantic tagging system is the USAS (UCREL Semantic Analysis System) (Wilson and Thomas 1997). This semantic tagset was originally loosely based on McArthur's (1981) *Longman Lexicon of Contemporary English* and contains 21 major fields, which are subdivided further. In the example below from Baker (2005), part of a script from the TV situation comedy *Will & Grace* has been semantically tagged. The word *kids* receives the code T3-. Here the code T3 refers to 'Time: Old, new and young; age', while the negative symbol refers to youth. However, words can also receive multiple tags under this scheme, so *kids* is also tagged as S2mf which places the word in the category of people. The letters m and f refer to gender (in this case, *kids* can refer to both males and females). For further information about types of tagging, see Garside et al. (1997).

<JACK> Why_Z5 is_A3+ n't_Z6 there_Z5 any_N5.1+ coffee_F2 ?_PUNC </JACK>

<KAREN>Same_A6.1+++ reason_A2.2 you_Z8mf do_Z5 n't_Z6 have_A9+ a_Z5 wife_S4f and_Z5 three_N1 kids_T3–/S2mf ._PUNC It_Z8 's_A3+ the_Z5 way_X4.2 God_Z4 wants_X7+ it_Z8 ._PUNC </KAREN>

5.4 Types and applications of corpora

A range of different types of corpora are in existence. First, a distinction needs to be made between general and specialized corpora. A *general corpus* is one which aims to be representative of a particular language (such as the British National Corpus, The Bank of English or the American National Corpus). These corpora tend to be extremely large (usually millions of words in size) and can take a long time to collect and annotate. However, they are useful resources when completed and can be used for a wide range of research purposes. A *specialized corpus*, however, can be smaller and contains a more restricted set of texts. For example, there could be restrictions on genre (e.g. just newspaper reporting), time (e.g. just texts that were published in May 1990) and/or place/language variety (e.g. just texts that were published in Singapore). Specialized corpora are generally easier than general corpora to collect and are used to answer specific research questions. However, specialized corpora are often used in conjunction with *general corpora*, with the general corpus acting as a 'benchmark' about typical language, being compared to the specialized corpus in order to show what forms of language (e.g. lexis, grammar, topics) are over- or underrepresented in the smaller corpus.

Another distinction involves whether a corpus contains spoken, written or computer-mediated texts (such as emails, text messages or websites) or a mixture of all three. *Spoken corpora* generally tend to be smaller than written or computer-based corpora, due to complexities surrounding gathering and transcribing data. The British National Corpus contains almost 10 million words of spoken British English (collected in the early 1990s), whereas the Diachronic Corpus of Present Day Spoken English contains 800,000 words of spoken British English from 1960 to 1992. Some spoken corpora are also specialized corpora, such as the 2 million word Corpus of Spoken Professional American English or the 1.7 million word Michigan Corpus of Academic Spoken English. *Written corpora* are generally easier to build (and large archives of texts that were originally published on paper can be found on the internet, meaning that such texts are already electronically coded). However, unless specifically encoded, formatting information such as font size and colour, as well as pictures can be absented from written corpora. Corpora of computer-mediated texts are expected to become increasingly popular, as societies make more use of electronic forms of communication. Such texts can be very easy to gather – mining programs can store whole websites at a time, although it ought to be pointed out that computer-mediated texts can contain a lot of 'noise' such as spam, hidden keywords designed to make a page be attractive to search engines and navigation menus which may need to be stripped out of individual pages before the text can be included in the corpus.

A third distinction involves the language or languages which a corpus is encoded in. A growing area of corpus linguistics involves the comparison of different languages, which is useful in fields such as language teaching, language testing and translation. A *multilingual corpus* usually contains equal amounts of texts from a number of different languages, often in the same genre. Such texts do not need to be direct translations from one language into another. However, a *parallel corpus* is a more carefully designed type of multilingual corpus, where the texts are exact equivalents (i.e. translations) of each other. Parallel corpora are often sentence-aligned (i.e. tags are added to the corpus data which act as markers to indicate which sentences are translations of each other). With the right software, these tags allow readers to view translations of sentences, side by side. Such corpora have enabled researchers to identify the differences between translations and the original text, which helps to point to features of 'translationese'. For example, Mauranen (2000) notes that translators tend to make optional cohesive markers explicit in the translated text even though they are absent in the source text, which suggests that translators have a tendency to spell things out rather than leave them implicit. In addition, Malmkjaer (1997) notes that in translations, punctuation often gets strengthened, with commas often being replaced with semicolons or full stops, and semicolons being replaced with full stops. This results in long, complex sentences being broken up into shorter and less complex clauses in translations, thereby reducing structural complexity.

Finally, a *learner corpus* is a corpus of a particular language produced by learners of that language. Learner corpora can be useful in allowing teachers to identify common errors at various stages of development, as well as showing over- and underuses of lexis or grammar when compared to an equivalent corpus of native speaker language. Many learner corpora consist of written essays or letters produced in classroom environments. The Longman Learner Corpus and the International Corpus of Learner English both contain contributions from a wide range of learners across the world, allowing researchers to identify the extent to which a student's first language is likely to impact on the way they learn English.

As stated at the beginning of this chapter, as corpus linguistics is mainly characterized as a methodology, it can be used in a number of different applications. For example, it can aid linguistic description, such as providing dictionary makers with real-life examples of words in use. Hunston (2002) compares three dictionaries: the 1987 *Longman Dictionary of Contemporary English*, which was created without the aid of a corpus; the 1995 version of the *Longman Dictionary*, which did use a corpus; and the *COBUILD 1995 Dictionary*, which also uses a corpus. She notes (2002: 97) that 'Longman 1987 gives 20 senses of KNOW. Longman 1995 gives over 40 and COBUILD 1995 gives over 30.'

Corpora can also aid language teaching, for example, Mindt (1996) looked at a corpus of spoken English and found that native speakers tend to use the modal verb *will* most frequently for future time reference. However, in German textbooks used to teach English, Mindt found that *will* was introduced to students about halfway through the second year, whereas other modal verbs, that were less frequent in corpus data, were introduced earlier. Such studies have implications for textbook and syllabus design. Other applications of corpus linguistics involve stylistics (Semino and Short, 2004), forensic linguistics (Coulthard, 1994) and Critical Discourse Analysis (CDA) (Baker, 2006).

For example, in forensic linguistics, Coulthard (1993) reports on his analysis of witness statements that had been used as evidence in the trial of Derek Bentley, who was executed in the United Kingdom in 1953 for his involvement in the death of a policeman. Coulthard compared the frequencies of words in Bentley's own statement with their frequencies in general written and spoken English, and other police and witness statements. His analysis pointed to some odd aspects of Bentley's statement: for example, it contained the word *then* much more frequently than expected when compared to spoken English or other witness statements. However, *then* was a very typical feature of police statements. This, and other corpus-based evidence, was used to argue that Bentley (who had a mental age of 11) had not produced his own statement, but that it had been written for him.

In stylistics, corpus methods of analysis have been used in order to add systematicity to and reduce subjectivity in stylistic analysis. For example, Malhberg (2009) argues that Charles Dickens often references the ways that characters use household objects as a way of drawing attention to their emotional states. Starting with a number of individual examples which involve objects like a watering-pot or a knife and fork, she searches in a corpus consisting of all of Dickens' novels in order to show how these objects are consistently used by Dickens to highlight emotions.

Finally, in the area of CDA, Baker (2006: 13) shows how corpus techniques can be used to show the 'incremental effect of discourse'. He argues (2006: 13) that 'an association between two words, occurring repetitively in naturally occurring language, is much better evidence for an underlying hegemonic discourse which is made explicit through the word pairing than a single case.' In addition, Mautner (2007) draws on CDA to examine how the elderly are constructed (as victims, in ill health and in need of care – more often than as empowered or independent) in a corpus consisting of language from a wide range of sources.

Most research questions in corpus linguistics are based around one over-arching question: 'how do people *really* use language?' This research question can often be related to specific fields in linguistics – for example, with the language teaching example above, Mindt (1996) wanted to know whether the language used in textbooks actually reflected the language that people encounter in everyday life. This is also a research question guiding many of the descriptive studies carried out on language (especially English) using corpus-based approaches: 'Most of these descriptive studies include quantitative information on the distribution of linguistic features in particular genres or for different functions in speech and writing' (Kennedy 1998: 88). As stated in section 5.1, some research questions involve tests of existing claims or theories about language, for example, 'has written language become more informal over recent years?'

Many research questions within corpus linguistics also tend to have a comparative aspect to them, such as 'how does the use of linguistic feature X differ in usage between language varieties A and B in terms of frequency and/or typical usage?' It is important not to overlook the concept of similarity, however – if a small difference, or no difference is found, then this is still a finding. In addition, corpus linguistics approaches can be used to ask research questions about language patterns that we are unaware of but may still have the power to influence us. For example, Stubbs (2001) notes that many words tend to hold semantic prosodies, based on their repeated uses in particular contexts. So, for example, if the word *illegal* strongly collocates with *immigrant*, then we may be primed to think of illegality whenever we encounter the word *immigrant*, even on the occasions where it occurs without the word *illegal*. So a research question that corpus linguists could ask would be 'what associations are triggered by the use of linguistic item X, based on its typical uses?'

5.5 Corpus software and analysis

A stand-alone corpus is not particularly useful in terms of aiding linguistic enquiry. For this reason, corpora are normally used in conjunction with analysis software, which are able to carry out the counting, sorting and presentation of language features (the results of which must then be interpreted by humans). Some corpora come with their own analytical interfaces (e.g. BNCweb is a web-based platform for use with the British National Corpus). However, other software (such as WordSmith Tools,[3] Xaira,[4] Wmatrix[5] and AntConc[6] can be used in conjunction with a range of corpora. This section illustrates some of the ways in which corpora can be manipulated in order to carry out linguistic analyses. I will be mainly using two corpora, the LOB (Lancaster-Oslo/Bergen) corpus of British English from 1961, and the FLOB corpus of British English from 1991. Both corpora are a million words in size, containing 15 genres of writing (including press, religion, science fiction and humour). In order to carry out comparisons of these corpora I will be using WordSmith Tools. Because the LOB and FLOB corpora are equivalent corpora, with a 30-year time span between them, they can be used in order to answer research questions regarding language change, as well as giving us a general profile regarding written British English.

Many forms of corpus-based analysis are based around the concept of frequency (and attendant statistical tests allowing us to compare frequencies). The most basic aspect of frequency analysis simply allows us to derive frequencies of particular words (or phrases or tags), or lists of all of the words in a corpus, presented alphabetically or in order of frequency. Table 5.1 below shows the ten most frequent words in the LOB and FLOB corpora respectively. I have also presented their percentage frequencies – so the word *the* accounts for 6.67% of all words in LOB. Presenting frequencies as percentages is often useful, particularly when making comparisons between multiple corpora (especially of different sizes).

Table 5.1 Top 10 word frequencies in LOB and FLOB

	LOB (1961)		FLOB (1991)	
1	THE	68,379 (6.67%)	THE	64,813 (6.35%)
2	OF	35,769 (3.49%)	OF	34,147 (3.35%)
3	AND	27,932 (2.72%)	AND	27,292 (2.67%)
4	TO	26,907 (2.62%)	TO	27,058 (2.65%)
5	A	23,170 (2.26%)	A	23,168 (2.27%)
6	IN	21,338 (2.08%)	IN	20,880 (2.05%)
7	THAT	11,197 (1.09%)	THAT	10,481 (1.03%)
8	IS	10.995 (1.07%)	IS	10,923 (1.01%)
9	WAS	10.502 (1.02%)	WAS	10,039 (0.98%)
10	IT	10,031 (0.98%)	FOR	9,344 (0.92%)

It ought to be clear from Table 5.1 that, in terms of the most frequent words at least, there is not a great deal of difference between LOB and FLOB. The ordering of words in both columns in the table is almost identical (apart from line 10). There are also similar frequencies, with *the* having an extremely high frequency (above 6%), then a set of words with frequency at around 2–3% (*of, and, to, a, in*) and then another set of words with frequencies around the 1% mark (*that, is, was, it, for*). It might help to be able to distinguish between different grammatical uses of some of these words (e.g. *that* can be a conjunction, a determiner or a gradable adverb), which is where consulting tagged versions of these corpora would be handy. It is also interesting to note that high frequency words tend to be grammatical words (conjunctions, determiners, prepositions), but in terms of exploring language change, the table doesn't offer much of interest.

A related form of frequency analysis involves calculating keywords. A keyword, put simply, is a word which occurs statistically more frequently in one file or corpus, when compared against another comparable or reference corpus. For example, we could derive a list of keywords by comparing a small learner corpus of English against a much larger corpus of general native-speaker of English. The keywords would be words which occurred relatively more frequently (taking into account overall sizes) in the learner corpus. Among such keywords we are likely to find simple adjectives and adverbs like *nice*, *big* and *very*, which learners tend to over-rely on, particularly in the early stages of their development. Regarding LOB and FLOB, because they are the same size, we would obtain two lists of keywords – one which gives words which are statistically more frequent in LOB (when compared to FLOB), the other giving words that are more frequent in FLOB (when compared to LOB). Table 5.2 shows some of these keywords.

The words in Table 5.2 are much more suggestive of differences. Some keywords can perhaps be explained due to events or people who were particularly in vogue at the time when the corpora were collected. For example, *Thatcher* and *Major* were British Prime Ministers in the early 1990s. In 1980, *Rhodesia* gained independence from Britain and then changed its name to Zimbabwe, so it is hardly surprising that Rhodesia is a keyword in the LOB corpus – Rhodesia only existed as a historical concept by the time we get to the period of the FLOB corpus. Similarly *Kenya* became independent from Britain in 1963 – so Kenya as a subject would have been in the British news a lot in the 1960s, because of this change in its status. The FLOB keywords *privatisation* and *market* are suggestive of a growing capitalist discourse (along with a number of other FLOB keywords, not shown in the table).

Table 5.2 Some keywords in LOB and FLOB when compared against each other

LOB (1961)	FLOB (1991)
COMMONWEALTH	THATCHER
MISS	MAJOR
MAN	WOMEN
THE	OK
HE	FUCKING
GIRL	AROUND
MUST	ET
SHALL	PRIVATISATION
RHODESIA	MARKET
KENYA	BLOODY

Other words suggest more subtle social changes. For example, the LOB corpus shows a tendency for keywords which indicate male bias (*man* and *he*), whereas FLOB has *women* as a keyword. However, we also find some female keywords in LOB (*miss* and *girl*) which could be argued as contributing towards male bias (see below). It is conceivable that we could argue that FLOB actually shows a female bias rather than LOB having a male bias (we would need to refer to actual frequencies to see if that was the case), but for the moment, we could refer to our own knowledge of social changes (such as women's liberation movements and greater awareness of sexism towards the last half of the twentieth century), in order to hypothesize explanations for our results. It should be noted that hypotheses are not always validated upon closer investigation, meaning that we should not take frequencies at face value. For example, consider the word *ET*, which is key in FLOB. I hypothesized that this was a 'cultural keyword', referring to the Steven Spielberg film *ET* from 1982. However, upon investigation of the corpus, it transpires that it is always used to refer to academic references such as Tunwell et al., 1991.

A number of keywords are more indicative of changes in style, which can also ultimately be linked back to social change. For example, the keywords *fucking*, *bloody* and *OK* suggest that written language has become more informal in the 30-year period between LOB and FLOB. In addition, the modal verbs *shall* and *must* are key in the 1961 LOB corpus. Both these modal verbs suggest strong modality, indicating that a more authoritarian tone of language was used in the 1960s, compared to the 1990s. A detailed study of modal verbs in these corpora by Leech (2002) confirms this (the only modal verbs which actually increased in usage over time were *can* and *could*, which suggest weaker modality).

Interestingly, both Leech (2002) and McEnery and Xiao (2005) found evidence to show that British English was becoming more similar to American English, by comparing frequencies in the LOB and FLOB corpora to their American equivalents (the Brown and Frown corpora). Leech demonstrated that between 1961 and 1991 both American and British English users showed a trend towards decrease in use of modal verbs, with an increase in semi-modals (such as *have to*, *need to*, *want to* and *got to*). However, the changes appeared to be more advanced in American English, with British English appearing to lag behind. McEnery and Xiao looked at change and variation in infinitive use (i.e. use of the full infinitive as in 'help him to forget' vs use of the bare infinitive as in 'help him forget'. They found that both American and British English users were showing a tendency over time to use fewer full infinitives, instead preferring bare infinitives. Again, this trend appeared to be more advanced in American English, with British English lagging behind.

As I have noted above, it is often not enough to simply extrapolate explanations based on the presence of keywords alone. They need to be investigated in more detail and in context. So how can we investigate context? This is where the concept of the concordance is useful. A concordance is simply a list of a word or phrase, with a few words of context either side of it, so we can see at a glance how the word tends to be used. Corpus analysis software normally allows concordances to be sorted alphabetically in various ways (e.g. one, two, three, etc. words to the left or right of the word under examination), which allows humans to recognize patterns more easily. Table 5.3 presents an unsorted random sample of concordance lines of *girl* from the LOB corpus.

From a close examination of the concordance lines we can start to get an idea of some of the ways that *girl* is used. For example, it is often preceded by adjectives or other words which relate to appearance (*fat*, *coloured*), occupation (*army*, *sales-*, *call-*), morality (*good*) or sexuality (*heterosexual*). The words to the right of *girl* also indicate similar groups (*civil servant*, *young*, *tall*, *pretty*). Such words can therefore be grouped in order to indicate what Louw (1993) calls 'semantic preference', for example, *girl* holds a semantic preference for physical appearance. The examination of concordances also helps to reveal discourse prosodies, this being 'a feature which extends over more than one unit in a linear string' (Stubbs, 2001: 65). Discourse prosodies are often indicative of attitudes. One discourse prosody that could be noted from the concordance is the way that *girl* tends to be used to refer to adult females, as seen for example in lines 5, 6, 9 and 11 above, which tend to refer to females involved in more 'adult' activities. This use of *girl* could be suggestive of a patronizing

Table 5.3 Sample concordance of girl (LOB Corpus)

1	ung people except with sports programmes. A	girl	civil servant of 17 likes TV for showing olde
2	a fuss all over again Charlotte, there's a good	girl	, Esmond said. Save your breath. You've got
3	that it was wrong to impregnate an unmarried	girl	for to do so would reduce her bride-price and
4	othing, even if it wasn't much of a match for a	girl	as young and pretty as that. You may have so
5	rner, covered by stony indifference. The army	girl	, tall and demurely pretty, threw a quick side
6	ars. There could be a lot of money in the call-	girl	racket, and not many expenses either, just a t
7	How old are you? Peter asked stiffly. The fat	girl	stared at him; pulling him around the floor as
8	, and her elder sister, Georgina, who is a sales-	girl	for the firm. Georgina does not envy her sist
9	ly to Simone. As Gay watched he offered the	girl	a cigarette and lit it, his hands cupping hers i
10	y scripted), is remarkable. There is a coloured	girl	who pretends to sophistication but is horrifi
11	are that Gavin would make love to the French	girl	on the sands, and no doubt he would come ba
12	and Albertine a perfectly normal heterosexual	girl	, the novel would have been, qua novel, neith

attitude towards women (see also Sigley and Holmes, 2002), at least in the LOB corpus. When *boy* is used in the LOB corpus, it tends to be used on children, rather than adult males. It is interesting that *girl* is key in the LOB corpus – perhaps users of British English are refraining from using it so much in contexts where it could refer to adults (again, concordance analyses would be required to confirm this).

A concordance analysis therefore combines aspects of quantitative and qualitative analyses together. In the case of *girl* above, there were 334 concordance lines to read, which is where sorting the corpus alphabetically would prove to be handy in helping the analyst to digest the large amount of information on display. In addition, Sinclair (1999) suggests that we take 30 lines at random, examine them to see what patterns or prosodies are present, then examine another 30 lines, then another, until we do not find anything more of interest. Hunston (2002: 52) advocates that 'a small selection of lines is used as a basis for a set of hypotheses about patterns. Other searchers are then employed to test those hypotheses and form new ones'. For example, based on the above concordance we could specify searches for terms like *pretty girl* or try to see which other sorts of nouns tend to occur with words like *pretty* or semantically related words like *attractive* and *beautiful*.

Because corpora can contain thousands or millions of words, this can often result in an overwhelming amount of information to analyse by hand. A statistical procedure which helps to reduce this information to more manageable chunks is collocation. Collocation refers to the statistically significant co-occurrence of words. For example, *bank* will collocate with lexical words like *blood*, *account* and *river* which tell us something about its semantic uses, but it is also likely to collocate with grammatical words like *the, to* and *of* (indicating grammatical patterns). Most words collocate to some degree with grammatical words because their frequencies are so high. There are a number of different ways of calculating collocation. Some, like the mutual information score (i.e. which take into account exclusivity of collocation – for example, words must always appear together and not apart), tend to give precedence to low frequency collocations involving nouns, adjectives and verbs. For example, using mutual information to calculate the collocates of *bank* in the British National Corpus, we find that most of the resulting collocates are low frequency nouns or proper nouns like *Jodrell, Barclays, Gaza, balances* and *lending*). Other ways of calculating collocation, such as log likelihood (which gives precedence to highly frequent collocates, tend to favour grammatical relationships. So collocates of *bank* calculated with log likelihood are *the, of, a, and, to* and *in*. There is clearly no 'best' way of working out collocation, but certain techniques favour certain types of words, so it makes sense to determine which sorts of collocates you wish to focus on.

In the British National Corpus, *girl* occurs over 14,000 times. Looking at its strongest collocates (using the log-log statistic, which gives a good compromise between high and low frequency collocates), we find words like *little, young* and *dark-haired*. Table 5.4 shows the most frequent 20 collocates for *girl* (for comparative interest, the collocates of *boy* are also presented).

Most of the collocates listed in Table 5.4 are adjectives or nouns, tending to occur one or two places to the left of the search word. There are some similarities between the two lists (*little, 14-year-old, 15-year-old, clever*) as well as the equivalent *guides* and *scouts*, but also some interesting differences. As noted above, a number of collocates of *girl* refer to appearance (*dark-haired, pretty, beautiful, blonde*) whereas no such collocates occur with *boy*. Instead we find collocates to do with jobs (*errand, messenger, rivet*). Such findings echo non-corpus based research on gender representations (e.g. Sunderland, 2004).

Table 5.4 Strongest 20 collocates of *girl* and *boy* in the British National Corpus using log-log

girl	boy
little, young, dark-haired, boy, 15-year-old, teen-age, raped, 14-year-old, 16-year-old, clever, pretty, mclaren, guides, golden, beautiful, blonde, nine-year-old, raping, five-year-old, poor	scouts, naughty, scout, scano, girl, waterloo, little, 12-year-old, 15-year-old, 14-year-old, clever, bonanza, errand, dear, old, wee, kritian, bistro, rivet, messenger

Some of the collocates are difficult to make sense of, requiring concordance analyses, for example, *waterloo* is a collocate of *boy* due to the name of a horse called Waterloo Boy in a text about horse racing. *Kritian* is from references in the corpus to the 'kritian boy', a famous sculpture in Greek Art, while Scano is a character in a novel in the corpus called *Death in Springtime*. Such collocates, when limited to numerous citations in a single text, or small number of texts, might be best discarded, unless, taken as a group, they contribute towards some other pattern. It is recommended that concordance analyses of collocates are undertaken, even in cases which look obvious. For example, the collocates *raped* and *raping* suggest that it is girls who are described as victims rather than perpetrators, but a quick concordance analysis could confirm this.

5.6 Critical considerations

As with all methodologies, corpus linguistics is not able to answer every research question in the area of linguistics. In this section I outline a few criticisms of corpus approaches and identify, where possible, ways of defending such positions.

First, corpora can be time-consuming, expensive and difficult to build, requiring careful decisions to be made regarding sampling and representativeness. There is a continuing need to create up-to-date balanced reference corpora, especially in languages other than English. More corpus users are turning to the internet for data (and a number of web concordancers[7] are in existence, offering researchers access to much larger sources of data than even the most ambitious corpus builders can conceive). However, internet data is a genre of language in itself, and should not be considered to be necessarily representative of general language use, although as many texts are being deposited on the internet, the task of building balanced corpora is now often less arduous than in previous decades.

Second, researchers who are not computer literate may initially find it off-putting to have to engage with analytical software or statistical tests. Although corpus linguistics is often seen as a quantitative form of analysis, in fact human input is required at almost every stage, from corpus building (deciding what should go in the corpus) to corpus analysis (what research questions should be asked, what should be looked for, what analytical procedures should be carried out, how the results can be interpreted). With that said, the software tools which are currently available are reasonably easy to learn how to use and are certainly no more complicated than a typical piece of word processing software. In addition, the software carries out the statistical tests for the user, so corpus linguists do not need to be mathematical wizards. Instead, knowledge of what the tests do rather than how to carry them out is more important.

Third, corpus analysis works best at identifying certain types of patterns. For example, BNCweb CQP edition allows users to search for patterns such as any adjective followed by an optional noun, followed by a conjunction occurring somewhere later in the same sentence. But identifying the absence of something is more difficult – for example, with McEnery and Xiao's (2005) study of infinitives, it is not so easy to instruct corpus software to identify all the cases where the infinitive *to* is implied but missing. More complex phenomena such as agency or metaphor are also difficult to automate, necessitating analysis of concordance lines by hand. With that said, analytical software is continually improving, meaning that fairly complex patterns can be searched for, particularly on tagged data, and the problem of identifying absence is not unique to corpus methods but to all forms of research. In addition, some advances have been made in the automatic identification of metaphor, see Sardinha (2002) and Charteris-Black (2004).

As mentioned earlier, corpus data tends to work at the textual level. For many forms of linguistic analysis this may be sufficient, but for more applied forms of analysis (such as visual analysis or CDA) it is often important to consider texts at other levels, such as their methods of production and reception, whether texts refer to or are referred by other texts, and the social, historical and political contexts within which texts occur. For example, in Baker (2008) I examined linguistic patterns around the word *bachelor*, finding ultimately that there were three sets of collocates: those which referred to the sense of bachelor as a university degree; those which referred to a young unmarried man (and tended to suggest positive constructions to do with eligibility); and those which referred to an old unmarried man (and tended to suggest more negative constructs of loneliness, domestic incompetence and eccentricity). However, the corpus did not reveal anything about the etymology of the word, and it was only by investigating other sources that I found that the 'university degree' and 'unmarried man' meanings are likely to be due to historical polysemy rather than being accidental homonyms.[8]

Similarly, a corpus analysis may produce interesting findings about language, but as with many other methodologies, it is a task for humans to provide explanations for those findings. For example, a corpus analysis tells us that *girl* collocates with *pretty* and *beautiful*, but it does not tell us why. Both a qualitative analysis which involves examining concordance lines to see in what contexts girls are being referred to in this way, and a further qualitative analysis which steps outside the corpus to examine gendered relationships in society, would help to provide explanations.

However, these criticisms should not preclude corpus analysis (all methods have limitations), but should instead make users aware of potential limitations, giving them information about when corpora should be used alone, when they could be combined with other methodological approaches and when they might be best avoided. My personal feeling is that the positives far outweigh the negatives (which can often be dealt with via triangulation). The strength of the corpus approach is in using fast and accurate techniques to identify patterns that human analysts would not notice. And in using large amounts of naturally occurring data, corpus analysis offers a high degree of reliability and validity to linguistic research.

Notes

1. The full tagset is at http://ucrel.lancs.ac.uk/claws5tags.html
2. A free trial service offers automatic part of speech tagging at http://ucrel.lancs.ac.uk/claws/trial.html
3. http://www.lexically.net/wordsmith/
4. http://www.oucs.ox.ac.uk/rts/xaira/
5. http://ucrel.lancs.ac.uk/wmatrix/
6. http://www.antlab.sci.waseda.ac.jp/software.html
7. http://www.webcorp.org.uk and http://www.kwicfinder.com/KWiCFinder.html
8. The term *bachelor* was used in the thirteenth century to refer to a young monk, someone belonging to the lowest stage of knighthood or the younger members of a trade guild, so while there are now distinct meanings, the term originally referred to a young person (always male), who was at the start of their profession.

Further reading

Garside, Leech and McEnery (1997) – An edited collection discussing a variety of aspects of corpus annotation.

Kennedy (1998) – An excellent overview, with a focus on corpus building and software tools

Hunston (2002) – A book which focuses on applications of corpus analysis, particularly relating to language teaching

McEnery and Wilson (1996) – This book provides a good overview of the field and an interesting discussion of its historical antecedents, for intermediate readers.

McEnery, Xiao and Tono (2006) – A comprehensive account of the field, suitable for advanced readers.

Sinclair (1991) – For those who are new to the field, this book gives an accessible account of concordancing and collocation.

Stubbs (1996, 2001); Hoey (2005) – Both use corpus-based methods in order to start to develop a theory of linguistics, based around concepts such as priming and prosodies.

References

Baker, P. (2005), *Public Discourses of Gay Men*. London: Routledge.

—. (2006), *Using Corpora in Discourse Analysis*. London: Continuum.

—. (2008) *Sexed Texts*. London: Equinox.

Biber, D. (1993), 'Representativeness in corpus design' *Literary and Linguistic Computing* 8, 4: 243–57.

Charteris-Black. J. (2004), *Corpus Approaches to Critical Metaphor Analysis*. Basingstoke Hants: Palgrave Macmillan.

Coulthard, M. (1993), 'On beginning the study of forensic texts: corpus concordance collocation', In M. Hoey (ed.) *Data, Description, Discourse*. London: Harper Collins.

—. (1994), 'On the use of corpora in the analysis of forensic texts' *International Journal of Speech, Language and the Law: Forensic Linguistics* 1: 27–44.

Garside, R., Leech, G. and McEnery, A. (1997), *Corpus Annotation*. London: Longman.

Hoey, M. (2005), *Lexical Priming. A New Theory of Words and Language*. London: Routledge.

Hunston, S. (2002), *Corpora in Applied Linguistics*. Cambridge: Cambridge University Press.

Kahneman, D. and Tversky, A. (1973), 'On the psychology of prediction', *Psychological Review*, 80, 237–51.

Kennedy, G. (1998), *An Introduction to Corpus Linguistics*. London: Longman.

Leech, G. (2002), 'Recent grammatical change in English: data, description, theory', in K. Aijmer and B. Altenberg (eds), *Advances in Corpus Linguistics. Papers from the 23rd International Conference on English Language Research on Computerized Corpora (ICAME 23)*, Gothenburg, 61–84.

Louw, B. (1993), 'Irony in the text or insincerity in the writer? The diagnostic potential of semantic prosodies', in M. Baker, G. Francis and E. Tognini-Bonelli (eds), *Text and Technology*. Amsterdam: Benjamins, pp. 157–76.

Malhberg, M. (2009), 'Corpus stylistics and the Pickwickian watering-pot', in Baker (ed.), *Contemporary Approaches to Corpus Linguistics*. London: Continuum, pp. 47–63.

Malmkjær, K. (1997), 'Punctuation in Hans Christian Andersen's stories and in their translations into English', in F. Poyatos (ed.), *Nonverbal Communication and Translation. New Perspectives and Challenges in Literature, Interpretation and the Media*. Amsterdam and Philadelphia: Benjamins, pp. 151–62.

Mauranen, A. (2000), 'Strange strings in translated language: a study on corpora', in M. Olohan (ed.), *Intercultural Faultlines. Research Models in Translation Studies 1: Textual and Cognitive Aspects*. Manchester: St. Jerome Publishing, pp. 119–41.

Mautner, G. (2007), 'Mining large corpora for social information: the case of elderly', *Language in Society*, 36 (1), 51–72.

McArthur, T. (1981), *Longman Lexicon of Contemporary English*. London: Longman.

McEnery, T. and Wilson, A. (1996), *Corpus Linguistics*. Edinburgh: Edinburgh University Press.

McEnery, T. and Xiao, Z. (2005), '*Help* or *Help To*: what do corpora have to say?', *English Studies*, 86 (2), 161–87.

McEnery, T., Xiao, R. and Tono, Y. (2006), *Corpus-Based Language Studies: An Advanced Resource Book*. London: Routledge.

Mindt, D. (1996), 'English corpus linguistics and the foreign language teaching syllabus', in J. Thomas and M. Short (eds), *Using Corpora for Language Research*. London: Longman, pp. 232–47.

Mynatt, C. R., Doherty, M. E. and Tweney, R. D. (1977), 'Confirmation bias in a simulated research environment: an experimental study of scientific inference', *Quarterly Journal of Experimental Psychology*, 29, 85–95.

Sardinha, T. B. (2002), 'Metaphor in Corpora: A Corpus-driven Analysis of Applied Linguistics Dissertations'. Paper given at the International Conference on Metaphor in Language and Thought, PUCSP.

Semino, E. and Short, M. (2004), *Corpus Stylistics: Speech, Writing and Thought Presentation in a Corpus of English Narratives*. London: Routledge.

Sigley, R. and Holmes, J. (2002), 'Watching girls in corpora of English', *Journal of English Linguistics*, 30 (2), 138–57.

Sinclair, J. (1991), *Corpus, Concordance, Collocation*. Oxford: Oxford University Press.

—. (1999), 'A way with common words', in H. Hasselgård and S. Oksefjell (eds), *Out of Corpora: Studies in honour of Stig Johansson*. Amsterdam: Rodopi, pp. 157–79.

Stubbs, M. (1996), *Text and Corpus Analysis*. London: Blackwell.

—. (2001), *Words and Phrases: Corpus Studies of Lexical Semantics*. London: Blackwell.

Sunderland, J. (2004), *Gendered Discourses*. London: Palgrave Macmillan.

Tognini-Bonelli, E. (2001), *Corpus Linguistics at Work*. Amsterdam: John Benjamins.

Vallone, R. P., Ross, L. and Lepper, M. R. (1985), 'The hostile media phenomenon: biased perception and perceptions of media bias in coverage of the "Beirut Massacre"', *Journal of Personality and Social Psychology*, 49, 577–85.

Wilson, A. and Thomas, J. (1997), 'Semantic annotation', in R. Garside, G. Leech and A. McEnery (eds), *Corpus Annotation: Linguistic Information from Computer Texts*. London: Longman, pp. 55–65.

Part III
Qualitative Research Methods

Discourse-Analytic Approaches to Text and Talk   6

Judith Baxter

Chapter outline

This chapter explores the different ways in which discourse-analytic approaches reveal the 'meaningfulness' of text and talk. It reviews *four* diverse approaches to discourse analysis of particular value for current research in linguistics: Conversation Analysis (CA), Discourse Analysis (DA), Critical Discourse Analysis (CDA) and Feminist Post-structuralist Discourse Analysis (FPDA). Each approach is examined in terms of its background, motivation, key features, and possible strengths and limitations in relation to the field of linguistics. A key way to schematize discourse-analytic methodology is in terms of its relationship between *micro*analytical approaches, which examine the finer detail of linguistic interactions in transcripts, and *macro*analytical approaches, which consider how broader social processes work through language (Heller, 2001). This chapter assesses whether there is a strength in a discourse-analytic approach that aligns itself exclusively with either a micro- or macrostrategy, or whether, as Heller suggests, the field needs to find a way of 'undoing' the micro–macro dichotomy in order to produce richer, more complex insights within linguistic research.

6.1 Introduction

In the last few decades, there has been a sea change in the field of linguistic research. Today, the study of real samples of speech and writing as evidence of the way in which people in the world use language in a range of social contexts is manifestly the business of linguistics. But it wasn't always so.

Historically within linguistic research, the study of 'text' (written discourse) or 'talk' (spoken discourse) was not considered worthy of serious research (see

Litosseliti and Sunderland 2002, for a discussion of terms). A key strand of linguistic research evolved from the writings of Noam Chomsky (1965), who argued that the goal of linguistics should be to study underlying 'linguistic competence': the rules that inform the production of grammatical sentences. For Chomsky, the focus of study was the abstract system: the underlying structure of language. Linguistic performance – speaker's actual utterances – were regarded as disorderly, chaotic and of no value in offering an understanding of language as a system. A significant challenge to Chomsky's theories was made by the applied linguist, Del Hymes (1972) who offered the term '*communicative* competence' in deliberate contrast to 'linguistic competence'. As Hymes observes, a person who has only linguistic competence would be quite unable to communicate – a 'social monster' producing grammatical sentences disconnected from the context in which they occurred. This notion of a communicatively competent speaker and writer, who knows the rules of how to communicate appropriately in different social settings, has had a profound effect on linguists with an interest in the field of discourse analysis. For the conversation analyst, Harvey Sacks (1992), ordinary, mundane speech exhibits an exceptional level of orderliness, and apparent instances of non-fluency are not viewed as the product of mistakes or speech errors, but have a meaning and a purpose. This chapter will look at the different ways in which discourse-analytic approaches have re-evaluated the 'meaningfulness' of text and talk within linguistics.

In terms of conducting research more broadly, there is a clear distinction between analysing text or talk (hence, 'discourse') as a means to an end, and analysing it as an end in itself. Many *non*-linguists – sociologists, psychologists and researchers in education, cultural studies and media studies – draw upon language as just one of many sources of evidence about their research subjects. Interviews, focus group discussions and observation data all involve verbal interactions that must be transcribed and analysed. In short, many non-linguists view discourse as data. For some, the language itself becomes a source of fascination, but for others, it is often seen within a 'realist'[1] paradigm as a transparent medium to external reality, or as a direct index of subjects' feelings and meanings (see also Chapter 8, for a discussion).

Alternatively, many linguists view 'data as discourse' (Cameron, 2001: 145) alongside 'discourse as data'. According to Wooffitt (2005), whenever we produce a description or refer to a place, object, event or state of affairs in the world, we invariably select from a range of possible words and phrases. Consequently it follows that 'discourse can never be taken as simply descriptive of the social action to which it refers, no matter how uniform particular segments of that discourse appear to be' (Gilbert and Mulkay, 1984: 7). Language is not simply a neutral medium for generating subject knowledge, but a form of social practice that acts to *constitute* as much as to reflect social realities (Silverman, 2000). Indeed, some post-structuralist linguists (e.g. Barthes, 1977; Baxter, 2003) go further than this in advocating that the language of research is a textualizing practice which requires analysts to be constantly self-reflexive about the constitutive power of their linguistic data.

In line with the post-structuralist view, different discourse-analytic approaches, situated as they are within different epistemological paradigms, are likely to produce varying sets of accounts of the same data. The chapter will review four approaches to discourse analysis considered to be of particular significance for current research in linguistics: namely, Conversation Analysis (CA), Discourse Analysis (DA), Critical Discourse Analysis (CDA) and Feminist Post-structuralist Discourse Analysis (FPDA). This is a small selection of a rich and diverse range of analytic approaches in the field that also includes Speech Act Theory, Interactional Sociolinguistics, Ethnography of Communication, Pragmatics, Variation Analysis and Discursive Psychology.

A key way to schematize discourse-analytic methodology is in terms of its relationship between *micro*analytical approaches, which examine the finer detail of linguistic interactions in transcripts, and *macro*analytical approaches, which consider how broader social processes work through language (Heller, 2001). The four approaches have been selected here not only because they have become highly influential in the field, but also because they manifest interesting differences and contrasts between microanalytical or 'bottom-up' approaches (CA); macroanalytical or 'top-down' approaches (CDA); and methods which aim to combine (DA), or indeed challenge aspects of both (FPDA).

Over the years, applied linguists such as Heller (2001) have suggested that the micro–macro dichotomy may not be the most helpful way in which to understand how the observable dimensions of linguistic interaction are linked to more durable structures which lie beyond the control of individual speakers and writers. Heller's (2006) own work in minority language education leads the way in showing how a 'big picture' approach which aims to identify larger issues can be interwoven with the fine detail of action research data in order to make sense of a significant linguistic problem. This chapter will consider whether there is a strength in a discourse-analytic approach that aligns itself exclusively with either a micro- or macrostrategy, or whether, as Heller suggests, the field needs to find a way of 'undoing' the micro–macro dichotomy in order to produce richer, more complex insights within linguistic research.

6.2 Four approaches to discourse analysis

The term 'discourse' is itself a contested term, which has generated a lot of debate among scholars about what it means and how it should be used. The first most straightforward definition – and the one that is still routinely used in linguistics textbooks – is that of 'language above the sentence' and refers to a sequence of sentences or utterances that constitutes a 'text' (Cameron, 2001). The second is its more functional and sociolinguistic definition as 'language in use', or 'language in social context', which is typically the implication of descriptive labels such as 'media discourse', 'legal discourse', 'educational discourse', and so on. This definition seems to cohere with Fairclough's (1992: 3) description of discourse as the 'situational context of language use' involving 'the interaction between reader/writer and text'. Finally, linguists whose work overlaps with post-structuralist and critical theory (as indeed, Fairclough's does) are also likely to understand discourse in the plural – as discourses. Such a usage reflects the influence of cultural historian, Michel Foucault, who famously defined discourses as 'practices that systematically form the objects of which they speak' (Foucault, 1972: 42). In simpler terms, discourses are more than just linguistic: they are social and ideological practices which can govern the ways in which people think, speak, interact, write and behave. Cameron (2001) gives the example of discourses on drug use, which can take multiple forms as dominant and resistant social attitudes, ways of speaking, formulaic behaviours, government policies, laws, anti- and pro-drug literature, and so on. The three definitions of discourse(s) above will be apparent in the discussion of the four approaches that now follow.

6.2.1 Conversation Analysis (CA)

Of the four approaches to discourse analysis, CA takes the most decisive departure from Chomsky's view that linguistic performance is of little relevance to the linguist. Indeed, proponents of CA would posit the reverse: that 'talk-in-interaction' provides extraordinarily rich evidence of the underlying rules of how language works.

The field of ethnomethodology with its interest in 'the study of methods used by a group of people' is a strong source of inspiration for CA. Its most famous pioneer, the sociologist, Harvey Sacks (1992) had been exploring a corpus of phone calls to the Los Angeles Suicide Prevention Centre, and noticed that, while members of staff were required to *elicit* callers' names during the course of the conversation, the callers themselves would use a range of strategies to *avoid* revealing their identity. Sacks began to wonder 'where in the course of conversation could you tell that somebody would not give their name' (Sacks, Vol. I: 3). With this examination of talk-in-interaction, Sacks raised the possibility of investigating utterances as social *actions* which speakers use to get things done (or to *avoid* getting things done) in the course of a conversation with others.

Increasingly linguists and social scientists are recognizing that the social world is pervasively a conversational one in which an overwhelming proportion of the world's activities are conducted through spoken interactions, whether it is taking part in a meeting, arranging an appointment, sealing a deal, making a complaint, enjoying a family meal or simply negotiating day-to-day relationships with people. In short, CA considers that ordinary conversations construct social realities. Through the use of audio or video recordings produced as transcripts, analysts can examine directly how talk organizes the world within specific social settings.

So, what are the key features of the CA approach? We shall consider the following:

- *Orderliness in talk-in-interaction*: Ordinary, everyday speech exhibits a high level of regularity or orderliness. This orderliness is not governed by innate cognitive structures of language (although grammatical features clearly inform the structure of utterances), but reflects a socially organized structure of interpersonal action. This orderliness, known as 'the speech-exchange system' is apparent in the pattern of sequential turn-taking, which, in Sacks et al.'s (1974) view, characterizes most spoken interaction. The following extract involves a conversation between three friends and Deborah Schiffrin, the researcher:

1 Henry:	Y'want a piece of candy?
2 Irene:	No.
3 Zelda:	She's not on a diet=
4 Debby:	= who's not on [a diet
5 Irene:	[I'm on- I'm on a diet²

  (Schiffrin, 1994: 62)

  Despite the apparent 'messiness' of this snatch of casual conversation, there is, nevertheless, an orderliness conducted by means of 'adjacency pairs': the question–answer sequence in lines 1–2, and the statement–response sequence of lines 3–4, and lines 4–5. In each adjacency pair, the second part of the pair becomes the first part of the next pair of exchanges, which produces a 'chain' of turns. In this way, the answer in line 2 is also the statement to which Zelda orients and responds in line 3, and so on.

- *A data-centred approach*: CA has a primary interest in transcript data and what these data reveal. Cameron (2001: 89) describes CA's microanalytical approach to spoken discourse as 'putting a snowflake under the microscope to examine its complexity and detail'. In order to enhance the quality of microanalysis, Jefferson (1984) evolved a detailed transcription system to help analysts provide a characterization of how meaning is produced through verbal, vocal, prosodic and paralinguistic means.

- *A neutral and objective stance*: Analysts are discouraged from bringing any theoretical or philosophical presuppositions to the data, in order to allow these to 'speak for themselves'. *A priori* speculation in terms of speaker 'orientations', motivations and identities, social settings and cultural norms, are regarded as distracting and irrelevant. Factors 'external' to the data, such as gender inequalities or cultural misunderstandings may be 'made relevant' by the participants in the transcript data. It is on this basis alone that external factors become available to the analyst for comment and interpretation.

Overall, the quest in most CA studies is to understand how turn-taking within a stretch of talk is negotiated between participants, in order to produce some form of social action or 'reality'. The turn-taking system provides a basic framework for the organization of talk, since it allows participants to interact in a co-ordinated way, rather than simply to make random, disconnected contributions. Interaction is often structured around pairs of adjacent utterances, or statement–response structures. Thus, if the first utterance is a question, the next utterance will usually be heard as an answer.

In one renowned study of news interview interaction by Heritage and Greatbatch (1991), clear patterns were discovered in the use of adjacency pairs leading to an ordered sequence of interactions. The interviewer was commonly found to use a preface, such as a statement of apparent fact, and then a question, which was routinely followed by an answer from the interviewee:

| Interviewer: | hhh the (.) price being asked for these letters is (.) three thousand pou::ds (.) are you going to raise it (0.5) |
| Interviewee: | at the moment it . . . (continues) |

(Heritage and Greatbatch, 1991: 99)

What emerges from this study is that, however combative the participants or adversarial the interview, participants tacitly expect this pattern within the interaction. In other words, it is a normative arrangement which confers expectations and obligations on the participants in predictable ways. Participants 'orient' to the obligation to produce questions and answers, and they orient to expectations of the way the activities within a news interview should be carried out.

Despite its name, therefore, CA does not concern itself only with social conversation. The approach has also been applied to talk in professional and workplace settings (Drew and Heritage, 1992), to political speeches (Atkinson, 1984), media genres such as radio phone-ins (Hutchby, 1996), and to understanding neighbourhood disputes (Edwards and Stokoe, 2007). Drew and Heritage (1992) have argued that there are structural differences between formal and informal settings. For example, within institutional talk, participation is focused on particular tasks and outcomes; the order of participation is fairly rigid; and the kind of turns expected of participants is relatively limited and to a certain extent, preallocated.

So, what is the contribution of CA to the field of linguistics? Primarily, the approach continues to demonstrate that fundamental rules govern the patterning of talk-in-interaction. Just as we can theorize the rules that underlie grammatical and syntactical choices, so we can make reasoned predictions – based on our knowledge of turn-taking rules and the ways these are occasionally broken or 'violated' – of the ways in which participants typically construct conversations within given social contexts. Schegloff (1997: 184) has posited that CA satisfies the need for a systematic form of discourse analysis that offers linguists an 'Archimedean point' which is 'internal to the object of analysis itself'. In other words, CA's data-centred approach possesses its own internal rule system, which allows linguistic data to be analysed neutrally and a single, reliable interpretation to be reached. CA focuses on what linguistic data reveal, rather than upon external, sociological theorizing, and additionally offers what it regards as a reliable set of instruments by which to describe, analyse and interpret spoken discourse within the field of linguistics. By the same token, CA can be deployed by researchers as an invaluable 'stand-alone' tool in cross-disciplinary studies. For example, Ehrlich (2006) uses CA as her analytical tool to examine question–answer sequences in a US courtroom rape case, to support her broader discussion of gender identities and power. Kitzinger (2002) has also evolved a version of CA known as Feminist Conversation Analysis whereby the methodology is harnessed to identify exactly how participants 'do' power and powerlessness, oppression and resistance within gendered contexts.

By using methods of microanalysis, working from the bottom up, CA attaches a very special value to the linguistic data itself and regards itself quasi-scientifically, as a caution against 'the relativisation and perspectivisation of cultural analysis' (Schegloff, 1997: 183). However, not all linguists using discourse analysis would agree that such a quest for neutrality or objectivity is attainable or even desirable, as we shall now see.

6.2.2 Discourse Analysis (DA)

Discourse Analysis (DA) has a strong focus on studying language in its own right, although it is often appropriated as an analytic tool by researchers from other disciplines. Like CA, this approach in its diverse strands recognizes that there is an orderliness, logic and meaningfulness to linguistic performance. The hallmark of DA, however, is its recognition of the variability in and the context dependence of participants' discourse. By far the most common sources of data for DA tend to be the accounts drawn from recordings of informal, spoken interviews between researchers and respondents, making it a popular, qualitative method of data analysis for linguists and social scientists alike (e.g. Lawes, 1999; Widdicombe, 1993). However, it has also been used to analyse a variety of data such as formal academic journal writing (Gilbert and Mulkay, 1984); newspaper reports and media interviews (Potter and Reicher, 1987), and accounts of journalists and politicians during a political controversy (Potter and Edwards, 1990).

Despite its clear focus on language, DA, like CA, has its origins in sociology. Social scientists Gilbert and Mulkay (1984) were investigating the sociology of scientific knowledge following a dispute in the field of biochemistry. Their analytical goal was to discover the systematic features of scientists' discourse but they came across strongly conflicting descriptions of experience. They had wanted to produce a single, definitive, sociological account of the social processes which were at work in the way this group of scientists resolved their dispute. The pair began to realize that accounts and descriptions cannot be treated as neutral representations of an 'objective' social reality but as linguistic *constructions* of a given experience (see also Chapter 8). In other words, they received a variety of different versions of ostensibly the same phenomenon: scientists' discourse in formal academic journals was systematically different from the discourse generated in informal interviews. The former appeared to be constituted through an 'empiricist repertoire', indexed by the use of formal language and terminology, a strict adherence to scientific procedure and its role in revealing an 'objective' reality, while the latter was constituted through a 'contingent repertoire', indexed by a more informal tone, biographical detail, personal comment and expression of feeling. In short, specific forms of language use were seen to construct different versions of reality.

So what are the key features of DA? Four are of interest to us here:

- *Principle of variability*: Language is used for a variety of functions and its use has variable consequences. The same phenomenon (such as a scientific experiment) can be described in a number of different ways according to audience, purpose and context, and thus there will be considerable variation in accounts. Accordingly, these will be received and interpreted in a range of contrasting but context-appropriate ways.
- *Constructed and constructive nature of language*: According to Gilbert and Mulkay (1984: 7), 'discourse can never be taken as simply descriptive of the social action to which it refers, no matter how uniform particular segments of that discourse appear to be.' Rather, any account of experience is a form of interpretation, constituting a new version of reality. Thus, the kinds of linguistic events that occur in interview data – descriptions, narratives, accounts, comments, jokes – are constructions that depend on the context in which they are produced and the purposes speakers wish them to serve. Indeed, the constructive and flexible ways in which language is used should themselves become a subject for study (Potter and Wetherell, 1987).
- *Interpretative repertoire*: Research accounts often provide evidence of regular, descriptive features or devices. The term 'repertoire' here denotes 'recurrently used systems of terms used for characterizing and evaluating actions, events and other phenomena' (Potter and Wetherell, 1987: 149). Repertoires are often signified by 'a distinctive vocabulary, particular stylistic and grammatical features, and the occurrence of specific features of speech, idiomatic expressions and metaphors' (Wooffitt, 2005).
- *A combination of micro- and macroanalytical approaches*: Micro- and macroanalytical approaches work together to produce an interpretation within DA. Its main conceptual tool, interpretative or linguistic repertoires are used to identify regular features in the data such as idioms, metaphors, figures of speech and professional terminology, which may signify wider patterns of language use. These in turn provide evidence for speculating about the role of contingent psychological, social or political factors that may inform the speech or writing of research participants. However, unlike CA, DA does not offer the same degree of formal methodological procedure (Wooffitt, 2005).

Overall, DA has principles in common with the Saussurian view that language constructs social realities through its use of culturally agreed sign systems. But DA takes issue with the positivist and empiricist basis to much traditional linguistic research that treats language data as available to objective or indeed, scientific forms of inquiry. Unlike CA, DA works from a hermeneutic, interpretative or social constructionist stance, which challenges the idea that there is a single 'Archimedean point' from which linguistic data can be analysed neutrally and a single, reliable interpretation reached. This positivist principle which underlies CA has been further challenged by the work of discourse analysts Potter and Wetherell (1987), who argue that ideologies are embodied in, and reproduced through everyday discourse practices. In their DA study of the racist discourse of white New Zealanders (1992), they draw upon methods of microanalysis to identify the textual evidence for linguistic repertoires which, they argue, signifies the macrostructuring role of dominant ideologies such as racism and unequal class relations.

What is the contribution of DA to the field of linguistics? Certainly, DA has evolved into a theoretical framework that potentially threatens tenets of linguistics as a 'science'. For many applied and sociolinguists working in interdisciplinary ways with various forms of cultural analysis, DA's social constructionist and interpretative stance is likely to make good epistemological sense. DA combines microanalysis of language with macrolevel discussion about how versions of social reality are constituted, and thereafter made resistant to criticism by the use of specific rhetorical strategies. This makes it a particularly effective method for deconstructing the linguistic accounts of political and media figures (e.g. Potter and Edwards, 1990). But Wooffitt (2005) argues that DA is limited by its lack of a formal apparatus by which to conduct such microanalyses, and tends to borrow methods eclectically from a range of fields such as Speech Act Theory, literary criticism and indeed, CA. Recent versions of DA have become more closely associated with Discursive Psychology (e.g. Harré, 1995), which in turn has some links with CDA (e.g. Billig, 1997).

6.3 Critical Discourse Analysis (CDA)

CDA is useful to linguistic scholars because, like CA and DA, it analyses real, and often extended, samples of spoken and written discourse. However, unlike CA in particular, CDA adopts a macroanalytical view of the world in that it takes the notion of *discourse* in its widest sense (see p. 120) as social and ideological practice. Thus CDA research specifically considers how language works within institutional and political discourses (e.g. in education, organizations, media, government), as well as specific discourses (around gender and class), in order to uncover overt or more often, covert inequalities in social relationships.

CDA does not regard itself as a coherent theory, a subdiscipline of discourse analysis or as a methodological approach like CA and DA. Rather, it views itself as a 'critical' perspective, or programme of scholarship which can be combined with other approaches and commissioned by scholars working in a range of disciplines related both to linguistics and to the social sciences more generally (van Dijk, 2001a). CDA evolved formally in the early 1990s as a perspective applied by a network of scholars with shared political concerns about social inequalities in the world but with widely differing interests in areas such as literature, politics, media studies, genre studies and information technology (see below). Since then, various branches of the movement have emerged. Among these, Critical Linguistics (e.g. Fowler et al., 1979) is the forerunner of CDA and looks closely at how features of grammar work ideologically within individual texts to undermine oppressed groups. French Discourse Analysis (e.g. Pecheux, 1982) looks at the ideological effects of discursive formations in positioning people as social subjects but does not emphasize practical applications of theory. Social Semiotics (e.g. Hodge and Kress, 1988) explores ways of analysing multimodal texts and practices of reading and interpreting. Socio-cognitive studies (van Dijk, 1991) focus on the reproduction of inequalities such as racism and ethnic prejudices in discourse and media communication, linking cognition with wider social processes. Lastly, the Discourse-historical method aims to 'integrate systematically all available background information in the analysis and interpretation of the many layers of a written or spoken text' (Fairclough and Wodak, 1997: 266). Whether analysts with a critical perspective prefer to focus on microlinguistic features as in the case of Social Semiotics, or macrolinguistic features as in the case of French Discourse Analysis, or combine the two as the Discourse-historical approach aims to achieve, a common reference point for all approaches is primarily a linguistic one: that of Halliday's systemic functional grammar. Halliday (1970: 142) stressed the relationship between the grammatical system and the social and personal needs that language is required to serve, through three meta-functions of language that are continuously interconnected: the ideational, the interpersonal and the textual. Hence, in Halliday's view as a linguist, text and context are inextricably linked in a dialectically constitutive relationship.

With its historical origins in mind, as well as its theoretical diversity, which key features are central to CDA's 'critical perspective'? The following are suggested here:

- *Language as social practice*: Language use in speech and writing is seen as a social practice, which 'implies a dialectical relationship between a particular discursive event and the situation(s), institution(s), and social structure(s) which frame it' (Fairclough and Wodak, 1997: 258). Thus, in this two-way relationship, discourse is considered to be socially constitutive as well as socially shaped.

- *Relationship between language and power*: Since discourses are so influential, they can help to produce and reproduce unequal power relations between different ethnicities, social classes, genders, ages, and professional groups.
- *A committed, emancipatory agenda*: Van Dijk (2001a: 96) has used the term 'critical' to mean 'discourse analysis with attitude'. Working from the opposite pole to CA, CDA starts from 'prevailing social problems, and thereby chooses the perspective of those who suffer most, and critically analyses those in power, those who are responsible, and those who have the means and the opportunity to solve such problems' (van Dijk, 1991: 4).
- *Text and context*: CDA largely draws upon a 'solid linguistic basis' (van Dijk, 2001a: 97) in that it examines textual features such as sentence structure, verb tense, syntax, lexical choice, the internal coherence and cohesion of discourse and so on. However, it places such microanalysis first, within a 'critical perspective', and second, within the contextual frame of the 'production' and 'consumption' of discourses. In practice this means that the analyst should consider the ways in which historical and cultural processes/structures give rise to the production of a text and the ways subjects within these processes/structures 'consume', or interact with texts. This implies a dialectical relationship between the reading of a particular text and the context, institution or social structure that frames this reading (Fairclough and Wodak, 1997).
- *Self-reflexivity*: Given CDA's commitment to an emancipatory agenda, an important self-correcting principle is that of self-reflexivity: the need for discourse analysts to be explicitly self-referential about their *a priori* assumptions, motivations and value systems in conducting linguistic research. Such value systems are often informed by Marxist critical theory, which in turn is viewed – in a curious reversal of CA logic – as offering analysts an objective reference point on social reality (Blommaert, 2005).
- *Interdiscursivity/intertextuality*: Interdiscursivity involves the ways in which one discourse is always inscribed and inflected with traces of other discourses. Chouliaraki and Fairclough (1999: 136) give the example of feminist political discourses which have 'internalised Marxist and poststructuralist discourses, incorporating some of their concepts, but appropriating them in ways which accord with their own logic'. Likewise intertextuality is where one text bears traces of a series of preceding texts, thus reinforcing historical presuppositions. Fairclough (2001: 127) gives the example of a magazine article on a royal wedding, which presupposes reader knowledge about participants, situational context and implicit power relations ('royal family are more important than readers').
- *Deconstruction*: CDA is concerned to unravel exactly how binary power relations constitute identities, subject positions and interactions within discourses and texts, and thus create social inequalities. One example is Wodak's deconstructive analysis of a series of interview narratives with Members of the European Parliament in order to ascertain whether gender mainstreaming policies were genuinely producing structural changes in equalizing gender roles (Wodak, 2005).

With its diverse range of theoretical approaches, no single research study can be considered prototypical of CDA, although common to many studies is an interest in institutional discourse and the language of the media. However, van Dijk's (1993) study of racism and political discourse contains some useful illustrative elements. The topic – the transcript of a speech made by a British Conservative Member of Parliament defending articles written by a right-wing head teacher from Bradford, UK, on multicultural education – is in keeping with CDA's aim to show how discourse enacts and reproduces the power of dominant groups. In this study, van Dijk's elaborate series of interpretative procedures is also fairly typical of the CDA tendency to produce complex, hierarchical models of linguistic analysis. Working from a top-down perspective, he first examines features of the broader context such as matters of access, setting and linguistic genre. He moves on to look at discourse dimensions of the speech itself, and then turns to 'macrosemantics': ways in which the debate is formulated, and the argumentative propositions within the speech. This leads finally to microanalytical matters of 'local meaning and coherence', involving the examination of lexical and grammatical features such as the use of words like 'mob' or 'Trots' to characterize the speakers' opponents (see Wooffitt, 2005: 142–3).

What is CDA's contribution to the field of linguistics? It is fair to say that 'the jury is out' in terms of how the field of linguistics has received CDA. On the plus side, CDA has been of immense value to researchers looking at institutional discourse, where differentials in power relations are often systemic. As we have seen, different theorists have provided models of analysis and sets of analytical tools with which to deconstruct public and media discourse. On the negative side, linguists have criticized CDA in terms of the vagueness of its method, methodology and analytical approaches; as well as in terms of 'its biased interpretations of discourse under the guise of critical analysis' (Blommaert, 2005: see p. 31 for a full discussion). For those linguists who continue to assess their subject primarily as a science governed by a positivist model of research, CDA will beg all sorts of questions about 'representativeness, selectivity, partiality, prejudice and voice' (2005: 31). For those linguists whose research has already embraced hermeneutic, interpretivist or social constructionist principles, CDA will be appreciated for its readiness to declare its principles and to marry ideological commitment to the pursuit of rigorous, replicable and retrievable research methods.

6.4 Feminist Post-structuralist Discourse Analysis (FPDA)

Like CDA, FPDA has its roots in DA approaches but more exclusively draws from post-structuralist theory (e.g. Bakhtin, 1981; Derrida, 1987; Foucault, 1972). Rather than taking a 'critical' perspective on the data based on Marxist social theory, it has embraced a 'feminist post-structuralist' perspective.

FPDA can be defined as:

> an approach to analysing intertextualised discourses in spoken interaction and other types of text. It draws upon the poststructuralist principles of complexity, plurality, ambiguity, connection, recognition, diversity, textual playfulness, functionality and transformation.
>
> The *feminist* perspective on poststructuralist discourse analysis considers *gender differentiation* to be a dominant discourse among competing discourses when analysing all types of text.
>
> (Baxter, 2008: 245)

FPDA originated from Post-structuralist Discourse Analysis (PDA) – see Baxter (2007). PDA adopts exactly parallel methods to its partner, but *without* the focus on a feminist perspective where gender differentiation is key. FPDA originally evolved in response to an ethnographic case study of teenage school children's assessed talk in a British classroom. During the long-term process of observing how these students interacted during a course module on public speaking, Baxter (2003) discovered that the ways in which children's talk was assessed as part of their GCSE[3] examination depended as much on the interplay of four ethnographically identified, dominant 'discourses' – in the widest sense of this term (see above) – as upon any formal assessment criteria. The discourses were labelled *gender differentiation, peer and staff approval, fair play* and a *model of collaborative talk*, which were seen to 'position' individual students in different and competing ways, at times as relatively powerful, and at other times as relatively powerless. Thus, Baxter's (2003) research evidence revealed that students who were awarded the top 'A' grade were not necessarily the most proficient speakers in the class. Rather, these students were more consistently positioned as powerful subjects among their classmates within and across the four discourses, which in practice meant that they tended to be male, popular with their peers, liked by their teachers, given more turns in class discussions, and able to use both presentational and collaborative forms of talk reasonably effectively. These positions of power were inscribed by hegemonic educational and social practices which appear to approve the ascendancy of males, the role of 'high status' students, and the abilities of speakers rather than listeners.

FPDA does share with CDA a number of defining features in keeping with its social constructionist origins: the idea of language as social practice; the relation between language and power; the importance of the self-reflexive researcher, the principle of intertextuality; and the role of deconstruction in conducting discourse analysis (see pp. 127–8). However, FPDA is not simply a sub-branch of the multidisciplinary and accommodating CDA, because it operates within a contrasting yet 'supplementary' theoretical paradigm (Derrida, 1987).

So, what are the key defining features of FPDA, which distinguish it from CDA? We can summarize these as follows:

- *Not an emancipatory agenda, but a 'transformative quest'*: In line with its post-structuralist origins, FPDA does not support an emancipatory agenda to discourse analysis because this is 'a will to truth' leading to 'a will to power', which will ultimately transmute into its own 'grand narrative' (Foucault, 1972). Alternatively, FPDA supports small-scale, bottom-up, localized social transformations that are vital in its larger quest to challenge dominant discourses (like gender differentiation, or indeed, an institutionalized method of linguistic analysis such as CDA.)
- *The diversity and multiplicity of speakers' identities*: For FPDA, many power variables construct speakers' identities such as regional background, ethnicity, class, age, though among these, gender is viewed as a significant force. According to context or moment, some of these variables are more or less salient in constructing identities through spoken interaction. FPDA also has the potential to analyse the multivoiced dimensions of *written* discourse, but as yet there is little such work in the field (e.g. see Warhol, 2005).
- *Complexity rather than polarization of subjects of study*: FPDA challenges binary thinking that tends to structure thoughts in oppositional pairs, placing one term over the other. Significantly, it takes issue with CDA's tendency to polarize subjects of study into two categories: the *more* powerful, those (people, groups, systems) who wield power over others; and the *less* powerful, or those who suffer its abuse (Baxter, 2007). So, for example, FPDA argues that most females are *not* helpless victims of patriarchal oppression, but that gender identities are complex, shifting and multiply located, continuously fluctuating between subject positions of powerfulness and powerlessness.
- *An interplay between micro- and macroanalysis*: FPDA draws upon both levels of analysis, or rather, an interplay between the two. The microlevel looks at the construction of meaning within localized or context-specific settings such as classrooms, board meetings and TV talk shows. Within these, it examines linguistic data in terms of turn-taking, sentence structure, verb tense, lexical choice, the internal coherence and cohesion of discourse, aspects which help analysts to

pinpoint the exact moments in discourse when a speaker shifts between states of relative powerfulness and powerlessness. Drawing on this finely grained evidence, dominant discourses are identified synchronically within individual transcripts, and diachronically, over a sequence of transcripts. Macroanalysis, drawing on the identified, dominant discourses, helps to explain major or more subtle shifts in the power relations between speakers within particular interactions and contexts.

What is the contribution of FPDA to the field of linguistics? While it is the newest and least established of the four approaches, FPDA is arguably a necessary antidote to the other three, in that it offers a 'supplementary' approach, simultaneously complementing and undermining other methods. Within linguistics, there is much value to be gained from a *multiperspectival* approach that combines different methodological tools in a pragmatic way as befits the task in hand. The textual interplay between competing terms, methods and sets of ideas allows for more multiple, open-ended readings of a piece of analysis. Thus while CDA in principle (e.g. van Dijk, 2001a) seeks to deconstruct hegemonic power relations inscribed within texts, and in so doing, may produce a single, oppositional reading that may eventually become authoritative, a post-structuralist, supplementary approach encourages the possibility of several competing readings. This means that no single reading of a text is regarded as fixed, but that every reading can be reviewed and perhaps contested in the light of competing perspectives or methods of analysis. Much exciting and challenging work within linguistics is being carried out by scholars prepared to experiment with multiperspectival and multimethod approaches. For example, Kamada (2008) combines discourse-analytic approaches including FPDA with Bourdieu's (1977) theories of cultural analysis to explore the linguistic construction of ethnic identities among six Japanese-Caucasian girlfriends. Castañeda-Peña (2008) makes FPDA his central approach for analysing the speech of preschoolers in Colombia, but also draws upon CA approaches to microanalyse sequences of conversational turns, as well as applying a CDA critique. In sum, it is the quest of FPDA to act as a kind of 'agent provocateur' to other more established approaches to discourse analysis, constantly questioning their status as 'grand narratives' (Baxter, 2008: 243) which may serve to impede new ways of thinking.

What are the possible limitations of FPDA? The first may lie in its *warrant* for identifying, naming and analysing significant discourses within classroom and other contexts. There are times when it seems that both CDA and FPDA are capable of randomly generating new discourses to suit their ideological

(CDA) or epistemological (FPDA) purposes. CA, in contrast, bases its own warrants on a systematic methodology: any larger patterns it claims to detect in its microanalysis of 'talk-in-interaction' can always be located, turn by turn, within specific speech exchanges. Secondly, FPDA may need to devise more linguistically distinctive methods of analysis. At present, its 'denotative' approach to analysis relies on eclectic methods more associated with Interactional Sociolinguistics, literary criticism and CA. The attribution of a rigorous and reliable method of analysis – a distinctive brand – still remains the preserve of CA.

6.5 Conclusion

This chapter has explored four approaches to analysing discourse that are of particular value to the field of linguistics. First, CA is a microanalytical approach which offers a theoretical framework, a terminology and a systematic *modus operandi* for analysing spoken discourse in particular. Furthermore, CA is a perfect instrument for linguists of any theoretical persuasion who are looking for a 'stand-alone' set of analytical tools in order to examine spoken interaction in relation to a clear model of the 'rules' of turn-taking. Secondly, DA offers linguists a bridge between micro- and macroanalytical approaches in its key concept of the 'interpretative' or 'linguistic repertoire'. It works 'above the sentence' in its exploration of how highly conventionalized patterns of language, constructed by characteristic stylistic features, help to construct different accounts of social reality. However, it does not offer such a clear and accessible 'stand-alone' approach as CA. Thirdly, CDA has always refuted that it is, in fact, a discourse-analytic approach. Linguists attracted to the use of CDA are likely to share the critical perspective that macrosocietal concerns, such as processes of inequality, transcend a scientific interest in 'language for language's sake'. In the past ten years, CDA exponents have done much to counter the charge that their top-down approach fails to 'explain how their perspective might apply to what is happening right now, on the ground, in this very conversation' (Wetherell, 1998: 395), but their research work has tended to result in higher level modelling of linguistic and social processes (Wodak, 2001; van Dijk, 2001a), in preference to data-centred studies. Finally, FPDA aims to demonstrate that the notion of a contradiction between micro- and macroanalysis is irrelevant. It has shown how its approach can 'undo the macro–micro dichotomy' (Heller, 2001: 212), by analysing transcripts microanalytically within a given time and space, and using these as a reference point for identifying how larger-scale discourses produce significant shifts in the power relations between speakers during a stretch of discourse.

Overall, linguists have a rich fund of discourse-analytic resources at their disposal, each of which challenges the Chomskyan shibboleth that 'linguistic performance' teaches us nothing about how language works.

Notes

1. See Silverman (2000) for a critique of the 'realist' paradigm of social science and linguistic research.
2. Transcription conventions are based on Jefferson (1984).
3. GCSE: General Certificate of Secondary Education, an examination for 15 to 16 year olds used in Britain and other English-speaking parts of the world.

Further reading

Baxter (2003) – This introduction to FPDA shows how the discourse-analytic approach works in relation to the social contexts of classroom discussions, and senior management meetings.

Blommaert (2005) – This book develops a constructive critique of CDA, which is made relevant to students of linguistics, linguistic anthropology and the sociology of language.

Cameron (2001) – Aimed primarily at students of linguistics, this is a useful introduction to the theory and practice of CA, CDA and a range of other approaches to spoken, rather than written discourse.

Wooffitt (2005) – This book systematically analyses the close and complex relationship between CA and DA in academic research, particularly as these methodologies apply to linguistics.

References

Atkinson, J. (1984), *Our Masters' Voices*. London: Routledge.

Bakhtin, M. (1981), *The Dialogic Imagination: Four Essays*. Austin, TX: University of Texas.

Barthes, R. (1977), *Image-Music-Text*. New York: Hill and Wang.

Baxter, J. (2003), *Positioning Gender in Discourse: A Feminist Methodology*. Basingstoke: Palgrave.

—. (2007), 'Post-structuralist analysis of classroom discourse', in M. Martin-Jones and A. M. de Mejia (eds), *Encyclopaedia of Language and Education: Discourse and Education*, vol. 3. New York: Springer, pp. 69–80.

—. (2008), 'FPDA – a new theoretical and methodological approach?', in K. Harrington, L. Litosseliti, H. Sauntson and J. Sunderland (eds), *Gender and Language Research Methodologies*. Basingstoke: Palgrave Macmillan, pp. 243–55.

Billig, M. (1997), 'Rhetorical and discursive analysis: how families talk about the Royal Family', in N. Hayes (ed.), *Doing Qualitative Analysis in Psychology*. Hove: Psychology Press, pp. 39–54.

Blommaert, J. (2005), *Discourse*. Cambridge: Cambridge University Press.

Bourdieu, P. (1977), *Outline of a Theory of Practice*. Cambridge: Cambridge University Press.

Cameron, D. (2001), *Working with Spoken Discourse*. London: Sage.

Castañeda-Peña, H. (2008), 'Interwoven and competing gendered discourses in a pre-school EFL lesson', in K. Harrington, L .Litosseliti, H. Sauntson and J. Sunderland (eds), *Gender and Language Research Methodologies*. Basingstoke: Palgrave Macmillan, pp. 256–68.

Chomsky, N. (1965), *Aspects of the Theory of Syntax*. Cambridge MA: MIT Press.

Chouliaraki, L. and Fairclough, N. (1999), *Discourse in Late Modernity: Rethinking Critical Discourse Analysis*. Edinburgh: Edinburgh University Press.

Derrida, J. (1987), *A Derrida Reader: Between the Blinds*. Brighton: Harvester Wheatsheaf.

Drew, P. and Heritage, J. (1992), *Talk at Work: Interaction in Institutional Settings*. Cambridge: Cambridge University Press.

Edwards, D. and Stokoe, E. (2007), 'Self-help in calls for help with problem neighbours', *Research on Language and Social Interaction*, 40 (1), 9–32.

Ehrlich, S. (2006), 'Trial discourse and judicial decision-making: constraining the boundaries of gendered identities', in J. Baxter (ed.), *Speaking Out: The Female Voice in Public Contexts*. Basingstoke: Palgrave, pp. 139–58.

Fairclough, N. (1992), *Discourse and Social Change*. London: Polity Press.

—. (2001), *Language and Power* (2nd edn). London: Pearson.

Fairclough, N. and Wodak, R. (1997), 'Critical discourse analysis', in T. van Dijk (ed.), *Discourse as Social Interaction*. London: Sage, pp. 258–84.

Foucault, M. (1972), *The Archaeology of Knowledge and the Discourse on Language*. New York: Pantheon.

Fowler, R, Hodge, R, Kress, G. and Trew, T. (1979), *Language and Control*. London: Routledge and Kegan Paul.

Gilbert, G. N. and Mulkay, M. J. (1984), *Opening Pandora's Box: A Sociological Analysis of Scientists' Discourse*. Cambridge: Cambridge University Press.

Halliday, M. (1970), *The Linguistic Sciences and Language Teaching*. London: Longman.

Harré, R. (1995) 'Agentive discourse', in R. Harré and P. Stearns (eds), *Discursive Psychology in Practice*. London: Sage, pp. 120–36.

Heller, M. (2001), 'Undoing the macro/micro dichotomy: ideology and categorisation in a linguistic minority school', in N. Coupland, S. Sarangi and C. N. Candlin (eds), *Sociolinguistics and Social Theory*. London: Longman, pp. 212–34.

—. (2006), *Linguistic Minorities and Modernity: A Sociolinguistic Ethnography* (2nd edn). London: Continuum International Publishing Group.

Heritage, J. and Greatbatch, D. (1991), 'On the institutional character of institutional talk: the case of news interviews', in D. Boden and D. H. Zimmerman (eds), *Talk and Social Structure*. Berkeley, CA: University of California Press, pp. 93–137.

Hodge, R. and Kress, G. (1988), *Social Semantics*. Cambridge: Polity Press.

Hutchby, I. (1996), 'Power in discourse: the case of arguments on a British radio talk show', *Discourse & Society*, 7 (4), 481–97.

Hymes, D. (1972), 'On communicative competence', in J. B. Pride and J. Holmes (eds), *Sociolinguistics*. London: Penguin, pp. 269–93.

Jefferson, G. (1984), 'Transcription notation', in J. Atkinson and J. Heritage (eds), *Structures of Social Interaction*. New York: Cambridge University Press.

Kamada, L. (2008), 'Discursive "embodied" identities of "half" girls in Japan: a multi-perspectival approach within Feminist Poststructuralist Discourse Analysis', in K. Harrington, L. Litosseliti, H. Sauntson and J. Sunderland (eds), *Gender and Language Research Methodologies*. Basingstoke: Palgrave Macmillan, pp. 174–90.

Kitzinger, C. (2002), 'Doing feminist conversation analysis', in P. McIlvenny (ed.), *Talking Gender and Sexuality*. London: John Benjamins.

Lawes, R. (1999), 'Marriage: an analysis of discourse', *British Journal of Social Pyschology*, 38, 1–20.

Litosseliti, L. and Sunderland, J. (2002), *Gender Identity and Discourse Analysis*. Amsterdam: John Benjamins.

Pecheux, M. (1982), *Language, Semantics and Ideology*. London: Macmillan.

Potter, J. and Edwards, D. (1990), 'Nigel Lawson's tent: discourse analysis, attribution theory and social psychology of fact', *European Journal of Psychology*, 20, 405–24.

Potter, J. and Reicher, S. (1987), 'Discourses of community and conflict: the organisation of social categories in accounts of a "riot"', *British Journal of Social Psychology*, 26, 25–40.

Potter, J. and Wetherell, M. (1987), *Discourse and Social Psychology: Beyond Attitudes and Behaviour*. London: Sage.

Sacks, H. (1992), *Lectures on Conversation, Vols I and II*. Oxford and Cambridge, MA: Blackwell.

Sacks, H., Schegloff, E. A. and Jefferson, G. (1974), 'A simplest systematics for the organisation of turn-taking for conversation', *Language*, 50, 696–735.

Schegloff, E. A. (1997), 'Whose text? Whose context?' *Discourse & Society*, 8 (2), 165–85.

Schiffrin, D. (1994), *Approaches to Discourse*. Oxford: Blackwell.

Silverman, D. (2000), 'Analyzing talk and text', in N. K. Denzin and Y. S. Lincoln (eds), *Handbook of Qualitative Research* (2nd edn). London: Sage.

van Dijk, T. (1991), *Racism and the Press*. London: Routledge.

—. (1993). '*Analyzing racism through discourse analysis. Some methodological reflections*', in J. Stanfield (ed.), *Race and Ethnicity in Research Method*. Newbury Park, CA: Sage, pp. 92–134.

—. (2001a), 'Multi-disciplinary CDA: a plea for diversity', in R. Wodak and M. Meyer (eds), *Methods of Critical Discourse Analysis*. London and Thousand Oaks, CA: Sage, pp. 1–13.

—. (2001b), 'Principles of critical discourse analysis', *Discourse & Society*, 4, 249–83.

Warhol, T. (2005), 'Feminist poststructuralist discourse analysis and biblical authority'. Paper delivered at BAAL/CUP Seminar: *Theoretical and Methodological Approaches to Gender and Language Study*, 18–19 November 2005, University of Birmingham, UK.

Wetherell, M. (1998), 'Positioning and interpretative repertoires: conversation analysis and post-structuralism in dialogue', *Discourse & Society*, 9 (3), 387–412.

Widdicombe, S. (1993), 'Autobiography and change: rhetoric and authenticity of 'gothic style', in E. Burnham and I. Parker (eds), *Discourse Analytic Research: Repertoires and Readings of Texts in Action*. London: Routledge.

Wodak, R. (1996), *Disorders of Discourse*. London: Longman.

—. (2001), 'What is CDA about – a summary of its history, important concepts and development', in R. Wodak and M. Meyer (eds), *Methods of Critical Discourse Analysis*. London and Thousand Oaks, CA: Sage, pp. 1–13.

—. (2005), 'Gender mainstreaming and the European Union: interdisciplinarity, gender studies and CDA' in M. Lazar (ed.), *Feminist Critical Discourse Analysis*. Basingstoke: Palgrave.

Wooffitt, R. (2005), *Conversation Analysis and Discourse Analysis: A Comparative Critical Introduction*. London: Sage.

7 Linguistic Ethnography

Angela Creese

Chapter outline

This chapter describes linguistic ethnography and its methodological and analytical contribution to the study of language and social life. It provides examples of its eclectic stance of combining different traditions of discourse analysis with ethnography and debates the opportunities and drawbacks of disciplinary and theoretical diversity. It describes two key issues in linguistic ethnography. The first relates to interdisciplinarity and the second to the challenges linguistic ethnography faces in the post-modern era. It also looks at the balance of different methods of data collection (ethnographic fieldnotes and interactional transcripts) and describes the relationship between the two. Several empirical studies are discussed in order to illustrate linguistic ethnography's application in the study of social contexts. Finally, team ethnography is put forward as a means to introduce voice, diversity and complexity into linguistic ethnographic accounts.

7.1 Background

Linguistic ethnography is a theoretical and analytical framework which takes an epistemological position broadly aligned with social constructivist and post-structuralist approaches by critiquing essentialist accounts of social life (Creese, 2008; Rampton, 2007). But it also draws widely on work in linguistic anthropology (Hymes, 1968; Erickson, 2004; Gumperz, 1982; Silverstein, 2003; Wortham, 2003). Rampton argues that linguistic ethnography is 'a site of encounter where a number of established lines of research interact, pushed together by circumstance, open to the recognition of new affinities, and sufficiently familiar with one another to treat differences with equanimity' (2007: 585). The mention of old familiarities and new affinities captures well linguistic ethnography's pedigree in anthropological linguistics with which it shares a theoretical base, as well as its more open and utilitarian approach to forging new connections.

Oriented towards these particular epistemological and methodological traditions in the study of social life, linguistic ethnography argues that ethnography can benefit from the analytical frameworks provided by linguistics, while linguistics can benefit from the processes of reflexive sensitivity required in ethnography (see section 7.2). This chapter will focus mainly on linguistic ethnography's contribution to interactional studies. However, in addition to the study of interaction, the study of situated literacy practices is also well represented in linguistic ethnography where the focus is on community-based literacy research (Barton and Hamilton, 1998; Gregory and Williams, 2000), multilingual literacy (Martin-Jones and Jones, 2000) and cross-cultural perspectives on literacy (Street, 1984). As with interactional studies in linguistic ethnography, such research starts from an understanding of literacy as social practice, that is, looks at how people actually use literacy in their lifeworlds and everyday routines, rather than viewing literacy as a measurable cognitive achievement concerned predominantly with educational success.

7.2 Linguistic ethnography and interaction

Linguistic ethnography conjoins two fields of study arguing that there is more to be gained in their unison than in their separation. Ethnography is said to be enhanced by the detailed technical analysis which linguistic brings, while linguistics is said to be enhanced by attention to context. Ethnography offers linguistics a non-deterministic perspective on data, while linguistics offers ethnography a range of established procedures for identifying discursive structures (Rampton, 2007). Rampton et al. (2004) argue for 'tying ethnography down and opening linguistics up' (p. 4) and for an enhanced sense of the strategic value of discourse analysis in ethnography. According to this argument, ethnography provides linguistics with a close reading of context not necessarily represented in some kinds of interactional analysis (such as Conversation Analysis (CA) and systemic functional discourse analysis (SFDA)), while linguistics provides an authoritative analysis of language use not typically available through participant observation and the taking of fieldnotes (p. 6).

The ethnographic approach is one which sees the analysis of small phenomena as set against an analysis of big phenomena, and in which 'both levels can only be understood in terms of one another' (Blommaert, 2005: 16). For example, Creese (2005) describes the interactional practices of teachers in multi-adult classrooms, and shows how teachers' interactional practices unwittingly reproduce structural hierarchies in schools. Using linguistic ethnography, she illustrates how facilitation pedagogies best suited for language teaching and learning hold little currency in a context where pedagogies of transmission dominate classroom practices. Creese's study shows how small phenomena, such as the interactional differences between teachers, can only be understood against an analysis of big phenomena: the systemic and structural privileging of curriculum transmission.

A linguistic ethnographic analysis then attempts to combine close detail of local action and interaction as embedded in a wider social world. A further example of this is Maybin's work (2006) on primary school classrooms, where she explores the relationship between the multilayered ecology of the classroom and the dialogic possibilities that intersecting children's voices create. Through a combination of linguistic and ethnographic analysis of children's voices in and out of schools, Maybin found that 'meaning-making emerges as an ongoing dialogic process at a number of different interrelated levels: dialogues within utterances and between utterances, dialogues between voices cutting across utterance boundaries and dialogues with other voices from the past' (2006: 24).

7.3 Questions and key issues in linguistic ethnography

This section will deal with two key issues in linguistic ethnography. The first relates to the interdisciplinarity of linguistic ethnography. The discussion here will focus on the possibilities and limitations of disciplinary openness. The second key issue is linguistic ethnography's social constructivist and postmodernist orientation and the challenge this presents for a methodology traditionally predicated on local and situated action.

7.3.1 Linguistic ethnography as interdisciplinary research

Linguistic ethnography's interpretative stance is shaped by a disciplinary eclecticism. It is the interdisciplinary nature of linguistic ethnography that allows us to look closely and look locally, while tying observations to broader relations of power and ideology. Recently, there has been an emphasis on the advantages of combining analytical approaches, rather than relying on only one approach or framework, for example, in the analysis of classroom interaction (see Rampton et al., 2002), or of professional talk (see Stubbe et al., 2003; also see Chapter 2). By combining different approaches, different perspectives can be brought to the same interaction. For example, a linguistic ethnographic approach might analyse a piece of classroom data using a range of discursive traditions, while keeping the ethnographic context central to its interpretation. Thus while ethnography holds that understandings of participants as social agents within contexts is central to any interpretation, the researcher might draw on other discourse approaches which do not necessarily view context in the same way. Below two examples are provided of how this might happen referring to SFDA and CA.

Systemic Functional Discourse Analysis (SFDA) (Eggins and Slade, 1997; Francis and Hunston, 1992) could be used alongside ethnography to provide 'delicacy' at the level of describing speech acts – by focusing on discoursal features such as 'follow-up moves' and 'question–answer sequences'. The SFDA could also be used alongside ethnographic fieldnotes to further an understanding of how language structures a context. For example, research on classrooms might use SFDA to understand structure/boundary exchanges among classroom participants, and at the same time rely on fieldnotes for detailed descriptions over time of the significance of such exchanges to the participants themselves and to the researcher. Fieldnotes would then be used to show how aspects of social practice become both meaningful for the participants and units of analysis for the researcher in the interpretative process.

Conversation Analysis (CA) (Schegloff et al., 2002: 13) could similarly be used with linguistic ethnography to reveal the subtle shifts and sequences in the social organization of 'conversation', or 'talk-in-interaction'. CA, through its repeated listening and precise transcription, enables subtle analysis of interactional features such as common adjacency pairs; openings and closings; speaker selection; wait-time; overlap; repair; interruptions; directives; hesitancy and uncertainty (see Chapter 6, for an overview). CA could be used alongside micro-ethnography to look 'closely and repeatedly at what people do in real time as they interact' (Erickson, 1996: 283), while ethnography would be used to provide the interpretative detail to explain and give depth to the linguistic analysis.

As illustrated in these examples, linguistic ethnography does not view different approaches as necessarily in conflict with each other; rather it seeks ways in which they can be complementary. Tusting and Maybin (2007) argue that linguistic ethnography particularly lends itself to interdisciplinary research, because of the increased interest across the social sciences in discourse. Blommaert similarly argues that the autobiographical-epistemic dimension of ethnography lends itself to interdisciplinary engagement and

> allows ethnography to be inserted in all kinds of theoretical endeavors, to the extent of course that such endeavors allow for situatedness, dynamics and interpretive approaches. Thus, there is no reason why ethnography cannot be inserted e.g. in a Marxist theoretical framework, nor in a Weberian one, nor in a Bourdieuan or Giddensian one.
>
> (Blommaert, 2001: 3)

However, just as there are strengths to be gained from disciplinary and theoretical diversity, there are dangers too. A word of caution can be found in Hammersley's (2007) discussion of linguistic ethnography. Hammersley's concern is with what he sees as a trend in the social sciences for 're-branding and relaunching' existing theory – a kind of 'hyper modernism' attempting to 'colonise intellectual territory' (2007: 690). Blommaert (2007: 685) too is concerned with disturbing long-established pedigrees and traditions in linguistic anthropology. He argues that there is no need in fact to separate linguistics from ethnography only to join them again under a new guise, and shows that a long pedigree already exists which conjoins linguistics and 'culture'/ethnography. This lineage links Boas, Sapir, Whorf, Hymes and Silverstein, and their research into language and culture as a single object rather than two distinct phenomena, as suggested by the term 'linguistic ethnography'.

In this important debate, both Hammersley and Blommaert are questioning what is to be gained by conjoining 'linguistics' and 'ethnography' although their concerns are slightly different. Hammersley's issue is that in 'relaunching' theory under the new guise of linguistic ethnography, new privileges are given to linguistics over ethnography which he points out are 'reminiscent of critiques of ethnography by conversation analysts' (Hammersley, 2007: 690). In other words, CA and ethnography do not share the same understandings of context and these might actually clash under the pluralist approach espoused in linguistic ethnography. The term linguistic ethnography implies, according to Hammersley, that 'without linguistics, ethnographic accounts will be speculative' (p. 693), that is, fieldnotes have less authority than electronically produced transcripts. Indeed, Rampton et al. seem to endorse this very point: 'The testimony of fieldnotes may sound quite authoritative in reports on exotic locations which few Westerners have ever visited, but evidentiary standards tend to be more demanding in social scientific accounts of social processes close to home' (2004: 6).

The evidentiary standards here refer to the confidence of claims made from fieldnote data. The quote suggests that warrants from linguistic data are more secure than those claimed from ethnographic data because fieldnotes cannot capture the complexity of social life and be held accountable in the same way as a linguistic analysis of interactional data can. However, I would argue that it is the very balance of these data methods which defines linguistic ethnography, and that retaining the importance of ethnographic fieldnotes as primary (and authoritative) data alongside recordings of interactional data is crucial. Technological advancement for recording linguistic data may have introduced new levels of surveillance which 'have allowed us to transport selected and carefully focused slices of life out of the original nexus of activity for collegial, peer-reviewable examination in richer more multimodal formats' (Scollon and Scollon, 2007: 620), but without a close account of context through the researcher's noticings and fieldnote commentary, we are no longer engaged in linguistic ethnography. Put simply, in linguistic ethnography interpretative assessments are built on locally or context-specific background knowledge recorded in fieldnotes or diaries. For example, in their study of the multilingual practices of young people and teachers in complementary schools in England, Blackledge and Creese (in press) show how study participants move between languages and their varieties to perform different values, affiliations and allegiances. They illustrate through transcripts, fieldnotes and interviews how language use both maps onto existing linguistic hierarchies but also challenges them. They also describe how fieldnotes are used to retain context, voice and contradiction; serve to make transparent the construction of arguments and the processes of representation; and provide evidence of theory building from the bottom up (see examples below).

7.3.2 Ethnography and post-structuralism

A second key issue developed in this chapter is linguistic ethnography's ability to 'keep up' methodologically in a field of study which has seen radical changes in its conceptualization of its key terminology (such as 'culture', 'community' and 'language'). Traditionally, ethnography has typically stressed a situated and contextually driven agenda of being 'on site' and geographically locatable (see Ochs Keenan's 1974 work on men's and women's speech in Madagascar for an example, and more recently, Jaffe's 1999 work on language and literacy practices in Corsica which spans 15 years). The ethnographer's observation of participants is very much part of the analysis and published accounts. That is, the researcher's 'being there' (Geertz, 1988) is part of the rich accounts provided.

The value of ethnographies describing geographically located communities is immense. However, Eisenhart points out that new global conditions of movements between nations, migration and immigration in what she describes as 'translocal times' (2001a: 21), requires ethnography to face up to new challenges. She notes:

> Although feminist, ethnic and postmodern critics have influenced the way ethnographers think about their relationships with study participants and the styles ethnographers use to write their accounts, methods of site selection, data collection and analysis remain virtually unchanged.
>
> (Eisenhart, 2001b: 218)

Eisenhart's argument is that ethnographic methodology has not kept pace with its core theoretical literature. She describes the advances in conceptualizing key constructs in post-modernity, such as 'culture', 'community', 'identity' and 'language', but a lack of simultaneous methodological advances in ethnography to research these features of contemporary life. She points to the difficulty of conceptualizing the participant, the community and the site, and argues that we need to adjust our conceptual orientations and methodological priorities to take into account changing human experiences such as migration, diaspora and the use of new technologies. She describes three 'muddles' in her account of ethnography past, present and future and then explores how these 'muddles' might be 'tidied up'. The first 'muddle' she explores is 'the trouble with culture'. She points out that we can no longer work with a view of culture 'as relatively enduring, coherent and bounded', for we cannot use the term 'culture' to identify social groups of people with a culture that is 'clearly bounded and determined, internally coherent, and uniformly meaningful' (2001b: 17). The second 'muddle' she explores is 'the enthusiasm (or not) for ethnography' (p. 19), focusing on the limitations for the sole ethnographer to participate in various settings, devote significant time to the research, and do justice to her areas of special interest and expertise. She points out that aspects of contemporary life, such as 'struggles within groups, movements of people across time and space, internet communications, extralocal networks, consumerism, and the mass media' (p. 19) can only be addressed superficially through current ethnographic methods. The third 'muddle' she raises concerns ethnography's responsibility to represent multiple and diverse perspectives or 'voices' (p. 19), suggesting, for example, that ethnographers of education should use their findings for positive educational intervention. The tension here lies in protecting those being researched while simultaneously meeting the need for detail and description required in ethnography. Eisenhart points out that in protecting some participants, the writer may also expose or privilege others. In describing how ethnography should 'tidy up' these three muddles, Eisenhart describes ways (synthesized here from 2001a, 2001b) in which ethnographers can respond:

1. Use of collaborative teams to broaden insights and perspectives.
2. Development of models stressing mutual and shared relationship between researcher and researched.
3. Experiments in writing that allow more perspectives or 'voices' to be revealed in final accounts.
4. Use of research narratives which show divisions, struggles or inconsistencies in the data.
5. Use of different media beyond 'textual writing' to represent the data; engaging audience through film, literature, television, computer.
6. A movement away from focus on individual people and an emphasis on new technologies, to understand the translocal rather than only the local.

Eisenhart concludes that we must be ready to extend or go beyond ethnography's conventional methods to meet new challenges. In the same vein, MacLure (2003) alerts us to the dangers of realism in ethnography. Her criticism is that ethnography presents its narratives as 'true' accounts of 'real' situations, with findings being offered as coherent and non-contradictory. Arguing from a post-structuralist perspective, MacLure claims that there are no such things as innocent texts and that we need to open up ethnographies to reveal different configurations, interpretations and contradictions.

7.4 Application of methods

This section will discuss methods of linguistic ethnography. It will describe 'traditional methods' in ethnography before focusing on team ethnography as a response to criticisms levelled against ethnography. Such criticisms argue for the need to move away from singular representations of situated contexts which ethnography has traditionally engaged in, and which create a singular 'reality' held up as 'true' (MacLure, 2003).

Traditional approaches in ethnography are summarized as follows (Eisenhart, 2001a: 218–19):

- Unobtrusive recorders of activity and faithful reporters of characteristic patterns
- Being empirical without being positivistic
- Offering an objective analysis of subjective meanings
- Representing meanings of participants
- Treating researchers as active, reflective subjects
- Providing first-hand knowledge of others
- Deliberately scrutinizing one's own view point in the light of others
- Seeing the others' worlds as 'reality'.

Traditionally in ethnography, one researcher works alone to collect the data, analyse the results and write up the findings. Analysis of the data focuses on the identification and interpretation of regular patterns of action and talk that characterize a group of people in a social context. This is achieved through participant observation, fieldnotes, ethnographic and open interviews, and often recordings/transcripts. Ethnography thus offers descriptions and per-spectives which are not only meaningful to the participants themselves, but also to the researcher. The investment of self in the writing of fieldnotes and the centrality of the researcher in ethnography is fundamental. Blommaert argues that fieldwork is more than data collection:

> [E]thnography is far more than a set of techniques or methods for field work and description. It cannot be reduced to ways of treating 'data' either, for 'data' in ethnography have a different status than in many other disciplines. Data are chunks of reality that have a (autobiographical) history of being known and interpreted.
>
> (Blommaert, 2001: 3)

But if the ethnographer's role in general and her use of fieldnotes in parti-cular are central in the interpretative processes of ethnography, there is also some criticism that these fieldnotes are often not made explicit in the building up of arguments through the interpretative process. MacLure (2003: 93) urges ethnographers to make 'the machinery' of writing (i.e. how texts are built and developed, and the contradictions and power struggles inherent in them) transparent in their ethnographic accounts. This is important because according to MacLure, realist ethnographic texts (representing reality through the ethnographer's account) are falsely coherent, non-contradictory, stripped of power relations and representing a frozen, dateless 'ethnographic present' (Fabian, 1983). From such accounts readers are invited to judge the 'truth' of the text, but in reality, MacLure describes how the worlds of the ethnographer and participant bleed into one another in the field, betraying the 'unofficial desires and demands' (p. 96) of 'self' in relation to 'other'.

We might consider team linguistic ethnography as one way to respond to these criticisms of ethnography as narrow realist texts presenting single-authored, non-contradictory accounts. Eisenhart (2001b) notes that increasingly, collaborative teams are being used to involve different kinds of people in designing the research process and creating final accounts. This collaboration requires the researchers to disclose more about their own views, commitments, and social positions (Eisenhart, 2001a). We can illustrate this process of social declaration below through some fieldnote examples from three researchers engaged in team ethnography (Creese et al., 2008a). Each researcher was observing at a Gujarati complementary school in Leicester, UK (Martin et al., 2004). Complementary schools are also known as community language schools, heritage language schools or supplementary schools. They are voluntary and community run. In this particular school, Gujarati language, 'culture' and 'heritage' were taught, once a week for 3 hours in the evening, to over 200 students.

In the three sets of fieldnotes which follow, we see the observations of three researchers (Angela Creese, Arvind Bhatt and Peter Martin[1]) in three different classrooms. Each fieldnote text was written independently and shows a developing interest in a key participant, Deepa, the school's headteacher and administrator. In our vignettes below, each researcher draws attention to Deepa's use of languages and in particular her English in relation to her Gujarati.

Extract 1

We stop the classes for around 10 minutes – I feel embarrassed by this. I also feel that the teachers might feel that their time with the students is being wasted. Deepa speaks in English throughout. I am not clear if this is for me or because she would usually do this. (AC 11/3)

Extract 2

Deepa walks in with a handful of documents and files. She consults with P (class teacher) and students chatter. Then Deepa asks students whether they learnt the prayer. She gets the class to recite the prayer. She claps her hands and says: star performers, but sing a little bit louder for the hall. Some of the students get excited and Deepa gives a 'high five' with nearest students. Other students also want to 'high five' with her but Deepa walks out saying 'I will think about it'. The teacher brings the class back to calmness and continues to revise. (AB, 18/3)

Extract 3

About 7.45 a whirlwind enters the room in the shape of Deepa. She comes in with a wodge of papers and comments 'Wow, what a lot of letters' referring to the 15 Gujarati letters on the whiteboard. She holds up a chart that she has prepared and asks the children what one or two of the letters are. She then proceeds to pass on some 'paper work' to the class teacher, new lesson plan documents and a number of policy documents (with ref. to discussion at Staff meeting). There are other documents that I cannot get a glimpse of, but one is for 'one minute feedback' on how the teachers thought the lesson went. On the new lesson plan Deepa makes the point that teachers had agreed to write in the additional resources that they use in class. Deepa counts out sheets for the children (number policy doc?) and I am surprised that this is done in English. After Deepa has gone the class returns to its usual quietness. Before break, the class teacher is talking about more letters. (PM, 29/4)

These fieldnote accounts of Deepa raise several issues. As researchers, we were particularly interested in Deepa's use of English to address the whole class, her compliments in English (star performers) and her use of gesture and signs (high fives) reminiscent of sport and youth contexts beyond the classroom. Her style was often in direct contrast to that of the teachers who were usually speaking Gujarati and attempting to maintain a quiet and calm learning atmosphere. This interest in Deepa's use of English and the register she chooses is recorded across our three sets of fieldnotes, where we begin to wonder whether she uses English because her own Gujarati proficiency is low and whether she uses a particular register of English because she is not a teacher herself and is unaware of the importance of calm in the classroom. In this way, we use our fieldnotes to 'close in' on our focus and signal to one another our interest in a particular phenomenon which later made its way into published accounts of 'flexible and dynamic bilingualism' (Creese and Blackledge, in press), linguistic variety, heritage and culture. Our fieldnotes were then used to narrow down our focus even further, looking at the relationship between Gujarati and English in classroom cohesion and identity performance. In other words, we brought to our analysis of complementary school classroom discourse our interpretations and constructions of Deepa as an agentive language user.

Although the examples of fieldnotes above have a focus in common, at times, our fieldnotes showed disagreement and contradiction or we noticed entirely different things (Creese et al., 2008a). The ethnographic team often used these notes as a resource to evidence divergent accounts and take them up for debate. In team ethnography, fieldnotes thus reveal the researchers' different voices and backgrounds, and at the same time they force researchers to look back on their own agendas, observations and representation of the research process and participants. A team of ethnographers is forced to do this more explicitly than the sole ethnographer through the buffeting of questionings that come up through sharing fieldnotes in a team. In our research (Creese et al., 2008b), we challenged, refuted, endorsed and refined one another's interpretations, carrying some forward and leaving others' behind. There was sometimes consensus in these writings but there was also contradiction which we attempted to hold onto rather than erase (and to carry into our published accounts). Through our team discussions of (*inter alia*) fieldnotes, some arguments and assertions made their way into different stages of the research, and influenced our analysis of other data sets (interactional and interview). In this way, fieldnotes play their part in theory building (Creese, 2008).

A further way in which teams of researchers can be used in linguistic ethnography to counter criticisms of singular texts, is the use of 'analytic vignettes' (see Erickson, 1990), to reveal relationships among researchers and research participants (Creese et al., in press). This involves describing aspects of researcher-identity negotiation, that is, how researchers use their linguistic, social and cultural resources to negotiate access and build relationships with participants in the research process and with one another in a research team. The vignettes below illustrate researchers negotiating shifting allegiances in positioning themselves towards research participants in complementary schools (teachers, parents and young people) and towards one another. These short extracts from two individual researcher accounts (by Shahela Hamid and Adrian Blackledge) come from the Bengali case study (one of four studies) on complementary schools. The full vignettes are one page each and can be found in Blackledge and Creese (in press), along with vignettes from the larger nine-member research team.

Vignette 1

As an insider (from the same ethnic and religious background with proficiency in native language varieties) I was able to gain the trust and confidence of the families. Positioning myself linguistically and culturally as a Bangladeshi woman

I was able to understand the norms and expectations of the families with whom I was negotiating. Developing a relationship with parents of key participants and teachers facilitated my status as an insider-participant observer. However, my insider status carried certain obligations with it. I had to be conscious at all times about the appropriateness of topics so that there was no loss of 'face'. Building a relationship with the participants' families was invaluable in understanding who key participants associated with, their network of friends and family, traditional values etc. [Shahela Hamid]

Vignette 2

My relationship to the participants in the case study frequently reminded me of the time I spent in the Bangladeshi community in Birmingham ten years ago, during data collection for my Ph.D. thesis. At the same time, it reminded me of the years I spent as a teacher in multicultural, multilingual Birmingham primary schools where the teaching staff were encouraged to visit the pupils' families at home during feasts and festivals. In all of these instances I felt both welcomed, and yet like an intruder, treading in domestic worlds where I was unfamiliar, and with which I was unfamiliar. On this occasion, without the collaboration and lead of my research partner Shahela Hamid, negotiating access to the domestic worlds of our participants would have been much more difficult, or even impossible. [Adrian Blackledge]

The researchers' accounts show an interest in the subtleties of the insider/outsider debate and acknowledge how feelings, attitudes and stances towards insider and outsider categories vary. Researchers here negotiate shifting allegiances and priorities in their positionality with the researched (teachers, parents and young people). They also show how the research pair with their different backgrounds comes to rely on one another. A team of researchers offers different instantiations of micro-experiences resulting in the production of divergent and overlapping views of the social order. We can use these overlapping and divergent accounts in ethnography to reveal not only the different voices of the researchers themselves, but also the interpretative processes that come to position the research participants in particular ways. Through such accounts, it is possible to present healthier, more contested and contradictory ethnography, capturing the complexity of social practices.

In this section, I have argued that team ethnography goes some way towards addressing some of the concerns expressed by MacLure (2003) and Eisenhart (2001a, 2001b). Team ethnography brings a variety of different, and often contradictory, voices into the production of ethnographic accounts, refuting clear coherent and non-contradictory accounts of social life. In this way, it can make explicit different views, commitments and social positions not necessarily made evident in the accounts of sole ethnographers. Team ethnography can also involve theory building, in allowing arguments to develop over time in fieldnote accounts (including some being privileged over others), and in influencing what is brought to the analysis of other data sets. However, as Creese et al. (2008a: 212) argue, it is important not to overinflate fieldnotes as interpretative resources; like other data in qualitative research, they are 'ephemeral' 'partial and incomplete', and need 'to be contested' and 'further analyzed in relation to other data sets'. Finally, on the issue of data and datasets, it is important to consider Erickson's argument that the corpus of materials collected in the field (notes, videotapes, even interview transcripts) 'are not data themselves, but resources for data', 'documentary materials from which data must be constructed through some formal means of analysis' (1990: 161). Although I have used the term 'data sets' throughout this chapter, I am persuaded by Erickson's argument that researchers use the interpretative process to construct 'materials' into data through their own participation in the research process.

7.5 Concluding remarks

While heavily indebted to early work in the ethnography of communication, linguistic ethnography offers a new perspective relevant to researchers working in the social sciences in post-modernity. Substantial developments in US linguistic anthropology, and the turn to post-structuralist accounts of discourse and meaning making in the research literature in the United Kingdom and Europe, have allowed linguistic ethnography to draw on more hybrid literatures in its analytical frameworks than those traditionally associated with the ethnography of communication (Hymes, 1968). Linguistic ethnography argues that the combination of linguistics with ethnography – and their different analytical tools – offers a greater set of resources than each field of study could offer on its own. Rampton et al. (2004) describe the linguistic ethnography endeavour as an 'enabling mechanism', and argue for leaving the intellectual space in linguistic ethnography open in terms of the kind of work which might emerge. In addition to this enabling potential, this chapter has also outlined dilemmas and criticisms facing ethnography, including the need to move forward methodologically, given the radical changes in key conceptualizations in the field.

Note

1. In April 2009, during the process of writing this chapter, Prof. Peter Martin died suddenly. He is sorely missed.

Further reading

Creese (2008) – An introductory text which gives a history of linguistic ethnography. Written in an encyclopaedia format, it provides a short summary of early developments, major contributions, problems and difficulties, as well as future directions for linguistic ethnography.

Tusting and Maybin (2007) – A special issue titled 'Linguistic ethnography and interdisciplinarity: Opening the discussion', which includes a paper by Ben Rampton offering an in-depth account of linguistic ethnography. It also contains chapters by leading social scientists commenting on linguistic ethnography in relation to their own theoretical and methodological orientations, and two discussion papers by Hammersley and Blommaert which develop a critical perspective on all the papers included.

Wortham and Rymes (2003) – This edited collection includes nine chapters which provide examples of how linguistic anthropology is used in empirical research in educational contexts. Linguistic anthropology and linguistic ethnography share much of their founding literature and this collection contains a rich collection of papers illustrating theoretical and methodological examples of these two closely related fields of study.

References

Barton, D. and Hamilton, M. (1998), *Local Literacies: Reading and Writing in One Community*, London and New York: Routledge.

Blackledge, A. and Creese, A. (in press), *Multilingualism: A Critical Perspective*. London: Continuum.

Blommaert, J. (2001), 'Reflections from overseas guests. Linguistic ethnography in the UK'. A BAAL/CUP seminar. University of Leicester 28–29 March 2001. Paper available at: http://www.lancs.ac.uk/fss/organisations/lingethn/leicesteroverseasreflections.rtf. Accessed October 2008.

—. (2005), *Discourse: A Critical Introduction*. Cambridge: Cambridge University Press.

—. (2007), 'Commentaries: on scope and depth in linguistic ethnography', *Journal of Sociolinguistics*, 11 (5), 682–8.

Creese, A. (2005), *Teacher Collaboration and Talk in Multilingual Classrooms*. Clevedon: Multilingual Matters.

—. (2008), 'Linguistic ethnography', in K. A. King and N. H. Hornberger (eds), *Encyclopedia of Language and Education*, 2nd Edition, Volume 10: Research Methods in Language and Education. Springer Science and Business Media LLC, pp. 229–41.

Creese, A. and Blackledge A. (in press), 'Translanguaging in the bilingual classroom: a pedagogy for learning and teaching', *Modern Language Journal*.

Creese, A., Bhatt, A., Bhojani, N. and Martin, P. (2008a), 'Fieldnotes in team ethnography: researching complementary schools', *Qualitative Research*, 8 (2), 223–42.

Creese, A., Baraç, T., Bhatt, A., Blackledge, A., Hamid, S., Li Wei, Lytra, V., Martin, P., Wu, C. J. and Yağcıoğlu-Ali, D. (2008b), *Investigating Multilingualism in Complementary Schools in Four Communities*. Final report to ESRC (RES-000-23-1180).

Creese, A., Bhatt, A. and Martin, P. (in press), 'Multilingual researcher identities: interpreting linguistically and culturally diverse classrooms', to appear in J. Miller, M. Gearon and A. Kostogriz (eds), *Linguistically and Culturally Diverse Classrooms: New Dilemmas for Teachers*. Clevedon: Multilingual Matters.

Eggins, S. and Slade, D. (1997), *Analysing Casual Conversation*. London: Cassell.

Eisenhart, M. (2001a), 'Changing conceptions of culture and ethnographic methodology. Recent thematic shifts and their implications for research on teaching', in V. Richardson (ed.), *Handbook of Research on Teaching. 4th Edition*. Washington, DC: American Educational Research Association, pp. 209–25.

—. (2001b), 'Educational ethnography past, present and future: ideas to think with', *Educational Researcher*, 30 (8), 16–27.

Erickson, F. (1990), 'Qualitative methods', in R. L. Linn and F. Erickson (eds), *Research in Teaching and Learning*. Volume 2. New York: Macmillan.

—. (1996), 'Ethnographic microanalysis', in S. L. McKay and N .H. Hornberger (eds), *Sociolinguistics and Language Teaching*. New York: Cambridge University Press, pp. 283–306.

—. (2004), *Talk and Social Theory: Ecologies of Speaking and Listening in Everyday Life*. Malden: Polity Press.

Fabian, J. (1983), *Time and the Other: How Anthropology Makes Its Object*. New York: Columbia University Press.

Francis, G. and Hunston, S. (1992), 'Analysing everyday conversation', in R. M. Coulthard (ed.), *Advances in Spoken Discourse Analysis*. London: Routledge.

Geertz, C. (1988), *Works and Lives: The Antrhopologist as Author*. Cambridge: Polity Press.

Gregory, E. and Williams, A. (2000), *City Literacies*. London: Routledge.

Gumperz, J. (1982), *Discourse Strategies*. Cambridge: Cambridge University Press.

Hammersley, M. (2007), 'Reflections on linguistic ethnography', *Journal of Sociolinguistics*, 11 (5), 689–95.

Hymes, D. (1968), 'The ethnography of speaking', in J. Fishman (ed.), *Readings in the Sociology of Language*. The Hague: Moulton, pp. 99–138.

Jaffe, A. (1999), *Ideologies in Action: Language Politics on Corisca*. Berlin: Mouton de Gruyter.

MacLure, M. (2003), *Discourse in Educational and Social Research*. Buckingham: Open University Press.

Martin, P. W., Creese, A, Bhatt, A. and Bhojani, N. (2004), *Final Report on Complementary Schools and their Communities in Leicester*. University of Leicester/University of Birmingham. (ESRC R000223949). Also available at: http://www.uel.ac.uk/education/staff/documents/complementery_schools.pdf

Martin-Jones, M. and Jones, K. (eds) (2000), *Multilingual Literacies*. Amsterdam: John Benjamins.

Maybin, J. (2006), *Children's Voices. Talk, Knowledge and Identity*. Basingstoke: Palgrave.

Ochs, Keenan, E. (1974), 'Norm-makers, norm-breakers: uses of speech by men and women in a Malagasy community', in R. Bauman and J. Sherzer (eds), *Explorations in the Ethnography of Speaking*. Cambridge: Cambridge University Press.

Rampton, B. (2007), 'Neo-Hymesian linguistic ethnography in the United Kingdom', *Journal of Sociolinguistics*, 11 (5), 584–607.

Rampton, B., Roberts, C., Leung, C. and Harris, R. (2002), 'Methodology in the analysis of classroom discourse', *Applied Linguistics*, 23 (3), 373–92.

Rampton, B., Tusting, K., Maybin, J., Barwell, R., Creese, A. and Lytra, V. (2004), 'UK linguistic ethnography: a discussion paper'. Unpublished. www.ling-ethnog.org.uk

Schegloff, E. A., Koshik, I., Jacoby, S. and Olsher, D. (2002), 'Conversation analysis and applied linguistics', *Annual Review of Applied Linguistics*, 22, 3–31.

Scollon, R. and Scollon, S. W. (2007), 'Nexus analysis: refocusing ethnography on action', *Journal of Sociolinguistics*, 11 (5), 608–25.

Silverstein, M. (2003), 'Indexical order and the dialectics of sociolinguistic life', *Language and Communication*, 23, 193–229.

Street, B. (1984), *Literacy in Theory and Practice*. Cambridge, Cambridge University Press.

Stubbe, M., Lane, C., Hilder, J., Vine, E., Vine, B., Marra, M., Holmes, J. and Weatherall, A. (2003), 'Multiple discourse analyses of a workplace interaction', *Discourse Studies*, 5 (3), 351–88.

Tusting, K. and Maybin, J. (2007), 'Linguistic ethnography and interdisciplinarity: opening the discussion', *Journal of Sociolinguistics*, 11 (5), 575–83.

Wortham, S. (2003), 'Linguistic anthropology of education: an introduction', in S. Wortham and B. Rymes (eds), *Linguistic Anthropology of Education*. Westport, CT: Praeger Press, pp. 1–29.

Wortham, S. and Rymes, B. (eds) (2003), *Linguistic Anthropology of Education*. Westport, CT: Praeger Press.

Contemplating Interviews and Focus Groups

8

Nigel Edley and Lia Litosseliti

Chapter outline

In this chapter we look at the use of both interviews and focus groups within social science and linguistics research. Working on the basis that they are closely related methods, we begin by examining the arguments, put forward by a number of critical commentators, that they are fundamentally flawed in offering up artificial or contaminated data. In line with those criticisms, we agree that there are some serious problems involved where they are deployed and understood – in traditional terms – as means of mining particular 'nuggets of truth'. Rather, following a more constructionist stance, we recommend that interviews and focus groups are treated as collaborative or interactional events in which the interviewer or moderator plays an important, participative role. So conceived, we argue that there is still a legitimate case for employing either of these research methods – and we end by providing a critical review of what are widely considered to be their primary strengths and weaknesses.

8.1 Introduction

In recent years it's been claimed that the inhabitants of the 'Western' world (at least) are living in 'interview societies' (see Atkinson and Silverman, 1997: 309). In Britain, for example, by the time a person reaches adulthood, it is very likely that they will have had some first-hand experience of being interviewed – in either 'careers' interviews at school and/or, of course, later on in interviews for jobs. But, more to the point, the claim rests on the assumption that, as a third party, the typical adult will have been witness to hundreds, if not thousands, of interviews broadcast by the media, in things like news and current affairs programmes, sports' reports and in feature articles found in both newspapers and magazines. To the 'Western' eye, interviews are incredibly familiar – and presumably, therefore, tremendously useful. It's generally assumed that the main benefit of interviews is that they give us privileged access to a person; that they allow us an intimate – or 'first-hand' – sense of what, say, a politician or a celebrity both thinks and is like as a person. By comparison, wider society is nothing like as familiar with focus groups. A person could watch television non-stop for weeks or months without ever seeing one. Likewise, readers are unlikely to find a journalist reporting explicitly on a focus group meeting in a newspaper or magazine article. That's not to suggest, however, that the general public are oblivious to the existence of focus groups. Many people will recognize the term, and some may have even taken part in one (organized, perhaps, by a marketing organization or a political party), but they still do not enjoy the same degree of presence as interviews, in ordinary, everyday culture.

Within the world of academia, however, the use of both interviews and focus groups is widespread. Over the course of the last few decades, their employment within the social and human sciences has increased significantly, partly as a consequence of a more general shift from quantitative towards qualitative methods (in response to a growing disenchantment with positivistic, laboratory-style experiments – see Armistead, 1974; Hepburn, 2003; Pancer, 1997 for a discussion of the so-called crisis debates). Within Psychology, one of the principal drivers of that shift – Rom Harré – once came out with a memorable injunction: that the basic principle for any social research should be to 'treat people as if they were human beings' (Harré and Secord, 1972). Harré's point was that people are not robots; their behaviour is *meaningful* rather than mechanical. So instead of concocting all kinds of weird and wonderful experiments in attempting to track down the causes of human behaviour, why don't we simply *talk* to people, he said? Ask them to account for their own actions because, he went on, it is very likely that people will be able to provide us with good or, at least, plausible explanations. Since then, it seems that many social researchers have opted to speak to those in whom their interests lie. Not only has focus group methodology become popular within many social research projects (in education – e.g. Lederman, 1990; linguistics – e.g. Myers, 1998; health research – e.g. Kitzinger, 1995; Powell and Single, 1996; feminist research – e.g. Wilkinson, 1998) but, in some quarters of the academy, interviews have emerged as *the* method of choice (Potter and Hepburn, 2005a – see also Wray and Bloomer, 2006, chapter 13).

Given the above, it should come as no surprise to find that there are a good number of available texts providing guidance on how to conduct interviews and focus groups and to analyse the resulting data (see Further Reading for some useful suggestions). What this also means, of course, is that there is not much point in us dedicating a whole chapter to providing yet another step-by-step or practical guide. So what we want to do here instead is to concentrate on some of the debates that have emerged in recent years, which raise pertinent questions about the merits or value of conducting language research using data generated by these closely related means. We want to examine why it is that some qualitative researchers (e.g. Potter and Hepburn, 2005a, 2005b; Silverman, 2001, 2007) are now arguing that we should move away from our current reliance on these particular methods of data collection. In preparation for that task, it is necessary for us first to review and interrogate some of the basic assumptions concerning research interviews and focus groups.

8.2 The logic of the research interview/focus group

Despite the obvious etymology of the term, most *interviews* are understood, not as reciprocal or two-way exchanges, but as a mechanism by which one party (i.e. the interviewer) extracts vital information from another (i.e. the interviewee). As Patton (1980) explains, they are usually seen as a means of accessing stuff that cannot be got at by direct observation. So, for example, in the context of a job interview, the series of questions put by the interviewing panel will be designed to elicit all kinds of information; including factual details about such things as the applicants' formal qualifications and previous work experience, but also more intangible phenomena like their motives for applying and enthusiasm for the post in question. As already mentioned, the interview is seen as providing us with a *window* onto the mind or 'life-world' (see Kvale, 1996) of the interviewee. Of course, any interviewing panel worth its salt will be aware that the characters parading before it will be trying to cast themselves in a positive light; but it will be assumed, nonetheless, that the central business at hand is, in theory at least, a basic fact-finding mission.

According to Silverman (2001), these same assumptions underpin most research within the social and human sciences that uses either interviews or focus groups as the primary means of data collection. Of the many thousands of studies that have done so, the majority presuppose that these tools are (at least ideally) neutral devices, facilitating the assembly of so many facts. Accordingly, the main methodological concerns expressed in many of these studies are about ensuring the neutrality of the interviewer or 'moderator' – through the eradication of leading or ambiguous questions and through the standardization of their delivery. One of the ways of responding to these concerns has been the development of the so-called structured interview. Here the interviewer's task is to work through a series of prescripted questions, ensuring that both the order and the wording used is identical on each and every occasion. In many structured interviews the questions are 'closed' or restricted in terms of how an interviewee can respond – either by using 'yes/no' formats, multiple choice questions or rating scales of one kind or another. Within more semi- or unstructured interviews (see Dörnyei, 2007; Hughes, 1996; and Grebenik and Moser, 1962 for further discussion of these differences), the process is more free-flowing and indeterminate. As with focus groups, in these cases, an interviewer/moderator may possess a set of guide questions, but they would not usually seek to impose them. Instead, they are encouraged to improvise; allowing the interview or focus group to follow whatever course it takes. Nevertheless, the interviewer or moderator is often implored still to remain neutral during the data gathering process; to withhold their own opinions vis-à-vis the questions and to remain impassive in the face of their respondents' answers. Common to both of these approaches, then, is the assumption that interview/focus group data are essentially free-standing or independent of the (discourse of the) interviewer/moderator. This is evident, not only in terms of the appeals to interviewers/moderators to remain neutral (i.e. to have no bearing or impact upon what a respondent might say), but also in the fact that, in the presentation of empirical data, the contributions of the convenor are often omitted or ignored.

8.2.1 Recent challenges

During the early 1990s, however, a number of academics began to raise questions about the validity of these underlying assumptions; and so too, therefore, about the legitimacy of interviews and focus groups as prime social research tools. In this regard, one of the landmark publications was an article written by two anthropologists, Lucy Suchman and Brigitte Jordan (Suchman and Jordan, 1990), which drew attention to some of the unfortunate consequences that may arise from failing to understand interviews, in particular, as a form of social *interaction*. More specifically, their article looked at some of the misunderstandings that can accrue when interviewers adhere strictly to a fixed schedule of questions. A short article by Antaki (2000) can help to illustrate the kind of point they were making. In the extract reproduced below (see Extract 1 – NB see end of the chapter for a key to the transcription notation), a psychologist is seen posing a question in a way that conforms to a very common 'structured' survey method. The interviewee ('Anne') is given a range of potential answers from which to select her response ('never'/'sometimes'/'usually'); but, as we can see from the transcript, she doesn't wait for the provision of the three standardized options. Instead, she provides a response immediately after the completion of the initial question (i.e. at the end of line 2). Seemingly undeterred, the psychologist forges ahead with the set protocol. On three successive occasions Anne denies that she feels uncomfortable 'in social situations', before she eventually comes out with a different response (in line 9) – which just happens to coincide with the psychologist coming to the end of that protocol. 'Sometimes I do' Anne says – which is then summarily accepted and translated into an 'equivalent' numerical score.

Extract 1

1 Psy: d'you feel out of place (0.4) out an about
2   in *social* (0.2) situations
3 Anne: n[o
4 Psy: [Anne (0.2) *never?*
5 Anne: no
6 Psy: sometimes?
7 Anne: °no°
8 Psy: or usually
9 Anne: *sometimes I do:*
10 Psy: yeah? (0.4) OK we'll put a two down for that one then (*sniff*)

(Antaki, 2000: 242–3)

The question is, of course, what are we to make of those three previous denials? Was it prudent of the psychologist to ignore them in this way? The answer, surely, is no. But, as Antaki (and Suchman and Jordan) point out, the source of this seemingly fundamental error is that the researcher fails to appreciate the encounter as a stretch of dialogue. In this case, for example, Antaki explains that the psychologist fails to appreciate how, in everyday conversational interactions, if a person is repeatedly asked the same question, they will usually infer that their previous responses are wrong or somehow inappropriate. The normal response, therefore, would be to come up with a new or different answer. For many linguists, it is precisely these responses (by Anne in the example above) that would constitute a topic of investigation (with CA analysts, for example, focusing specifically on aspects of this interaction such as sequencing, adjacency pairs or pauses) – more on this below.

The case for treating interview data as social interaction was given significant further impetus with the publication of Holstein and Gubrium's book *The Active Interview* (Holstein and Gubrium, 1995). The crucial contribution made by these two sociologists was to apply various social constructionist insights, regarding the nature of language, to the consideration of interviewing. In particular, drawing upon the work of Berger and Luckmann (1967), Garfinkel (1967) and Cicourel (1964), they tried to emphasize that language is a form of social *practice*; that it doesn't just describe a world 'out there', but rather, that it is a means of *acting* in the world. In addition, they argued that language has a *constitutional* as well as a representational function; that both the interviewee and the interviewer are, during the real time of the interview itself, in the process of creating knowledge and understanding. As they put it:

> Both parties to the interview are necessarily and unavoidably *active*. Each is involved in meaning-making work. Meaning is not merely elicited by apt questioning nor simply transported through respondent replies; it is actively and communicatively assembled in the interview encounter. Respondents are not so much repositories of knowledge – treasures of information awaiting excavation – as they are constructors of knowledge in collaboration with interviewers.
>
> (Holstein and Gubrium, 1995: 4)

In keeping with a constructivist stance, Holstein and Gubrium saw interview discourse as their central *topic* of interest – rather than as a simple *resource* (i.e. as a route through to the 'treasures' mentioned above). That said, they maintained, nonetheless, a distinction between what they referred to as the '*hows*' and the '*whats*' of meaning or knowledge construction; in other words, a difference between the *performative* and the *referential* aspects of discourse. More specifically still, Holstein and Gubrium claimed that it is possible to disentangle – or at least keep simultaneous track of – what people are both *doing* and talking *about* when they take part in an interview (or, for that matter, in any other kind of verbal interaction). So, in Gubrium's own work looking at the life histories of nursing home residents (Gubrium, 1993), attention was paid, not just to how the residents' discourse was designed both to respond to and function within the local context of the interview itself, but also to what their discourse said about their actual lives, their sense of self and so on and so forth.

In that respect, Holstein and Gubrium's position echoes that of other discourse theorists, such as Freeman (1993: 16), who described the analytical challenge as one of '[trying] to maintain and embrace [the] primacy of the word without losing the world in the process'.

There are others, however, who take a very different stance in relation to these issues. Silverman (2001, 2007), for example, argues that any data emanating from interviews or focus groups is 'got up' or 'manufactured', and should only be used as a last resort. Likewise, Potter and Hepburn (2005a, 2005b) regard these forms of data as contrived and so compromised; preferring, instead, what they, and others, refer to as *naturalistic* or *naturally occurring* data. Previously, Potter (1996) has suggested that discourse analysts ought to be able to apply what he called the 'dead social scientist test' as a means of assessing the appropriateness (or otherwise) of their data. For him, naturally occurring data emerge out of social interactions that would have taken place even if the researcher set to gather that data had been run over and killed some time earlier in the day. Needless to say, interview and focus group data tend, therefore, to fail Potter's test – insofar as they are prompted by the initiative of the social researcher her- or himself. Indeed, for Potter, the only truly legitimate grounds for using data from either interviews or focus groups is when those very forums are, themselves, the topic of one's analysis. For instance, in his work with Claudia Puchta (Puchta and Potter, 1999, 2004), the meaning and knowledge-producing practices of focus groups were the object of study. So, for Potter, interviews and focus groups can supply us with 'natural' data, but only in these very particular circumstances.

According to Potter and Hepburn (2005a, 2005b), there are several problems inherent in using 'manufactured' data; the most serious of which derive from the fact that, in setting up any interview or focus group, the social researcher sets the whole agenda. Volunteers are recruited, in the first instance, to talk about a given theme or topic. As such, they will usually come along on the understanding that they are to speak on behalf of whatever group or category of person is the focus of the researcher's interest (i.e. as an immigrant, single mother, school governor, etc.). What is more, the researcher's concerns and concepts will also tend to be foregrounded, as embodied in the scripting of the questions. The authors claim that all these things put unnecessary constraints upon the parameters of what gets said and that they also tend to draw people into talking about the world around them in strange and artificial ways.

Now, before proceeding any further, it might be worth trying to provide an illustration of at least some of these issues. To that end, we have chosen some data that comes from a series of interviews conducted with a small group of sixth-form (i.e. 17–18 years) students who, at the time (during the early 1990s), were attending a single sex boys' school in the United Kingdom (see Wetherell, 1994 for a full account of this project). The data that constitute Extract 2 comes from a discussion about heterosexual relationships. Just prior to this stretch of talk, Phil had been recounting a story about a weekend in which his friend (Aaron) had purportedly 'struck it lucky' with a number of young women. Indeed, it was claimed that he had 'got off' with four in one night. Line 73 sees Phil bringing that story to an end.

Extract 2

73	Phil:	So that like took me aback somewhat (0.3) so that was
74		a good weekend for you
75		(.)
76	Nigel:	Is that *good*?
77	Phil:	Well in his books *yes* you know–
78	Aaron:	=hhhh.h [yeah]
79	Phil:	[The thing] is you got so much stick for it
80	Aaron:	Well yeah I could take the stick because it was
81		almost like (0.2) a good ego trip when everyone was
82		taking the stick oh you got off with her ah ha ha
83		yep I did so what's your problem? [Oh, er..errr]
84	Nigel:	[Hm mm]
85	Aaron:	[Errr]
86	Phil:	[None of them] were particularly pikey so you were
87		alright really
88	Aaron:	No (.) they weren't .hh none of them were like majorly
89		pikey .hh (.) one or two perhaps could have like
90		(.)
91	Phil:	I don't know I don't know I think I know this Cathy
92		bird I know Jenny I know Cathy thing I don't know who
93		the other one was and neither do you so can't tell=
94	Nigel:	=Yeah I mean I wasn't sort of saying is four in two
95		days good I mean it's *impressive* [you know]
96	Aaron:	[hh [hhh] hh
97	Phil:	[hhhhh] hhhh
98	Nigel:	But I me:an like (.) it presu:mes that erm that's:: a
99		creditable thing (.) yeah? Is it?
100		(0.2)
101	Phil:	°No because you're on the moral low ground°
102	Aaron:	But I don't mi↑nd being on the moral [low ground]
103	Phil:	[Oh no you don't]

104		mind I I it didn't fuss me at all you know and I wasn't I
105		thought it was quite (.) it was quite impressive you
106		know you're sort of thinking that's shocking because it
107		never happens to me um:: .h hhh
108	Aaron:	Hhhh

There are, of course, many things that one could say about this extract; but, for now, we want to focus upon just three aspects. First of all, this slice of interaction, like all of these interviews, was framed in terms of the topic of masculinity. As a consequence, the participants are all being invited to speak *as* members of that gender category. As it happens, the 'jury' still appears to be 'out' as to whether or not gender is an omni-relevant feature of all discursive encounters (see Garfinkel, 1967; Schegloff, 1997; Stokoe and Smithson, 2001; Weatherall, 2002); but in any case, in instances such as this, it is clear that speaking as a gendered subject is a structural requirement of the task. In other words, it's not something that the participants could easily avoid. The second feature worthy of comment takes us back to a point made earlier – regarding the conventional understanding of repeated questions. Across lines 76 and 98/99, Nigel (in?)effectively poses the same question twice over. Little wonder, then, that Phil comes back with two different answers. As is evident from the transcript, the second formulation of the question is an attempted clarification (or 'repaired' version) of that posed on line 76. But, as Potter and Hepburn (2005a) pointed out, it would be unwise to take Phil's answer on line 101 as the more reliable (or authentic) opinion – because, in effect, the shape of the dialogue makes it difficult for him to just repeat his previous answer. The third aspect of the data is also concerned with line 101. Note how *quietly* it is produced. Moreover, it is delivered in a somewhat monotonic fashion. Listening to the tape, one gets the distinct impression (particularly as an experienced teacher) that what we have here is akin to a bit of *seminar* interaction; where Phil is supplying what he imagines is the 'right' or 'sought after' response. How much more dangerous, therefore, to presume that this is what Phil really thinks!

Such an illustration allows us to appreciate better the force of Potter and Hepburn's arguments, as we can begin to see how, in various ways, the framing of an interview or focus group can impact on one's data. The idea of either method as a neutral mechanism for generating data is thoroughly unsettled. Instead, we come to see interview and focus group talk as more like forms of 'institutionalized' discourse (see Heritage, 1997), rather than identical to the kind of material that emerges over the phone, down at the pub or in the privacy of people's own homes. However, are Potter and Hepburn (as well as Silverman) entirely justified in treating interview and focus group data as fatally compromised or second-rate (in comparison with 'naturalistic' data)? Should we, in effect, just write them off as a 'bad job' – or are there any positive reasons for wanting to hang on to these most popular of research methods?

8.2.2 In defence of interviews and focus groups

Of course, one of Potter and Hepburn's central objections regarding interviews and focus groups – that such events are 'flooded' by the interviewer's/modera-tor's research agenda – has often been seen as one of their great strengths or advantages. If a person is interested in analysing how people perform greetings or negotiate invitations, it's all very well using (naturalistic) data taken from, say, a telephone exchange. But if one is interested in looking at people's under-standings of, say, the British royal family (see Billig, 1991) or of 'lad mags' (see Benwell, 2003), then things aren't always that simple. One might record thou-sands of hours of casual conversation without encountering even a single snippet on either of these topics. Silverman (2007) has suggested that, with a bit of thought and imagination, it is often easy to solve these problems of access – and that researchers should resist falling back on the interview (or focus group) option. But it's hard to ignore the economies made by setting the agenda – in terms of time, money and patience! What these examples also sug-gest is the fact that interviews and focus groups can come into their own, as useful research methods, when, in Holstein and Gubrium's (1995) terms, we are interested in *what*, as opposed to *how*, questions (see also Smith, 2005). In other words, they can be seen, for the purposes of some research projects, as very useful in examining the content, as opposed to the form of people's talk (but see below). Potter and Hepburn (2005b) have argued that the analysis of what people are *doing*, interactionally, with their discourse should come before any consideration of what they are talking 'about' (see also Wooffitt, 2005) – and it's a point worth considering (not least because our idea of what that something *is* may change as a result). But that doesn't mean that an analysis of the performative dimensions of language displaces or exhausts all issues of 'reference'. Exploring the limits of the 'sayable' in terms of such things as human sexuality (Hollway, 1984), 'race' (Wetherell and Potter, 1992) or feminism (Edley and Wetherell, 2001) is not the same as analysing what people are *doing* via the invocation of those different discourses. As it turns out, interviews and focus groups seem to be well suited to exploring both of these angles. Within linguistics, some researchers may use interviews and focus groups to investigate the 'what' or content of people's responses or narratives (e.g. Wagner and Wodak, 2006; Anderson, 2008); others will want to explore a web of responses and 'how' these are pursued, grounded, clarified and interlinked through group interaction (e.g. Petraki, 2005; Tilbury and Colic-Peisker, 2006); and others focus explicitly on the interplay between these (e.g. Litosseliti, 2002).

A final reason for exercising caution over the dismissal of interviews and focus groups centres on the legitimacy of the very distinction between 'natural(istic)' and contrived or 'got up' data. As Speer (2002) has pointed out, discourse analysts have been at the forefront of attempts to highlight the *indexical* or context-specific nature of spoken (and other discourse) data. In studying the 'expression' of attitudes (Potter and Wetherell, 1987), memories (Middleton and Edwards, 1990) and emotions (Edwards, 1997), they have shown how none of these activities involves the simple reporting of some prior state of mind (or 'heart'); but that all such accounts are designed in ways that are sensitive to the contexts in which they make their appearance. In other words, they have shown that all discourse data is 'got up' for something; there is no such thing as a context-free domain. According to this view, the discourse stemming from interviews and focus groups is no more contaminated or compromised than any other data set – and, as such, it should continue to be respected.

In summary, it would appear that there are some clear grounds for seeing both interviews and focus groups as legitimate and valuable research tools. On the proviso that they are understood as interactional events (rather than a simple mechanism for 'harvesting' people's ideas and opinions), they can be used as a basis for examining a whole range of issues – from the way that accounts are designed to do a range of social activities to looking at both the shape and limits of people's understandings of the world. Moreover, in coming to terms with the idea of these methods as forms of social interaction, a fresh perspective is opened up regarding the role of the convenor. Instead of conceiving of them as a potential liability and putting into practice all kinds of measures aimed at limiting or nullifying their impact, they become re-specified as another participant whose contributions are also open to analytical scrutiny. In considering Extract 2, for example, there's nothing essentially wrong in the fact that Nigel (as interviewer) queries the valorization of male promiscuity evident in Phil's previous narrative. In no sense is he speaking out of turn. Of course, the fact that the query came from the interviewer – rather than a member of Phil's own peer group – could be significant; that is, it might have an impact upon the shape of the talk that follows. But it doesn't *invalidate* those turns as an object of interest; indeed, it could become the focus of one's analysis. Moreover, as an intervention, it can help us to see other important things – such as the rhetorical resources that may be brought to bear in the defence of what has become here, temporarily at least, a form of 'troubled' identity (see Wetherell and Edley, 1999; Caldas-Coulthard and Iedema, 2007).

8.3 Going ahead with interviews and focus groups

Having given them, in effect, the 'green light', it is appropriate now to move on to consider the conducting of both interviews and focus groups. As we have already mentioned, our intention is not to provide a step-by-step guide to either methodology, rather our aim is to raise some of the issues involved in their use as well as to highlight some of their particular strengths and weaknesses. As is implied by the very framing of this chapter, interviews and focus groups are seen as closely related. Some researchers maintain that they are similar but nevertheless distinctive (see Dörnyei, 2007), whereas others tend to treat one (i.e. focus groups) as a subcategory of the other (e.g. as in the phrase 'focus group interviews'). To us, they are best thought of as two related forms of practice that often overlap or bleed into each other. In section 8.3.1 below, we'd like to say a little bit more about the nature of focus groups (as the less well known-about methodology) and how they might differ, if at all, from research interviews. We will then move on to consider the pros and cons of both interviews and focus groups.

8.3.1 A focus on focus groups

The most obvious feature of focus groups is given away by the very name; focus groups always feature multiple respondents (typically 6–10). Interviews, however, can be one-to-one affairs – although it is by no means unusual for researchers to interview several people at once. The other half of the label – 'focus' – refers to the fact that, in focus groups, talk constitutes a collective activity centred around a small number of issues (debating particular questions, reading a text, etc.), but, once again, this tends not to distinguish them too clearly from interviews, particularly those that are topic driven. One of the key claims made about focus groups is that they are genuinely *interactive*, in the sense that a group takes shape by – indeed depends on – the synergistic dynamics of participants responding to and building on each other's views. However, it's important to recognize that this is also a feature of many group interviews, where the aim (and hope) is for a dialogue to take off between the participants – instead of every interaction either issuing from or being directed towards the interviewer. What this gives both focus groups and group interviews is a more 'natural' and unpredictable feel, where participants 'are influencing and influenced by others' (Krueger, 1994: 19; see also Morgan 1997; Gibbs 1997). What this also means, of course, is that, compared to *structured* interviews, the moderator/interviewer in these more group-based settings has less control over the research agenda. The person convening the session may initiate topics through the provision of specific questions, but the ensuing talk may spiral off in all kinds of directions and down different kinds of avenues. Importantly, this is usually seen as a strength of both focus groups and group-based interviews – particularly within more ethnographic studies (where a priority is placed upon encouraging the emergence of participants' concerns and issues) and among feminist academics (who have been at the forefront of questioning the power relationships that exist between the researcher and the researched – see Wilkinson, 1999).

One characteristic feature of focus group research is the use of multiple meetings – although, again, this doesn't mark a clear point of distinction from interviews. Typically, each group represents a different constituency. For example, in a study on the topic of animals and biotechnology, the researcher may convene one group of farmers, another group of hunters, a third group of pet owners and a fourth of animal rights activists. Through working with these different groups, such a study may be able to shed some light on a 'communication or understanding gap between groups or categories of people' (Krueger, 1994: 44) – as might also be the case, for example, between policy makers and the public, physicians and patients, employers and employees. Although less common, it is not unknown for the 'same' focus group to meet on more than one occasion (i.e. either in terms of actual personnel or in terms of the particular constituency). This may be deemed necessary because the outcome of a single session may not be seen as sufficient, or because researchers wish to hear from several such 'representative' users. But, even in such cases, researchers will generally assume (and explicitly acknowledge) the fact that each focus group meeting in a series will vary from the next. One group may turn out to be exciting and energetic, another may be much more quiet or low-key, while another may be affected in unexpected ways by a dominant or 'difficult' participant. Experience has shown that it is extremely rare that the same 'topic guide' will lead different focus groups (however defined) down the exact same conversational pathways.

In terms of selecting participants, focus group researchers seem to have placed more emphasis, than those conducting interviews, on finding 'homogeneous, like-minded individuals from the same gendered, ethnic, sexual, economic or cultural background' (Kitzinger, 1995: 300 – although, as Kitzinger goes on to suggest, it is often beneficial to have participants from diverse backgrounds, as it increases the chances of seeing the emergence of and interaction between various different perspectives). Of course there will be many subtle distinctions within each 'category' of participants – such as social and occupational status, income, educational level or expertise – and, insofar as they are perceived by participants themselves, these can sometimes make people 'hesitant to share' or 'defer their opinions' to those perceived to be more knowledgeable or influential (Krueger, 1994). For different reasons, writers of the step-by-step guides sometimes caution against including friends, spouses, relatives and colleagues in the same focus group, as they can affect group cohesion and inhibit other participants by, for example, entering into essentially private conversations (Templeton, 1987). Familiarity can both promote and limit self-disclosure and also discourage disagreement, as interaction is likely to rely on past experiences, and shared or assumed knowledge (Myers, 1998).

Finally, as we've already seen, in focus group research, the notion of the 'interviewer' gives way to that of a 'moderator'. Implicit within this role is the idea that the moderator's job is to facilitate and guide the participants' discussion without themselves playing too active a part. It is assumed that a good moderator will keep the discussion 'on track', without inhibiting the flow of ideas, and that they will ensure that all group participants have opportunities to contribute to the discussion. However, as we've also seen, once we re-specify the focus group as a locus of knowledge *creation* or *construction* – rather than as a means of data collection – then the presence and impact of the moderator (on the data) becomes more a matter of academic interest than a 'concern' that has to be acknowledged and 'allowed for'. As mentioned above, it is assumed that the moderator is another participant whose presence, contributions, perceived background, etc. influence the group discussion; and that different data are produced by different degrees of structure and flexibility in moderating (e.g. allowing for topics to be revised, and deciding what contributions to pursue in more depth and detail – see also Myers, 2007). Similarly, there are countless other factors that influence the amount, kind and quality of interaction in an interview or focus group: the location, the seating and recording arrangements, the presence of observers, perceptions of confidentiality and other ethical issues (as discussed in Litosseliti, 2003).

8.3.2 Interviews and focus groups: Assessing the pros and cons

One of the great advantages of interviews and focus groups is their tremendous flexibility. On the one hand, they can be used as the primary source of data. For instance, Myers and Macnaghten (1998) used focus groups to explore how people talk about environmental sustainability; similarly, Edley and Wetherell (1999) used interviews to look at how young men constructed the role of the father. On the other hand, they can be employed just as easily as *supplementary* sources of data, or, indeed, in *multimethod* studies (which, as the name suggests, combine different data gathering methods – see Morgan, 1997). In the latter case, for example, Litosseliti (2002) analysed people's argumentation around the topic of marriage, by combining focus group data with the analysis of relevant debates in the British media.

Within any given study, both focus groups and interviews can be useful at different stages of the project. One of the ways in which they can be used is towards the end of a study – in assessing, for example, the development, effectiveness or impact of a programme of activities. However, some academics feel that both methodologies truly come into their own more at a preliminary or exploratory stages of a research project – in the generating of 'hypotheses' (NB loosely defined – see Kitzinger, 1994). For example, Skeggs et al. (1998–2000) conducted focus groups meetings with gay men, lesbians and single women in both city and rural areas, in an attempt to get a feel for these groups' different perceptions of violence and space. The outcome of these meetings did not, in itself, form the 'findings' of their study; rather, it helped them in formulating and designing a subsequent research programme.

Many of the advantages of both interviews and focus groups – over other research methods – can be gleaned from the paragraphs above. Specifically, they are both seen as providing multiple views on any given subject or topic; they encourage the exploration of 'members' or 'participants' (i.e. *emic*) own experiences or 'life-world' and, as a consequence, they also tend to generate a sense of *empowerment* for those taking part (Goss and Leinbach, 1996). For the likes of Wilkinson, they help 'shift the balance of power away from the researcher [and] towards the research participants' (1999: 64), in allowing participants to contribute to the research agenda (particularly if they come from minority, underrepresented or disadvantaged groups). In addition, focus groups and interviews can have a range of other, more practical, benefits. For instance, they are useful in obtaining information from illiterate communities; they can be used to gather data on activities that span many days or weeks; and, in the case of virtual focus groups, they can facilitate the participation of people (e.g. busy professionals, government officials) who are hard to reach or to get together in one place, or who are unwilling to contribute in person (e.g. on sensitive or controversial topics).

Alongside the above, there seems to be a general consensus in key discussions of the merits of both focus groups and interviews (see Gibbs, 1997; Hughes, 1996; Krueger, 1994; Race et al., 1994; Morgan and Krueger, 1993; Powell and Single, 1996; Wray and Bloomer, 2006) that they are particularly useful for:

- discovering new information and consolidating old or established knowledge
- obtaining different perspectives on the 'same' topic (sometimes described as multivocality) in participants' own words
- gaining information on participants' views, attitudes, beliefs, responses, motivations and perceptions on a topic; 'why' people think or feel the way they do
- examining participants' shared understandings of everyday life, and the everyday use of language and culture of particular groups
- brainstorming and generating ideas
- gaining insights into the ways in which individuals are influenced by others in a group situation (group dynamics)
- generating a sense of rapport between the researcher(s) and the researched.

(adapted from Litosseliti, 2003: 18)

Within projects in linguistics and in disciplines where language plays an important role, interviews and focus groups have been used to do all of the above in relation to a range of different topics: people's attitudes towards language in general; people's attitudes towards particular language aspects (e.g. accents and dialects, specific language use, language teaching and learning); people's perceptions of a linguistic experience (see, for example, Kitzinger, 1994, 1995 on audiences' perception of media messages around HIV/AIDS); and people's discursive construction of self and identity (e.g. gender identity – e.g. Litosseliti, 2002; national identity – e.g. Wodak et al., 1999; or ethnic identity – e.g. De Fina, 2007). A common feature of most of these projects is an interest in the way that the groups interact (Kitzinger 1994). Group discussions go through stages of 'forming', 'storming', 'norming', 'performing' and 'adjourning' (Tuckman, 1965; Tuckman and Jensen, 1977), during which participants variously negotiate opinions, arguments, responses, consensus and disagreement. In other words, there is a whole range of fairly unpredictable group dynamics. In relation to focus groups, Stewart and Shamdasani (1990) argue that the direct, open-response interaction among participants and between the moderator and the participants allows for a whole range and variety of responses, probing, connections between points made, nuances and deeper levels of meaning. So again we can see that, interaction in such groups is not just important for what it tells us about people's views (or their language), but also because it involves participants responding to each other – in having to reconsider or re-evaluate their own understandings and experiences (Kitzinger, 1994, 1995). Meanings are constantly negotiated, renegotiated and co-constructed in interaction with others in the group. Common sense leads us to imagine that participants will come to such meetings 'armed' (or 'minded' perhaps) with certain opinions, however, experience in conducting both focus groups and (group) interviews reveals that 'opinions' are emergent and dynamic, rather than established and fixed (see Agar and MacDonald, 1995, for example). While this may prove disconcerting to a researcher determined to 'pin down' what a particular group or individual thinks (NB which is the way that focus groups have been traditionally used within commercial organizations), it will seem a blessing for the linguist who both expects, and is interested in, those very dynamics. As Myers and Macnaghten (1999) put it (in relation to focus group research):

> Focus groups offer a practical way of eliciting such complex talk, and in analysing the conversation we acknowledge the situatedness of opinion, and recover some of the richness and complexity with which people express, explore and use opinions. . . . Focus groups are typically designed to elicit something less fixed, definite and coherent that lies beneath attitudes, something that the researcher may call feelings, or responses, or experiences, or world-views. [They also] provide richer accounts of how people understand particular issues in the context of wider social concerns. . . . The great strength of focus groups as a technique is in the liveliness, complexity and unpredictability of the talk, where participants can make sudden connections that confuse the researchers' coding but open up their thinking. (pp. 174–5)

It should go without saying that some of the benefits of interviews and focus groups can be re-construed as weaknesses or problems. As we've just noted, their open-endedness and unpredictability can be a source of dismay, as much as a source of delight. This might be particularly true of those who see interviews and focus groups as a quick and easy method for testing hypotheses (see Merton, 1987) – a perception that may stem both from the sheer ubiquity of interviews and from the legacy of focus group use in time-intensive marketing or advertising projects. In contrast, however, a considerable amount of time and skill has to go into conducting these types of projects. As Stewart and Shamdasani (1990) point out, rather than being ad hoc or atheoretical exercises, interviews and focus groups should be both theoretically grounded and rigorously planned. Equal care and attention should be dedicated to the actual conducting of these events, as well as to the analysis of any resulting data (see Krueger (1994), Bloor et al. (2001) and Litosseliti (2003) for some specific guidance to each of these stages). That said, as above, it is useful to list some of the more commonly mentioned limitations of interviews and focus groups as they appear in the literature (see Krueger, 1994; Morgan, 1997, 1993; Gibbs, 1997; Hughes, 1996). They include the following:

- Bias and manipulation, due to the interviewer/moderator either leading participants directly in terms of what they say in the meetings, or where participants end up saying what they think the convenor (or others in the group) want to hear.
- 'False' consensus, which may be the result of some participants with strong personalities and/or similar views dominating the discussion, while others remaining silent.
- Other effects of group dynamics – such as group polarization (see Myers and Lamm, 1976) – where a group may respond collectively in a more exaggerated way than any individual member.
- Problems with making generalizations from these groups to a wider population.
- They are intensive in terms of both time and resources and usually require a high level of commitment from one's participants.

(adapted from Litosseliti, 2003: 21)

Some of these problems are practical issues that can be addressed through careful planning and skilful moderation. For example, regarding the issue of dominant participants, the interviewer/moderator can establish a code of conduct at the start of the discussions, for instance, asking people not to talk at the same time and to respect each others' views. It is also possible, through the use of eye contact and gentle probing, to minimize the influence of dominating participants and to encourage the other parties. The careful design of the questions and topics to be developed during the discussion will help the interviewer/moderator to steer clear of leading or loaded questions (e.g. 'yes/no' and 'why' questions) and promote a balance of contributions among the different participants (for discussions of questions, see Litosseliti, 2003; Stewart and

Shamdasani, 1990; Puchta and Potter, 1999). Finally, many social researchers will 'check' their practices and interpretations through the use of pilot groups, an observer or assistant present during their group discussions, and/or via post-discussion interviews with the participants themselves.

However, it is important to understand that most of the 'problems' listed above are limitations only if one assumes, in the first place, that it is possible to achieve a veridical or authentic account of a person's opinion (which treats such 'things' as stable or fixed), or that the 'name of the game' is to identify a representative sample of participants whose views can be safely generalized to a wider population. Again, as Silverman (2001) points out, this would be to adopt a 'positivist' approach to one's research data – which stands at odds with the more 'constructionist' framework assumed by many contemporary practitioners (including us), which treats the interview or focus group as a space in which opinions are (re)constituted, rather than simply reported. Contrary to the positivist position, the constructivist researcher uses focus groups and interviews, not to achieve a representative 'sample' of talk, but to create bodies of data that are indicative or illustrative of particular social phenomena. Likewise, in relation to the 'charges' of bias and manipulation, the constructivist researcher sees interviews and focus groups as offering insights into what participants *say* they believe or do – not into what they 'actually' think or do. This is not to imply, however, that there is necessarily a clear distinction between what a person says and thinks – indeed, constructionists have been at the forefront of challenging precisely this divide (see Burr, 2003; Edwards, 1997). So while the positivist researcher may fret about participants telling the interviewer/moderator what they think she wants to hear, or about participants not wanting to disclose certain information about themselves or their lives (because they perceive it to be too personal or embarrassing), this tends not to be such a concern for the constructionist. Many would maintain that there is no 'underlying truth' that may be hidden or concealed. Instead, they'd tend to treat any or all resulting data as designed for the context in which it emerges. In other words, the constructivist researcher *expects* their participants to tailor their discourse in response to the demands of the situation.

As we can see, many of the most commonly understood limitations of interviews and focus groups involve them being either theorized or implemented in ways that are somehow problematic: by treating the interviewer/moderator as 'neutral'; by ignoring the many contextual parameters that help to shape any discourse; by taking what people say at face value; by not placing enough emphasis on the interaction and group dynamics; and by generalizing or trying to quantify the data gathered. What we are promoting here is a different epistemological warrant for both interview and focus group data, in response to observations (see, for example, Wilkinson, 1999) that such warranting is often missing from many studies. We'll end by quoting Krueger – whose point about focus groups extends just as well to interviews. He states: 'it is important to keep in mind that the[ir] intent . . . is not to infer but to understand, not to generalize but to determine the range, not to make statements about the population but to provide insights about how people perceive a situation' (1994: 87). So conceived, they are a positive boon to the field of linguistics.

8.4 Transcription notation

This transcription notation represents a simplified version of that developed by Gail Jefferson (see Atkinson and Heritage, 1984):

(1.0)	Timed pause (in tenths of seconds)
(.)	Micropause (i.e. too short to time)
No=	Indicates the absence of a discernable gap between the end of one
=gap	speaker's utterance and the beginning of the next
Wh [en]	Marks overlap between speakers. The left bracket indicates the
[No]	beginning of the overlap while the right bracket indicates its end
No::w	One or more colons indicate the extension of the previous sound
> <	Indicate talk produced more quickly than surrounding talk
text	Word(s) emphasized
CAPITAL	Noticeably louder talk
°hush°	Noticeably quieter talk
↑↓	Rising and falling intonation
?	Indicates rising inflection (but not necessarily a question)
.	Indicates a stopping fall in tone (but not necessarily the end of a turn)
hh	Indicates an audible out-breath (the more 'h's the longer the breath)
.hh	Indicates an audible intake of breath (the more 'h's the longer the breath)
(( ))	Non-verbal activity (e.g. Banging)
[text]	Clarificatory information

Further reading

Interviews

Holstein and Gubrium (1995) – Although in no way a 'how to do' guide, this compact book provides an excellent introduction to a constructivist approach to theorizing (and conducting) interviews. It thoroughly unsettles what Silverman (2001 – see below) refers to as the 'positivist' and 'emotionalist' interpretations of interview data.

Hughes (1996) – This is a very straightforward account of the use of interviewing in the Social Sciences and Humanities. Hughes runs through the 'pros' and 'cons' of interviewing; he delineates the various types or styles of approach and he describes the basic stages involved in an easy, step-by-step, manner.

Silverman (2001) – Chapter 4 (pp. 83–118) provides an insightful critique of the routine use of interviews in social research – by drawing attention to the various epistemological framings which commonly (but often implicitly) underpin such work. As noted above, Silverman has been quite outspoken in his reservations about the overall value of interview-based studies – so he is an important voice to consider.

Wray and Bloomer (2006) – Chapter 13 (pp. 152–167) provides an overview of various research methods – including interviews, focus groups and, indeed, questionnaires. Detailed and practical, this chapter – like ours – underlines the connections between interviews and focus groups. However, like Hughes's chapter (see above), this one sits within a firmly positivist frame.

Focus Groups

Barbour and Kitzinger (eds) (1999) – A collection of articles on the theory, practice and politics of focus group research. Particularly useful for its critical thinking around participation and community views, its discussion of often neglected areas (e.g. sensitive topics, feminist research) and its useful perspectives on analysis.

Bloor, Frankland, Thomas and Robson (2001) – An introductory book on the key issues and practical requirements for planning, conducting and analysing focus groups within the social science context. It offers a basic overview of the methodology, and can be used as a supplementary text.

Krueger (1994) – An established, easy-to-read book with useful examples and guidelines. It includes discussions of focus groups outside marketing research, and as part of evaluation research.

Litosseliti (2003) – An accessible overview of the methodology and the key issues, and a step-by-step guide to planning and conducting focus groups. Particularly useful for looking at focus groups from a linguistic/discursive perspective. Full of examples throughout and useful tables of different types of questions and different probes (for developing a discussion, for encouraging different viewpoints and for managing particular types of participants).

References

Agar, M. and MacDonald, J. (1995), 'Focus groups and ethnography', *Human Organization*, 54 (1), 78–86.

Anderson, K. (2008), 'Constructing young masculinity: a case study of heroic discourse on violence', *Discourse & Society*, 19 (2), 139–61.

Antaki, C. (2000), 'Why I study talk-in-interaction', *The Psychologist*, 13 (5), 242–3.

Armistead, N. (ed.) (1974), *Reconstructing Social Psychology*. Harmondsworth: Penguin.

Atkinson, P. and Heritage, J. (1984), *Structures of Social Action: Studies in Conversation Analysis*. Cambridge: Cambridge University Press.

Atkinson, P. and Silverman, D. (1997), 'Kundera's immortality: the interview society and the invention of the self', *Qualitative Inquiry*, 3, 304–25.

Barbour, R. and Kitzinger, J. (eds) (1999), *Developing Focus Group Research: Politics, Research and Practice*. London: Sage.

Benwell, B. (ed.) (2003), *Masculinity and Men's Lifestyle Magazines*. Oxford: Blackwell (Sociological Review Monograph Series).

Berger, P. and Luckmann, T. (1967), *The Social Construction of Reality*. New York: Doubleday.

Billig, M. (1991), *Talking of the Royal Family*. London: Routledge.

Bloor, M., Frankland, J., Thomas, M. and Robson, K. (2001). *Focus Groups in Social Research*. Introducing Qualitative Methods Series. London: Sage.

Burr, V. (2003), *Social Constructionism* (2nd edn). London: Routledge.

Caldas-Coulthard, C. R. and Iedema, R. (eds) (2007), *Identity Trouble: Critical Discourse and Contested Identities*. London: Palgrave.

Cicourel, A. V. (1964), *Method and Measurement in Sociology*. New York: Free Press.

De Fina, A. (2007), 'Code-switching and the construction of ethnic identity in a community of practice', *Language in Society*, 36 (3), 371–92.

Dörnyei, Z. (2007), *Research Methods in Applied Linguistics: Quantitative, Qualitative, and Mixed Methodologies*. Oxford: Oxford University Press.

Edley, N. and Wetherell, M. (1999), 'Imagined futures: young men's talk about fatherhood and domestic life', *British Journal of Social Psychology*, 38 (2), 181–94.

—. (2001), 'Jekyll and Hyde: analysing constructions of the feminist', *Feminism & Psychology*, 11 (4), 439–57.

Edwards, D. (1997), *Discourse and Cognition*. London: Sage.

Freeman, M. (1993), *Rewriting the Self: History, Memory, Narrative*. London: Routledge.

Garfinkel, H. (1967), *Studies in Ethnomethodology*. Englewood Cliffs, NJ: Prentice Hall.

Gibbs, A. (1997), 'Focus Groups', *Social Research Update, Issue 19*. Department of Sociology, University of Surrey. http://www.soc.surrey.ac.uk/sru/SRU19.html

Goss, J. D. and Leinbach, T. R. (1996), 'Focus groups as alternative research practice', *Area*, 28 (2), 115–23.

Grebenik, E. and Moser, C. A. (1962), 'Society: problems and methods of study', in A. T. Welford, M. Argyle, O. Glass and J. N. Morris (eds), *Statistical Surveys*. London: Routledge and Kegan Paul.

Gubrium, J. F. (1993), *Speaking of Life: Horizons of Meaning for Nursing Home Residents*. Hawthorne, NY: Aldine de Gruyter.

Harré, R. and Secord, P. F. (1972), *The Explanation of Social Behaviour*. Oxford: Basil Blackwell.

Hepburn, A. (2003), *An Introduction to Critical Social Psychology*. London: Sage.

Heritage, J. (1997), 'Conversation analysis and institutional talk: analyzing data', in D. Silverman (ed.), *Qualitative Analysis: Issues of Theory and Method*. London: Sage.

Hollway, W. (1984), 'Gender difference and the production of subjectivity', in J. Henriques, W. Hollway, C. Urwin, C. Venn and V. Walkerdine (eds), *Changing the Subject: Psychology, Social Regulation and Subjectivity*. London: Methuen, pp. 227–63.

Holstein, J. A. and Gubrium, J. F. (1995), *The Active Interview*. London: Sage.

Hughes, M. (1996), 'Interviewing', in T. Greenfield (ed.), *Research Methods: Guidance for Post-Graduates*. London: Arnold.

Kitzinger, J. (1994), 'The methodology of focus groups: the importance of interaction between research participants', *Sociology of Health*, 16 (1), 103–21.

—. (1995), 'Introducing focus groups', *British Medical Journal*, 311, 299–302.

Krueger, R. A. (1994), *Focus Groups: A Practical Guide for Applied Research*. London: Sage.

Kvale, S. (1996), *Interviews: An Introduction to Qualitative Research Interviewing*. London: Sage.

Lederman, L. C. (1990), 'Assessing educational effectiveness: the focus group interview as a technique for data collection', *Communication Education*, 39 (2), 117–27.

Litosseliti, L. (2002), 'The discursive construction of morality and gender: investigating public and private arguments', in S. Benor, M. Rose, D. Sharma, J. Sweetland and Q. Zhang (eds), *Gendered Practices in Language*. Stanford: Center for the Study of Language and Information, Stanford University, pp. 45–63.

—. (2003), *Using Focus Groups in Research*. London: Continuum.

Merton, R. K. (1987). 'The focussed interview and focus groups: continuities and discontinuities', *Public Opinion Quarterly*, 51 (4), 550–66.

Middleton, D. and Edwards, D. (eds) (1990), *Collective Remembering*. London: Sage.

Morgan, D. L. (ed.) (1993), *Successful Focus Groups: Advancing the State of the Art*. Newbury Park, CA: Sage.

—. (1997), *Focus Groups as Qualitative Research* (2nd edn). London: Sage.

Morgan, D. L. and Krueger, R. A. (1993), 'When to use focus groups and why', in D. L. Morgan (ed.), *Successful Focus Groups*. London: Sage.

Myers, D. G. and Lamm, H. (1976), 'The group polarization phenomenon', *Psychological Bulletin*, 83, 602–27.

Myers, G. (1998), 'Displaying opinions: Topics and disagreement in focus groups', *Language in Society*, 27 (1), 85–111.

—. (2007), 'Enabling talk: How the facilitator shapes a focus group', *Text and Talk*, 27 (1), 79–105.

Myers, G. and Macnaghten, P. (1998), 'Rhetorics of environmental sustainability: commonplaces and places', *Environment and Planning*, A 30 (2), 333–53.

—. (1999), 'Can focus groups be analysed as talk?', in R. Barbour and J. Kitzinger (eds), *Developing Focus Group Research: Politics, Research and Practice*. London: Sage, pp. 173–85.

Pancer, M. S. (1997), 'Social psychology: the crisis continues', in I. Prilleltensky and D. Fox (eds), *Critical Psychology: An Introduction*. London: Sage.

Patton, M. Q. (1980), *Qualitative Evaluation Methods*. Beverley Hills, CA: Sage.

Petraki, E. (2005), 'Disagreement and opposition in multigenerational interviews with Greek-Australian mothers and daughters', *Text*, 25 (2), 269–303.

Potter, J. (1996), 'Discourse analysis and constructionist approaches: theoretical background', in J. Richardson (ed.), *Handbook of Qualitative Research Methods for Psychology and the Social Sciences*. Leicester: BPS Books, pp. 125–40.

Potter, J. and Hepburn, A. (2005a), 'Qualitative interviews in psychology: problems and possibilities', *Qualitative Research in Psychology*, 2, 281–307.

—. (2005b), 'Authors' response' (Commentaries on Potter and Hepburn, 'Qualitative interviews in psychology: problems and possibilities'). *Qualitative Research in Psychology*, 2, 319–25.

Potter, J. and Wetherell, M. (1987), *Discourse and Social Psychology: Beyond Attitudes and Behaviour*. London: Sage.

Powell, R. A. and Single, H. M. (1996), 'Focus groups', *International Journal of Quality in Health Care*, 8 (5), 499–504.

Puchta, C. and Potter, J. (1999), 'Asking elaborate questions: focus groups and the management of spontaneity', *Journal of Sociolinguistics*, 3 (3), 314–35.

—. (2004), *Focus Group Practice*. London: Sage.

Race, K. E., Hotch, D. F. and Parker, T. (1994), 'Rehabilitation program evaluation: use of focus groups to empower clients', *Evaluation Review*, 18 (6), 730–40.

Schegloff, E. A. (1997), 'Whose text? Whose context?', *Discourse & Society*, 8 (2), 165–87.

Silverman, D. (2001), *Interpreting Qualitative Data* (2nd edn). London: Sage.

—. (2007), *A Very Short, Fairly Interesting and Reasonably Cheap Book About Qualitative Research*. London: Sage.

Skeggs, B., Moran, L. and Truman, C. (1998–2000), *Violence, Security, Space: A Study of the Practical and Policy Context of Substantive Safe Public Spaces*. ESRC research project, Lancaster University, UK.

Smith, J. A. (2005), 'Advocating pluralism' (Commentaries on Potter and Hepburn, 'Qualitative interviews in psychology: problems and possibilities'). *Qualitative Research in Psychology*, 2, 309–11.

Speer, S. (2002), '"Natural" and "contrived" data: a sustainable distinction?' *Discourse Studies*, 4 (4), 511–25.

Stewart, D. W. and Shamdasani, P. N. (1990), *Focus Groups: Theory and Practice*. London: Sage.

Stokoe, E. H. and Smithson, J. (2001), 'Making gender relevant: conversation analysis and gender categories in interaction', *Discourse & Society*, 12, 217–44.

Suchman, L. and Jordan, B. (1990), 'Interactional troubles in face-to-face survey interviews', *Journal of the American Statistical Association*, 85 (409), 232–41.

Templeton, J. (1987), *Focus Groups: A Guide for Marketing and Advertising Professionals*. Chicago: Probus.

Tilbury, F. and Colic-Peisker, V. (2006), 'Deflecting responsibility in employer talk about race discrimination', *Discourse & Society*, 17 (5), 651–76.

Tuckman, B. (1965), 'Developmental sequence in small groups', *Psychological Bulletin*, 63, 384–99.

Tuckman, B. and Jensen, M. (1977), 'Stages of small group development', *Group and Organizational Studies*, 2, 419–27.

Wagner, I. and Wodak, R. (2006), 'Performing success: identifying strategies of self-presentation in women's biographical narratives', *Discourse & Society*, 17 (3), 385–411.

Weatherall, A. (2002), 'Towards understanding gender and talk-in-interaction', *Discourse & Society*, 13 (6), 767–81.

Wetherell, M. (1994), 'Men and masculinity: a socio-psychological analysis of discourse and gender identity'. ESRC grant No. R000233129.

Wetherell, M. and Edley, N. (1999), 'Negotiating hegemonic masculinity: imaginary positions and psycho-discursive practices', *Feminism & Psychology*, 9 (3), 335–56.

Wetherell, M. and Potter, J. (1992), *Mapping the Language of Racism: Discourse and the Legitimation of Exploitation*. London and New York: Harvester Wheatsheaf and Columbia University Press.

Wilkinson, S. (1998), 'Focus groups – a feminist method', *Psychology of Women Quarterly*, 23 (2), 221–44.

—. (1999), 'How useful are focus groups in feminist research?' in R. Barbour and J. Kitzinger (eds), *Developing Focus Group Research: Politics, Research and Practice*. London: Sage, pp. 64–78.

Wodak, R., de Cillia, M. and Liebhart, K. (1999), *The Discursive Construction of National Identity*. Edinburgh: Edinburgh University Press.

Wooffitt, R. (2005), *Conversation Analysis and Discourse Analysis: A Comparative and Critical Introduction*. London: Sage.

Wray, A. and Bloomer, A. (2006), *Projects in Linguistics: A Practical Guide to Researching Language* (2nd edn). London: Arnold.

9 Multimodal Analysis: Key Issues

Jeff Bezemer and Carey Jewitt

Chapter outline

This chapter discusses multimodal approaches to the study of linguistics, and of representation and communication more generally. It draws attention to the range of different modes that people use to make meaning beyond language – such as speech, gesture, gaze, image and writing – and in doing so, offers new ways of analysing language. The chapter addresses two key questions. First, how can all these modes be handled theoretically? What are 'modes'? How do people use them? Second, how can all these modes be handled analytically? What are the methodological implications if one or more modes are excluded from the analysis? The chapter first highlights the ways in which multimodality is taken up in *social linguistic* research. It then describes a *social semiotic* approach to multimodality. The steps taken in such an approach are described and exemplified with case studies of classroom interaction and textbooks. It concludes with a discussion of the potentials and constraints of multimodal analysis.

9.1 Introduction

Multimodality refers to a field of application rather than a theory. A variety of disciplines and theoretical approaches can be used to explore different aspects of the multimodal landscape. Psychological theories can be applied to look at how people perceive different modes or to understand the impact of one mode over another on memory, for example. Sociological and anthropological theories and interests could be applied to examine how communities use multimodal conventions to mark and maintain identities. This chapter describes approaches to multimodality in studies in linguistics, and representation and communication more generally. These approaches are concerned with the socially and culturally situated construction of meaning, and can be applied to investigate power, inequality and ideology in human interactions and artefacts. The chapter is organized as follows. Section 9.2 discusses 'social linguistic' approaches to multimodality. Section 9.3 sets out a social semiotic approach to multimodality. Section 9.4 offers an analytical framework for analysing multimodal representation and communication. Sections 9.5–9.6 show how the framework was applied in two of our studies. Finally, section 9.7 deals with the potentials and limitations of multimodal analysis.

9.2 Social linguistic approaches to multimodality

Speech and writing are the central modes of representation and communication in a range of interrelated research traditions concerned with the social and situated use of language. These 'social linguistic' traditions include Conversation Analysis (Psathas, 1995), interactional sociology (Goffman, 1981), Interactional Sociolinguistics (Gumperz, 1999), linguistic anthropology (Duranti, 1997), micro-ethnography (Erickson, 2004) and linguistic ethnography (Creese, 2008). To varying degrees, all of these traditions have also been and are increasingly concerned with modes other than language, such as gesture or gaze. The interest in multimodality is enabled by the use of digital photography and video recordings of human communication which is becoming standard practice in qualitative research (Knoblauch et al., 2006).

Multimodality is differently construed in social linguistic work. Some studies are based on the assumption that speech or writing is always dominant, carrying the 'essence' of meanings, and that other, simultaneously operating modes can merely expand, exemplify or modify these meanings. This is reflected by fine-grained, moment-to-moment analysis of, for example, lexis, intonation, rhythm and tone, hesitations and restarts, alongside more occasional discussion of, for instance, hand movements or shifts in direction of gaze in talk (e.g. Erickson, 2004). The methodological privileging of particular linguistic resources is also reflected in notions like 'non-verbal', 'paralinguistic' or 'context'. Gumperz (1999), for instance, defines a 'contextualisation cue' as 'any verbal sign which when processed in co-occurrence with symbolic grammatical and lexical signs serves to construct the contextual ground for situated interpretation' (p. 461), thus treating lexis and grammar as 'text', other 'verbal' signs, such as intonation, rhythm and tone as 'paralinguistic' or 'context', and any other 'non-verbal' sign is either treated as context or placed beyond the scope of the analysis. Other studies foreground the significance of particular modes (e.g. pointing in Haviland, 2003), and transcribe them in conjunction with speech or writing. Yet other studies attend to a wide range of different modes and their mutually modifying effect, emphasizing their different potentials and constraints and essentially moving towards a semiotic perspective on representation and communication (e.g. McDermott et al., 1978; Goodwin, 2000; Scollon and Wong-Scollon, 2003).

Multimodality has been central to much theorizing in social linguistic traditions. Erving Goffman's notion of 'frame' (Goffman, 1974), for instance, suggests how people co-construct a 'definition of what goes on' in interactions using a range of different modes. Frames are bracketed through beginnings and endings marked in a range of different modes of communication. Goffman draws his example from Western dramaturgy, with the lights dimming, the bells ringing and the curtain rising signifying the beginning of a performance, and the curtains falling and lights going on at the end of it. In talk, such boundary markers may be realized through shifts in tone of voice and bodily orientation (Goffman, 1981). People are expected to respond or align themselves to such shifts: they 'not only organize themselves posturally in relation to what they are doing together, but they take on the postures characteristic to what they are doing together at exactly the same moment' (McDermott et al., 1978: 257).

Such practices of modal alignment can become rather complex when used for engagements within different, simultaneously operating frames (Scheflen, 1973; Norris, 2004). Kendon (1990) shows how a participant standing in a social circle with two others can temporarily turn his head away from the centre point of this 'f-formation', while sustaining his involvement in the talk. The participant keeps his lower body in line with the centre of the f-formation to express his engagement with the talk, and uses his upper body to engage, temporarily, with a frame situated outside the formation. When the speaker's gaze reaches his or her listener, however, the listener is expected to be oriented towards the speaker again (Goodwin, 1981). If not, a pause or a restart follows. The speaker, in turn, can look away from the listener without impacting on the structure of the conversation. In this way, shifts in multimodal displays of orientation can suggest varying levels of engagement within different frames operating at the same time.

While modes of communication other than language are, to varying degrees, being attended to in social linguistic work, its central units of analysis are usually linguistic units (e.g. 'intonation unit') or units defined in linguistic terms (e.g. a 'turn' is defined in terms of 'who is speaking'). Modes of communication other than language are increasingly seen as relevant in social linguistic research, given its concern with examining situated language and language use in interaction. Linguists working in CA and Ethnomethodology in particular have focused on the role of gaze, gesture, drawing and texts alongside language in interaction (Goodwin, 2001; Luff et al., 2009). In a social semiotic approach (see section 9.3), 'mode' is privileged as an organizing principle of representation and communication, and therefore treated as a central unit of analysis.

9.3 A social semiotic approach to multimodality

The starting-point for social semiotic approaches to multimodality is to extend the social interpretation of language and its meanings to the whole range of modes of representation and communication employed in a culture (Kress, 2009; van Leeuwen, 2005). Central to this approach are three theoretical assumptions.

First, social semiotics assumes that representation and communication always draw on a multiplicity of modes, all of which contribute to meaning. It focuses on analysing and describing the full repertoire of meaning-making resources which people use in different contexts (actional, visual, spoken, gestural, written, three-dimensional, and others, depending on the domain of representation), and on developing means that show how these are organized to make meaning.

Second, multimodality assumes that all forms of communication (modes) have, like language, been shaped through their cultural, historical and social uses to realize social functions. We, along with many others, take all communicational acts to be socially made, and meaningful about the social environments in which they have been made. We assume that different modes shape the meanings to be realized in mode-specific ways, so that meanings are in turn differently realized in different modes. For instance, the spatial extent of a gesture, the intonational range of voice, and the direction and length of a gaze are all part of the resources for making meaning. The meanings of multimodal signs fashioned from such resources, like the meanings of speech, are located in the social origin, motivations and interests of those who make the sign in specific social contexts. These all affect and shape the sign that is made.

Third, the meanings realized by any mode are always interwoven with the meanings made with those other modes co-present and co-operating in the communicative event. This interaction produces meaning. Multimodality focuses on people's process of meaning making, a process in which people make choices from a network of alternatives: selecting one modal resource (meaning potential) over another (Halliday, 1978).

Social semiotics assumes that resources are socially shaped to become, over time, meaning-making resources which articulate the (social, individual/ affective) meanings demanded by the requirements of different communities. These organized sets of semiotic resources for making meaning (with) are referred to as *modes*. The more a set of resources has been used in the social life of a particular community, the more fully and finely articulated it will have become. For example, the way in which gesture has been shaped into modes varies across diverse communities such as the hearing impaired, ballet dancers, deep-water divers and airport runway ground staff. In order for something to 'be a mode' there needs to be a shared cultural sense within a community of a set of resources and how these can be organized to realize meaning. Modes can also be understood in terms of Halliday's (1978) classification of meaning. He suggests that every sign simultaneously tells us something about 'the world' (ideational meaning), positions us in relation to someone or something (interpersonal meaning) and produces a structured text (textual meaning). Multimodality sets out to explore how these meanings are realized in all modes.

Modal affordance, originating in the work of Gibson (1977), is a concept describing what is possible to express and represent easily in a mode. For Gibson, affordance is a matter of the material perception of the physical world. By contrast, social semiotics approaches affordance in relation to the material *and* the cultural, social-historical use of a mode. Compare speech and image, for instance. Sound, the material basis of speech, unfolds in time; it is sequenced. This logic of sequence in time is unavoidable in speech: one sound has to be uttered after another, one word after another, one syntactic and textual element after another. Marks on a surface constitute a material basis of image, which does not unfold in time to its audience; the reader of an image can access the spatially organized constituents of the image simultaneously. These different material affordances of sound and marked surfaces are used to mean; out of their historical use new meaning potential arises. Meaning attaches to the order of words, for instance, or the layout of a page, and these meanings differ from (socio-cultural) context to context. As a result of these different material and cultural affordances, some things can be signified more easily in an image, others in writing. A number of studies have described modes in these terms, including Kress and van Leeuwen's (1996) work on image, Martinec's (2000) research on movement and gesture, and van Leeuwen's work on music (1999). As modes have different affordances, people always use different modes simultaneously to 'orchestrate' complex, 'multimodal ensembles'. We will demonstrate this point in sections 9.5 and 9.6. First we turn to a discussion of the steps involved in doing social semiotic research.

9.4 Collecting and analysing multimodal data

In this section we describe the steps taken in a social semiotic approach to multimodal research. In some respects these steps are similar to more general ethnographic procedures which are also adopted in much of the social linguistic work described above (cf. Erickson, 1986; Green and Bloome, 1997), but they differ in their systematic attention to *meaning* and the ways in which people use modes to represent the world and engage in social interaction.

Step 1: *collecting and logging data* If the focus is on face-to-face interaction, say, in a classroom, data are likely to include a mixture of video recordings, fieldnotes, materials and texts used during the interaction, participant interviews, and possibly policy documents and other texts related to what we have observed. In our own research, we view the video recording of a lesson along with the fieldnotes and the texts collected from the lesson. From this viewing we make a descriptive account of the lesson – a video log. The log is a synopsis of what was going on during the observations. We often include sketches of events, video stills, a map of the classroom layout and trails, and comments on the teacher and student movement. Alongside, but separate from this account, we note analytical thoughts, ideas and questions. If the focus is on 'static' texts, such as a book or a web page, the data are perhaps more readily available, but the logging process is similar in that the 'chapters' or 'web spaces' will be summarized, possibly including 'thumbnail' depictions of particular excerpts and provisional analytical notes.

Step 2: *viewing data* Multimodal analysis involves repeated viewing of the data. We watch video data as a research team, sometimes including visiting fellows and colleagues external to the project to get their insights and different perspectives. We view video data with both sound and image. We hone in on excerpts that we viewed with vision only, sound only, fast forward, in slow motion – all of which provide different ways of seeing the data. This helps recognize customary acts, patterns of gesture, for example, and routines across the time and space of the classroom. If the focus is on static texts, the procedure is similar, individually and jointly engaging with the collected materials, sometimes covering one mode and focusing on the other and asking 'what sense can I make of this text if I can't see the images?' or 'what sense can I make of the text if I change its layout?' Viewing the data alongside the logs and organizing it in light of the research questions serves to generate criteria for sampling the data, refining and generating new questions, and developing analytical ideas.

Step 3: *sampling data* Using video to collect data produces rich data and often a lot of it. Multimodal transcription and analysis are intensive. It can take hours to transcribe an excerpt of a few minutes. With a focus on all the modes in play it is generally not feasible nor necessary to analyse all the video of a lesson in detail. For this reason we sample the video data to select instances (episodes) for detailed analysis. With static texts, transcription works differently and may not be as laborious, but here too a fine-grained, multimodal analysis demands selection of focal texts – pages from books or websites. How to select these episodes or focal texts is a difficult question and one that is intimately guided by the research question; we tend to focus on those moments in the interaction or in the static text where the interaction order is disturbed or where a convention is broken, as it is on those occasions where power relations and ideologies become manifest (cf. a student contesting the teacher – in interaction or by using an unconventional layout for an assignment). We may focus on what stands out, but always return to the whole data corpus to test our analysis of the selected texts against it.

Step 4: *transcribing and analysing data* Linguistic notions of transcription refer to the 'translation' of speech into writing. In this tradition, transcription conventions are used to express features of speech, such as intonation, hesitations or pauses, which are not normally expressed in writing. But even if one adopts the most sophisticated set of conventions, the transcriber has to accept that there are details which are lost; the letters merely suggest the phonemic interpretation of sounds, not the actual sounds; 'accents' and voice quality is lost, and so forth. At the same time, what is gained from the transcript is the potential to rearrange speech units to enable certain aspects to come to the fore, such as the synchrony or asynchrony of speakers, their turn-taking patterns, or their repeated use of certain lexical items. From a multimodal perspective, the instance of communication originally produced and selected for further analysis is not necessarily limited to speech or writing, and the resulting entity is not necessarily limited to writing. The 'transductions' involved in a multimodal transcript are therefore potentially more varied than those involved in the transduction from speech to writing. As a consequence, where first we only had to attend to the gains and losses involved in a move from speech to writing, now we also need to address gains and losses resulting from a move from gesture, gaze, posture and other embodied modes of communication to image, writing, layout, colour and other graphic modes available in print.

Transcription may not seem to be an issue if the focus is on static texts, but the 'original' books or web pages are transformed for analytical and rhetorical purposes. Pages from the book may be digitized and read from the screen, and web pages may be printed out and analysed on paper. Some modes – image, writing, layout, colour – may be available in both media, but others – moving image – may get lost when moving from screen to print. In the case of video data, there are different ways of making multimodal transcripts (see Flewitt et al., 2009; Norris, 2004; Baldry and Thibault, 2005). We transcribe video data using a range of descriptive dimensions to describe gaze, gesture, movement, body posture, the semiotic objects of action, image and speech (Jewitt and Kress, 2003).

In the next sections we discuss two examples to show how the steps outlined above can be applied in research on classroom interaction and textbooks.

9.5 Speech in a multimodal world: A social semiotic study of classroom interaction

The case study presented in this section is drawn from the research project 'The Production of School English' (Kress et al., 2005), set in London. This project took a multimodal approach to address the following questions: 'How is English produced? What does English become when it is interactively constructed in classrooms marked by social, cultural and linguistic diversity?' Project data included teacher and student interviews, video recordings and observation of half-term topic units of nine teachers in three London schools.

Following the steps outlined in section 9.4, the video data and observation notes were used to produce descriptive accounts and video logs of each lesson: a multimodal commentary on curricular content, interaction and practices, sketches and maps of events, and so on. In the lesson discussed here, the teacher, Irene, is teaching a short story as part of the Key Stage Four National Curriculum requirements for 'wider reading'. The text she has chosen is a short story by William Trevor, *Teresa's Wedding*. It examines the relationships among an Irish Catholic family and their friends and partners, as revealed at a wedding reception. The teacher's curriculum objective is to develop students' skills in providing evidence from the text to justify their interpretations of these characters, including their (own) feelings and motives.

The video data was viewed with the video logs, in order to organize it thematically in light of the research questions and to generate criteria for data sampling. The video data was sampled to select instances (episodes) that showed how curriculum concepts and policy features (e.g. 'ability') were realized in the classroom. The episode discussed here appeared to be a critical incident – one of debate – where the discursive organization of the classroom changed significantly. At the start of this 'critical incident', the teacher moved from a formal posture and position (seated in an upright posture at a desk at the front-centre of the classroom) to an informal one (sitting on the edge of a desk at the front-left side of the classroom). This marked and, we argue, produced a significant change in the discourses adopted from then on by both the teacher and the students.

Once the video data was sampled into manageable 'chunks' of data, the video excerpts were viewed repeatedly. They were transcribed to provide a detailed multimodal account of the video data, using a column indicating the time, and a series of columns in which each mode was described. These descriptions included sketches and screen grabs to represent shifts in the position of participants. The analysis centered around three different 'starting-points', or steps, each of which is briefly described below.

The first starting-point foregrounds the idea of *mode*. A number of modes are key to the interaction in this episode (and this is typical of the multimodal interactions we observed in the data): gesture, gaze, body posture, movement, spatiality, talk, writing/diagram, the teacher's interaction with the textbook. For example, through gesture the teacher transformed a simple diagram she had drawn on the blackboard (the word 'women', followed by a vertical black line, followed by the word 'men') into an analytical grid for use on the text. Augmenting the 'line' acting as a division between 'women' and 'men' on the blackboard, the teacher gestured with her hand to create a barrier in front of her body between herself and a male student, Peter. As she did this she said, 'there's a line between male and female it seems . . .' Her gesture served to realize the 'line' between men and women as a physical, material one. She gestured back at the line of the diagram and by so doing, she linked the line on the board with the physical barrier she had created between herself and Peter: she *embodied* the separation of men and women. Later she repeated this gesture with reference to all the 'men' in the room, relating the violence and sexism of the male characters to the male students through her use of gaze. Moreover, she gazed directly at Christopher, who had earlier in the discussion made a punching gesture in response to the teacher's question of how he might feel with respect to the infidelity experienced by one of the male characters in the story.

Analysing modes individually, while analytically useful, is also problematic in the way it breaks up the interaction into separate modes. This problem is overcome by looking at all the modes together and asking how it is that they interact (this is the second analytical stage). In the example discussed above, for instance, looking at how *gaze* and *gesture* were used by the teacher showed that there was a pattern in how these two modes were used throughout the lesson. The teacher used gaze to nominate students to talk and to link her spoken statements to particular students – for example, when talking about male violence in the story she stared at one of the boys. She used gesture to orchestrate a debate which tacitly separated the class into girls and boys. Through her gesture and gaze the teacher restrained and encouraged individual students to talk and she was also able to carefully select which boys contributed to the debate.

The third analytical starting-point seeks to understand the communication practices of the teacher (i.e. why and how she set up a gendered debate) through the social principles at work across modes. We analysed how the teacher rhetorically 'orchestrated' the students, and deployed her knowledge of her students and their lives to construct a seemingly simple framework of gender which they could use in a successful 'personal response' and interpretation of the story for the purposes of assessment. The focus of this lesson is on drawing out and establishing ways of examining the construction of gender in the story being studied and also in relation to the lived experiences of the students in the class.

Each of the above three steps offers a different perspective for the analysis of meaning. Combining them overcomes the problems inherent in each. This framework also provides different scales of analysis: moving from semiotic resource and individual modes, to semiotic and social principles at the level of text and interaction. The short excerpts analysed are also then contextualized in the broader context of the series of lessons that they were taken from. Insights, findings or questions that emerged from the analysis of the critical instances of learning were later explored in relation to the larger data set where appropriate.

9.6 Writing in a multimodal world: A social semiotic study of learning resources

In this study on contemporary textbooks and learning resources (Bezemer and Kress, 2008) we addressed two questions. First, what exactly has changed in the graphic designs of learning resources for secondary school students over the last century? Second, what may have been gained and what may have been lost in potential for learning as a result of these changes? We compiled a corpus of multimodal, hyper- or interrelated 'texts' ('lessons', 'units', 'chapters', 'exercises' from textbooks, workbooks, websites), categorized according to variables that relate to the graphic design of these texts: subject and year group on the one hand, and era and dominant medium of dissemination (book or screen) on the other hand. We digitized all texts and kept an index of all materials with hyperlinks to their pfd-versions. We then browsed through the materials, comparing and contrasting texts from different eras and different subjects, before zooming in on particular sets of examples: excerpts covering different eras but the same topic; say, 'poetry' or 'digestion'.

The focal excerpts were then analysed in detail, attending to the different modes in operation. Figures 9.1 and 9.2 below, provide examples where analysis showed that the contemporary display in educational texts has changed from a one-dimensional, ruled *site of display* for writing (and possibilities

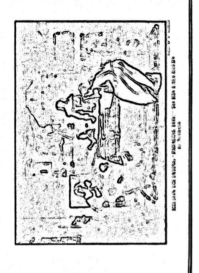

Figure 9.1 Drawing after Mamour (1934)

Figure 9.2 Drawing after Brindle et al. (2002)

for embedding image) to a two-dimensional, open site of display for graphic representation. We found that this change has had three effects (briefly discussed below): on the segmentation, the layout and the directionality of the text.

In Figure 9.1, from a textbook published in 1934, we identified different 'bits of text': an introduction, a poem, a painting, questions. The left-hand page shows a painting of John Milton dictating one of his seminal poems to his daughters. The introduction on the right-hand page sets the historical context for John Milton's 'l'Allegro'. The poem begins on the right-hand page and continues overleaf, up until page 88. Questions about the poem are then put. The next section of the textbook continues with 'language study', 'word study', 'writing', 'speech training', 'written composition' and 'illustration'. We can *graphically* identify these 'bits of text' – the segmentation of the text: their distinctive use of modes, titles, headings, margins, captions, numbering and placement on the page separates one bit of text from the other. Similarly, in Figure 9.2, from a textbook published in 2002, we recognize separate blocks of writing and photographs, through their distinctive use of modes, titles, margins, bullets and placement on the page, but also through the use of colour and font. The boundaries between different bits of text now present themselves much more profoundly. Written text is placed in boxes, and these boxes are placed at variable distances from each other. Different functions of different bits of text are marked off: 'Assessment objectives', for instance, are placed in a separate box and given a distinctive colour. Compared to the 1934 example, then, the text seems to be organized by different pedagogic categories, and these are much more distinctively marked. Where in the 1930s' textbook the boundaries between different units were realized as 'breaks', such as a small indentation at the beginning of a new paragraph, maintaining a fairly strong sense of 'continuity', in the contemporary textbook the boundaries are much sharper.

The change in the site of display has also given raise to the development of *layout* as a mode of representation. In Figure 9.2, the placement of five chunks on one and the same page and their shared background suggests that we are dealing with a unit of some kind: we know that these chunks are related somehow. The small overlaps of the various chunks strengthen these connections. The distribution of modes suggests a division of some kind: two parts use image, three parts use writing. This potential divide is reiterated through the tilted placement of the images as opposed to the straight positioning of the text blocks. Indeed, when 'reading' the chunks we engage in two different historical accounts. The writing produces a general, factual, hence somewhat distanced account, whereas the images produce a spatially and temporally more specific, personal account of these events. While the distribution of modes may suggest a *division*, the relative placement of the parts suggests that image and writing are not *contrasted*. The parts are placed in a *cross*, suggesting integration, whereas a contrast could have been realized by placing the images *next to* the written text blocks. Through cross-placement, a discourse of 'national histories' and a discourse of 'personal histories' are brought together. In the same way, the black-and-white and full colour images may suggest some kind of contrast, but the placement of these images does not. The difference in colour reiterates the contrast suggested by the ethnic differences of the people represented, while the layout reiterates the similarity suggested by the despair of the people represented. The people represented on the photographs were not enemies but going through the same ordeal.

The change in the site of display also means that *directionality* has changed. In Figure 9.1, the text is entirely sequentially organized (a 'first-then' principle): the learner was supposed to read from page one through to the last page, and to read, on each page, from the top left corner to the bottom right corner. The order in which learners engaged with the parts of the text was fixed, by the designer. In Figure 9.2, however, the reader is required to follow more of a 'back-and-forth' principle, moving between the text blocks and the images, but leaving room for learners to pursue their preferred navigation path.

This kind of analysis enables us to explore connections between the observed representational changes and changes in the wider educational and social landscape. The change in textual segmentation may be related to the increasingly detailed prescriptions of – in this case – the form and assessment requirements of the UK national curriculum into contents, learning objectives, themes (to which specific amounts of time are allocated). It may also be related to the shift in the site of knowledge production from the textbook to the classroom, where students are now required to participate in a range of different communal activities. The development of the mode of layout and its resources for the arrangement of 'chunks' of text on a site of display may be related to another change: where previously the open, two-dimensional site of display was found in 'informal' or 'unofficial' settings or specific genres only, it is now becoming a common display in many genres, for example, also in academic presentations. The shift from a first-then to a back-and-forth directionality, which makes the learners' navigation path less fixed, can be related to a shift within society from 'vertical' to 'horizontal' structures, from hierarchical to more open, participatory relations.

9.7 Potentials and limitations of multimodal research

Multimodality is an eclectic approach. Linguistic theories, in particular Halliday's social semiotic theory of communication (Halliday, 1978) have provided the starting-point for the social semiotic approach we set out in section 9.3. A linguistic model was previously seen as wholly adequate for some to investigate all modes, while others set out to expand and re-evaluate this realm of reference drawing on other approaches (e.g. film theory, musicology, game theory). In addition, the influence of cognitive and socio-cultural research on multimodality is also present, particularly in Arnheim's work on visual communication and perception (1969). A social semiotic approach to multimodality is still at an early stage of development, with much yet to be established, both in terms of theory and in terms of practices of transcription, language of description and analysis.

Like any analysis of representation and communication, multimodal analysis is limited in its scope and scale. In terms of *scope*, a 'Conversation Analysis' (see Chapter 6) may be based on moment-to-moment analysis of speech, including all intonational nuances, and largely ignore the direction of gaze; a 'multimodal' analysis may include speech as well as gaze patterns but largely ignore the intonational nuances of speech. Too much attention to many different modes may take away from understanding the workings of a particular mode; too much attention to a single mode and one runs the risk of 'tying things down' to just one of many ways in which people make meaning. As for potentials and limitations in *scale*, multimodal analysis is focused on micro-interaction, and therefore questions of how the analysis can speak to 'larger' questions about culture and society are often raised. This can be overcome, in part at least, by linking multimodal analysis with broader social theory, such as in the study discussed in section 9.5, and by taking into account historical contexts, such as in the study discussed in section 9.6. Many of the concerns that underpin multimodality indeed build on anthropological and social research, as seen in the work of Bateson (1987), and Goffman (1979), for example. It is through such links between *social* and *semiotic* theories that multimodal approaches can be developed further and continue to widen our understanding of human meaning making.

Acknowledgements

This chapter draws on our contribution to the Researcher Development Initiative, 'Ethnography, Language and Communication', funded by the Economic and Social Research Council (RES-035-25-0003). We would like to thank our colleagues on this project, Jan Blommaert, Adam Lefstein, Ben Rampton and Celia Roberts for the many ideas we exchanged about language, multimodality, social semiotics and linguistic ethnography. We are also grateful to Gunther Kress, whose ideas have been central to the development of this chapter. Section 9.5 draws on a research project carried out by Carey Jewitt, Gunther Kress, Ken Jones, and others, funded by the Economic and Social Research Council (R000238463). Section 9.6 draws on an ongoing research project (2007–2009) carried out by Jeff Bezemer and Gunther Kress, 'Gains and Losses: Changes in Representation, Knowledge and Pedagogy in Learning Resources', funded by the Economic and Social Research Council (RES-062-23-0224).

Further reading

Baldry and Thibault (2005) – This book sets out a systemic functional-linguistic approach to multimodal transcription using examples from print media, film and websites.

Jewitt (2009) – This is a 22-chapter edited volume on multimodal theory, data analysis and transcription. It includes chapters on multimodality in CA and early sociolinguistic approaches to 'non-verbal' communication.

Kress (2009) – In this book, language is theorized in a social semiotic framework of multimodal communication. It refers to a wide range of examples of text and talk.

Norris (2004) – A practical guide to understanding and investigating multiple modes of communication, which explores all aspects of data collection and analysis, including transcription.

Scollon and Wong-Scollon (2003) – In this book, the authors analyse how people interpret language as it is materially placed in the world, showing that the meanings of language are spatially as well as socially situated.

Van Leeuwen (1999) – This book explores speech, music and other sounds, and their common characteristics. It presents a framework for analysing rhythm and the material quality of voice, and shows how these communicate meaning.

References

Arnheim, R. (1969), *Visual Thinking*. Berkeley and Los Angeles: University of California Press.

Baldry, A. and Thibault, P. (2005), *Multimodal Transcription and Text Analysis*. London: Equinox.

Bateson, G. (1987), *Steps to an Ecology of Mind: Collected Essays in Anthropology, Psychiatry, Evolution, and Epistemology*. London: Aronson.

Bezemer, J. and Kress, G. (2008), 'Writing in multimodal texts: a social semiotic account of designs for learning', *Written Communication*, 25 (2), 166–95 (Special Issue on Writing and New Media).

Brindle, K., Machin, R. and Thomas, P. (2002), *Folens GCSE English for AQA/A*. Dunstable: Folens, pp. 100–1.

Creese, A. (2008), 'Linguistic ethnography', in K. A. King and N. H. Hornberger (eds), *Encyclopedia of Language and Education, 2nd Edition, Volume 10: Research Methods in Language and Education*. New York: Springer Science+Business Media LLC, pp. 229–41.

Duranti, A. (1997), *Linguistic Anthropology*. Cambridge: Cambridge University Press.

Erickson, F. (1986), 'Qualitative methods in research on teaching', in M. C. Wittrock (ed.), *Handbook of Research on Teaching*. New York: Macmillan, pp. 119–61.

—. (2004), *Talk and Social Theory. Ecologies of Speaking and Listening in Everyday Life*. Cambridge: Polity Press.

Flewitt, R, Hampel, R., Hauck, M. and Lancaster, L. (2009), 'What are multimodal data and transcription?' in C. Jewitt (ed.), *Routledge Handbook of Multimodal Analysis*. London: Routledge.

Gibson, J. J. (1977), 'The theory of affordances', in R. Shaw and J. Bransford (eds), *Perceiving, Acting and Knowing*. Hillsdale, NJ: Erlbaum.

Goffman, E. (1974), *Frame Analysis. An essay on the Organization of Experience*. Boston: Northeastern University Press.

—. (1979), *Gender Advertisements*. London: Macmillan.

—. (1981), *Forms of Talk*. Oxford: Blackwell.

Goodwin, C. (1981), *Conversational Organization: Interaction between Speakers and Hearers*. New York: Academic Press.

—. (2000), 'Action and embodiment within situated human interaction', *Journal of Pragmatics*, 32, 1489–522.

—. (2001), 'Practices of seeing, visual analysis: an ethnomethodological approach', in T. van Leeuwen and C. Jewitt (eds), *Handbook of Visual Analysis*. London: Sage, pp. 157–82.

Green, J. and Bloome, D. (1997), 'A situated perspective on ethnography and ethnographers of and in education', in J. Flood, S. B. Heath and D. Lapp (eds), *Handbook of Research on Teaching Literacy through the Communicative and Visual Arts*. New York: Macmillan, pp. 181–202.

Gumperz, J. J. (1999), 'On interactional sociolinguistic method', in S. Sarangi and C. Roberts (eds), *Talk, Work and Institutional Order. Discourse in Medical, Mediation and Management Settings*. Berlin: Mouton de Gruyter, pp. 453–71.

Halliday, M. (1978), *Language as a Social Semiotic*. London: Edward Arnold.

Haviland, J. (2003), 'How to point in Zinacantan', in Sotaro Kita (ed.), *Pointing: Where Language, Culture, and Cognition Meet*. Mahwah, NJ and London: Lawrence Erlbaum Associates, pp. 139–70.

Jewitt, C. (ed.) (2009), *Routledge Handbook of Multimodal Analysis*. London: Routledge.

Jewitt, C. and Kress, G. (2003), 'Multimodal research in education', in S. Goodman, T. Lillis, J. Maybin and N. Mercer (eds), *Language, Literacy and Education: A Reader*. Stoke on Trent: Trentham Books/ Open University, pp: 277–92.

Kendon, A. (1990), *Conducting Interaction: Patterns of Behaviour in Focused Encounters*. Cambridge: Cambridge University Press.

Knoblauch, H., Schnetter, B., Raab, J. and Soeffner, H. (2006), *Video Analysis: Methodology and Methods. Qualitative Audiovisual Data Analysis in Sociology.* Frankfurt am Main: Peter Lang.

Kress, G. (2009), *Multimodality: A Social Semiotic Approach to Communication.* London: RoutledgeFalmer.

Kress, G. and van Leeuwen, T. (1996), *Reading Images: The Grammar Of Visual Design.* London: Routledge.

Kress, G., Jewitt, C., Bourne, J., Franks, A., Hardcastle, J., Jones, K. and Reid, E. (2005), *English in Urban Classrooms: A Multimodal Perspective on Teaching and Learning.* London: RoutledgeFalmer.

Luff, P., Heath, C. and Pitsch, K. (2009), 'Indefinite precision: artefacts and interaction in design', in C. Jewitt (ed.), *Routledge Handbook of Multimodal Analysis.* London: Routledge.

McDermott, R. P., Gospodinoff, K. and Aron, J. (1978), 'Criteria for an ethnographically adequate description of concerted activities and their contexts'. *Semiotica*, 24 (3/4), 245–75.

Mamour, A. (1934), *The Complete English. Book II.* London: Macmillan, pp. 84–5.

Martinec, R. (2000), 'Construction of identity in Michael Jackson's Jam', *Social Semiotics*, 10 (3), 313–29.

Norris, S. (2004), *Analysing Multimodal Interaction: A Methodological Framework.* London and New York: Routledge.

Psathas, G. (1995), *Conversion Analysis: The Study of Talk in Interaction.* Thousand Oaks, CA: Sage.

Scheflen, A. E. (1973), *How Behavior Means.* New York: Gordon and Breach.

Scollon, R. and Wong-Scollon, S. (2003), *Discourses in Place: Language in the Material World.* London: Routledge.

van Leeuwen, T. (1999), *Speech, Music, Sound.* London: Macmillan.

—. (2005), *Introducing Social Semiotics.* London: Routledge.

10 Narrative Analysis in Linguistic Research

Julio C. Gimenez

People are always tellers of tales

Paul Sartre

Chapter outline

This chapter introduces the key elements of traditional and new emerging socio-linguistic approaches to the analysis of narratives, focusing specifically on *narrative networks*. It illustrates how a narrative networks approach examines narratives not only as texts, but also as representative of an array of social processes in their own contexts of production and consumption. The chapter first reviews the main definitions of narratives and illustrates traditional analytical perspectives, namely the componential and functional analyses. It then presents narrative net-works: its origins and theoretical principles. It outlines a step-by-step procedure for designing and analysing networks, showing how they can facilitate the critical analysis of narratives as sociolinguistic manifestations.

10.1 Introduction

Narrative, broadly defined as a 'recounting of things spatiotemporarily distant' (Toolan, 2001: 1), has been the focus of linguistic, sociolinguistic and discourse analysis for the past 40 years. In fact, a decade ago this ever growing interest in narrative was termed 'the narrative turn' in several human sciences (Brockmeier and Harré, 1997). Since then, narratives have been examined in a plethora of studies, covering fields as diverse as accounting (e.g. Sydserff and

Weetman, 1999), language and gender (e.g. Coates, 2003), health and illness (e.g. Balfe, 2007) and technology (Pentland and Feldman, 2007).

The beginnings of narrative analysis can be traced back to Aristotle who, in his work *Poetics*, outlined the structure of plots in narratives. More contemporary analyses have been influenced by Labov and Waletzky's (1967) seminal analytical framework. Labov and Waletzky (1967) identified the 'narrative clause' (e.g. '[She left the house] and [he called the police]') as the basic unit in personal narratives and indicated that the order of clauses represents the sequence of events as they actually happened. If, for example, the clauses in 'She left the house and he called the police' were changed to 'He called the police and she left the house', they would be implying a different sequence of events and thus a different narrative. They concluded that clauses in a narrative can perform five different functions. Labov (1972) further expanded the functions to six (abstract, orientation, complication, resolution, evaluation and coda), creating one of the most influential models for analysing personal narratives.

The emphasis on the structural analysis of formal elements in narratives suggested by these early models has created, however, a notable tendency to examine narratives as isolated, self-contained accounts of past experience. While this type of analysis has made invaluable contributions to various fields (e.g. linguistics, discourse studies and genre studies) and has been adequate for the analysis of individual narratives, it may not be sufficient to establish connections between personal narratives and the social issues they evoke. In this respect, analysing narratives in isolation has largely overlooked the discursive connections that can be made between groups of narratives or discourses produced in the same sociolinguistic context and the social patterns which frame and sustain them.

This chapter adopts the view that narratives are sociolinguistic manifestations as well as discursive constructions of an array of social processes. It argues that a sociolinguistic analysis of narratives should examine not only their formal elements but also the sociolinguistic elements that surround narratives, thus furthering our understanding of the social phenomena reflected in individual narratives. The chapter starts with a discussion of the main definitions used in narrative studies and a review of how narratives have traditionally been analysed with examples from the field of linguistics (section 10.2). It then focuses on narrative networks as an alternative method of analysis and presents a step-by-step procedure for designing and analysing the networks (section 10.3).

10.2 The study of narrative: An overview

In the Western tradition we have been fascinated with narratives since Greek times. Aristotle was the first to describe the structure of narrative plots as having a beginning, a middle and an end; a description that most guidelines for the composition and analysis of narrative still follow to date (Hogan, 2006). But before considering how narratives have been traditionally analysed, let us look at the definitions that have influenced narrative studies in linguistics.

10.2.1 Defining narrative

Our fascination with narrative is mirrored not only in the number of studies and books published in the past four decades but also in the multiplicity of terms that have been used to refer to narrative. *Narrative* is often used interchangeably with 'story', 'life story', 'account', 'discourse', 'narration' and 'tale' with little or no difference in meaning. The term 'narrative' itself also refers to various things: 'the telling of something', 'a story' or 'stories' and a method of analysis as in 'narrative inquiry'.

Coupled with this variety of terms, there are many definitions of narrative, of which the most oft-quoted is Labov and Waletzky's: 'any sequence of clauses which contains at least one temporal juncture' (1967: 28). The notion of temporal juncture is central to their definition as it is a distinguishing feature of narratives that creates a link between the sequence of events and the clauses that describe them. To illustrate this, consider Extract 1 below which includes 'and' (line 3) as a temporal juncture:

> **Extract 1**
> (1) I know a boy named Harry
> (2) Another boy threw a bottle at him right in the head,
> (3) and he had to get seven stitches.
>
> (Labov, 1972: 361)

Labov and Waletzky's definition is rather technical, primarily focusing on the formal elements that make up a narrative. It is, however, consistent with their analytical approach which examines the structural elements in narratives. This is described in more detail in section 10.2.2.

Working with life stories, Linde (1993: 21) offers a more sociolinguistic definition of narrative. She defines a life story as consisting of 'all the stories and associated discourse units, such as explanations and chronicles, and the connections between them, told by an individual during the course of his/her lifetime'. Linde further explains that life stories make a point about the speaker, not about the world, are tellable (i.e. they have a reason to be told) and are told and retold over a long period of time. Similarly, Ochs and Capps (1996: 21) define life histories as narrations in which people represent their 'selves' in relation to their physical and emotional environment and through which they 'come to know [themselves], apprehend experiences and navigate relationships with others'. Thus a 'multiplicity of selves', suggest Ochs and Capps (1996: 22), can be represented in the same story.

In their study of narrative research, Lieblich et al. (1998: 8) define narratives as stories which 'are usually constructed around a core of facts or life events, yet allow a wide periphery for the freedom of individuality and creativity in selection, addition to, emphasis on, and interpretation of these remembered facts'. Like Linde, Lieblich et al. focus specifically on the story and the narrator, which is also part of their new framework for narrative analysis (for more details, see section 10.2.2.3). Along similar lines, in their recent work on narrative as a research method Webster and Mertova (2007: 1) state that 'narrative records human experience through the construction and reconstruction of personal stories'. They add that because narrative presents complex issues, its analysis should move beyond the structural elements that make up a story into 'the underlying insights and assumptions that the story illustrates' (p. 4). To this purpose, Webster and Mertova's is another new analytical framework for narrative research, based on *critical events* within narratives, that is, incidents that reveal 'a change of understanding in worldview by the story teller' (2007: 73). Both Lieblich et al. (1998) and Webster and Mertova (2007) are important studies because they represent an attempt to reach a compromise between the two dominant approaches to the study of narrative described in sections 10.2.2.1 and 10.2.2.2.

The terms and definitions presented above reflect both the immense surge in the interest in narrative and how the study of narrative has evolved over time. Since Aristotle's definition of the structure of narratives, through Labov and Waletzky's analysis of their formal elements, to more sociolinguistics readings like those proposed by Ochs and Capps, narratives have been analysed mainly following either a componential or a functional analytical approach.

10.2.2 Analysing narrative

Componential analysis[1] aims to identify the different elements that constitute a narrative and how these elements interact and change as a result of their interaction (Hogan, 2006), while the *functional analysis* examines the purpose(s) of narrative. Although these are two inextricably linked approaches, what narratives describe and what they accomplish are two completely different things (Brockmeier and Harré, 1997). The sections that follow examine how these two broad divisions in narrative analysis have been used in linguistics.

10.2.2.1 Componential analysis of narrative

The *componential approach* has been highly influential in narrative analysis. It was the preferred approach in early studies (e.g. Labov and Waletzky, 1967). Here I will illustrate the main features of the componential approach with examples from Labov and Waletzky's (1967) and Linde's (1993) studies.

As stated above, the componential approach aims to identify the basic structure of a narrative and to examine the sequence of its clauses. This sequential arrangement can then be used to determine the functions of the clauses. One prominent example of the componential approach is Labov and Waletzky's (1967). Apart from narrative clauses, they identified three types of clauses which maintain the strict temporal sequence:

- *free clauses*: they can be displaced without disrupting the match between the clause and the event sequence, and are normally used to provide background information about a central action or situation in the narrative
- *co-ordinate clauses*: they can have a number of complex relations to the narrative sequence
- *restricted clauses*: they are less fixed to the sequence than a narrative clause, but less free to be displaced than a free clause.

In Extract 2 below the first three clauses are free clauses (lines 1–3). They set the scene for the narrative: the situation, the action and the characters. The fourth (line 4) and fifth clauses (line 5) are narrative clauses. Clauses six and seven (lines 6 and 7) are examples of co-ordinate clauses, related to the narrative clause which immediately precedes them. Lines 13–14 offer an example of a restricted clause which could have been placed before the narrative clause (line 5) without affecting the logical sequence of the narrative, but the word 'either' at the end of it restricts its position in the sequence.

Extract 2

(1) and so we was doing the 50-yard dash

(2) there was about eight or ten of us, you know,

(3) going down, coming back

(4) and, going down the third time, I caught cramps

(5) and I started yelling 'Help!'

(6) but the fellows didn't believe me, you know,

(7) they thought I was just trying to catch up

(8) because I was going on or slowing down

(9) so all of them kept going

(10) they leave me

(11) and so I started going down

(12) Scoutmaster was up there

(13) he was watching me

(14) but he didn't pay me no attention either

(Labov and Waletzky, 1967: 31)

As can be seen from the analysis above, by isolating the formal structure of narratives Labov and Waletzky identified the sequences in which clauses can be arranged in a narrative. This, in turn, enabled them to demonstrate the different functions the clauses performed. These functions were: orientation, complication, evaluation, resolution and coda, to which Labov (1972) added the abstract. The abstract, found at the beginning of the narrative, announces that the narrator has a story to tell. Orientation is used to orient the listener as to person, place, time and situation, and is usually found in the first clauses of a narrative which tend to be of the free type. In Extract 2 above, the first three free clauses (lines 1–3) serve the orientation function. Complication, the second function, is performed by the clauses in the main body of the narrative (lines 4–11) and denotes a series of events leading to a result. Evaluation reveals the attitude that the narrator holds towards the narrative. Most narratives, Labov and Waletzky explained, end with a resolution; the results of the complication of the narrative. Some, however, have an extra function called 'coda' which returns the verbal perspective of the narrative to the moment of narrating, that is, the present.

Linde's (1993) analysis of narratives about people's choice of profession also illustrates the componential approach. Linde focused on how different elements in a story and in the listener–speaker interaction combined to create coherence through *causality* and *continuity*. She defined causality as what 'is acceptable by addressees as a good reason for some particular event or sequence of events' (p. 127), whereas continuity has to do with the normal progression of events in a story. Both are necessary in order to explain how narrators manage to keep their narratives coherent in the face of discrepant events which may threaten the causality or continuity of their narratives. Thus narrators may use a series of strategies which include presenting accidents, for example, as unimportant, implying that in the end their choice was appropriate; distancing themselves from previous, sometimes younger and inexperienced selves; or suggesting that the discontinuity was only temporary. In Extract 3 below, taken from Linde (1993), the narrator uses the orientation function to explain how he went into Renaissance studies (lines 2–3). However, he later justifies this 'accident' by evaluating the complication as the right thing to do (line 9), thus making the accident look less important.

Extract 3
(1) That was more or less an accident.
(2) Uh, I started out in Renaissance studies,
(3) but I didn't like any of the people I was working with,
(4) and at first I thought I would just leave Y and go to another university
(5) uh but a medievalist at Y university asked me to stay or at least reconsider
(6) whether I should leave or not,
(7) and um pointed out to me that I had done very well in the medieval course
(8) that I took with him and that I seemed to like it,
(9) and he was right. I did
(10) And he suggested that I switch fields and stay at Y.
(11) And that's how I got into medieval literature.

(Linde, 1993: 84)

Although Labov and Waletzky's approach has been criticized for its insufficient attention to context and audience (Langellier, 1989) and Linde's for its lack of attention to linguistic details (Herman, 1996), their work has set an analytical standard for the componential approach.

10.2.2.2 Functional analysis of narrative

The other traditional way of analysing narratives is the *functional approach*, which mainly examines the purpose(s) of narratives. Among the multiple functions that narrative can serve, the most widely studied is the representational function: how narrators represent or interpret the world (Schiffrin, 1996); how they represent self and others (e.g. Dyer and Keller-Cohen, 2000); and how they construct their – gendered, ethnic or class identities (e.g. Goodwin, 2003).

Cheshire's (2000) study of narratives and gender in adolescent friendships follows an analytical framework which consists of three basic components: the tale (the narrative), the teller (the narrator) and the telling (the act of narration). Cheshire demonstrates not only that the way the tale structures experience differs between boys and girls and that the ways in which a teller represents self and other also differs according to gender but also, and probably most interestingly, that the telling is used by boys and girls for different purposes. Cheshire shows that in most of the boys' narratives there are elements of inclusion of other speakers and co-construction of familiar narrative which are used 'to create a sense of group identity through the telling of a story' (2000: 242). This sometimes results in narratives being told in a 'disorganized' way, but it reinforces the idea that boys are more interested in the telling of the story than in the story itself. Girls, however, narrate stories of a more individual nature, are not so inclined to co-construction, but produce narratives which are more coherent. This, suggests Cheshire, seems to emphasize the idea that girls are more interested in the story than in the act of narration.

Extract 4 below, shows how the act of telling serves Nobby, the main narrator, to create a sense of group identity. This is contrasted with Extract 5, Julie's personal narrative about how her brother burnt his leg (both transcripts and their transcription conventions can be found in Cheshire, 2000).

Extract 4

(1)	Nobby:	and then my dada had to keep it there for about two days I think it
(2)		was wasn't it Ben?
(3)	Ben:	yeah
(4)	Nobby:	cos it crashed outside your house didn't it? A lorry hit his wall . . . his
(5)		house wall
(6)	Ben:	we was sitting in there aren't we . . . me and her . . . watching the telly . . . and
(7)		it goes scrapping along our fucking wall . . . went in the back and went
(8)		'aah' the old man goes 'and what you been doing' . . . 'It's a
(9)		fucking . . . er well . . . it's a lorry'
(10)	Nobby:	and his dad thought it was him!

(Cheshire, 2000: 242)

Extract 5

(1)	Julie:	my brother he must have been daft cos he came back from Spain
(2)		and he was ever so tired . . . we was downstairs and anyway I went out and he

(3)	was fast asleep lying in the fire and . . . your know the fire was on full . . . and he
(4)	burnt his leg he had a big blister on it . . . he didn't even know he'd
(5)	done it didn't even feel it I thought ooh

(Cheshire, 2000: 242)

In Extract 4 Nobby includes Ben by using an addressee-oriented tag (wasn't it Ben?, line 2) and by encouraging Ben to co-tell the tale that is familiar to both of them. These are two ways in which boys usually constructed group identity in these narratives of adolescent friendship. In Extract 5, however, Julie narrates a personal story which shows no elements of co-construction or familiarity with the story on the part of the addressees.

The extracts above illustrate the analytical divide between the forms and the functions of narratives. In an attempt to avoid this analytical division, Lieblich et al. (1998) have combined both types of analyses, offering a framework based on two dimensions by which narratives can be read: the holistic – categorical, and the content – form dimensions (see Lieblich et al., 1998, for a discussion). Webster and Mertova's framework (2007), see section 10.2.1, also attempts to reach a compromise between the componential and functional analyses.

The approaches briefly reviewed in this section have examined narratives as individual and self-contained stories, sometimes making very little or loose connections with their larger sociolinguistic contexts. Placing narratives in their macrosociolinguistic context of production and consumption, however, can shed new light on the representational functions they serve in their local and social contexts. This is the focus of the next section.

10.3 Narrative networks

The term 'narrative networks' was first used by Bearman and his colleagues (Bearman et al., 1999; Bearman and Stovel, 2000) to describe how the structural elements in a narrative create an internal network of meanings which supports the holistic interpretation of a story. Despite carrying the label 'narrative networks', their work has also focused on isolated, discrete elements of narratives.

In this section, a different taking on the word 'network' is offered. A narrative network is defined as a group of stories, texts and artefacts collected around the emerging issues in a core narrative. The network shows not only what the stories, the texts, the artefacts and the core narrative have in common, but also how they differ, thus broadening the analytical perspective and helping tensions and contradictions emerge during analysis (Gimenez, 2005; Solis, 2004). Narrative networks can then help highlight the links between the local and social functions that narratives represent. The meanings and functions of personal narratives enacted in their local contexts normally reflect a more macro set of social meanings and patterns, which are best captured when local narratives are networked with other narratives, texts and artefacts produced in both local and global contexts.

10.3.1 Theoretical principles in narrative networks

From an epistemological perspective, narrative networks can be placed within Critical Discourse Analysis (CDA; see Chapter 6). Although a thorough review of CDA is beyond the scope of this chapter,[2] I will here define it and review some of the criticism it has attracted.

In Chouliaraki and Fairclough's words (1999: 6), CDA establishes a dialogic connection between 'critical social science and linguistics' in a single theoretical and analytical framework. Wodak further (2001: 2) points out that CDA is concerned with 'analysing opaque as well as transparent structural relationships of dominance, discrimination, power and control as manifested in language'. Thus, CDA takes a particular interest in the relationship between language and power and moves beyond the linguistic boundaries of the written or spoken texts it analyses to examine the multiplicity of historical, political and institutional forces (including values, interests and beliefs) operating in a single given text.

CDA has created immense interest in fields such as media communication (Chouliaraki and Fairclough, 1999), business and economy (Fairclough, 2001), education (Baxter, 2002), and language and gender (Lazar, 2005). It has also attracted a good deal of criticism, mainly in connection with its terminology, methodology and data analysis procedures. Widdowson (2004) has been especially critical of the fuzziness with which concepts such as 'text', 'discourse' and 'context' are used in CDA. He suggests that making a theoretical and analytical distinction between them will help analysts avoid confounding analysis, interpretation and explanation, an arguable shortcoming of some CDA analyses. Coupled with the ambiguity of its concepts, CDA has also been criticized for failing to establish a clear methodology, and lacking theoretical rigour in its formal analysis (Schegloff, 1997). The third area of concern relates to the way CDA analyses and interprets data. Some CDA analysts seem to confound two related but still different processes in data analysis: interpretation and explanation (Widdowson, 2004). Interpretation results from assigning meaning to specific features of a text in relation to particular contextual factors. Explanation, however, refers to assigning significance to the text being analysed in broader socio-cultural terms.

Narrative networks provide a framework for the critical analysis of narratives that attempts to accommodate some of the criticism presented above. The framework is based on the following four theoretical principles:

1. *Representation*: The narrative chosen for analysis should represent the problem rather than how the analyst theorizes and interprets it. It should also represent the values, norms and behaviour of all those involved in the social problem. Misrepresentation can be avoided by creating a network of representative texts, documents and artefacts around the core narrative.

2. *Falsifiability*: To prevent argumentative circularity, the analysis of the narrative should consider counter-evidence, avoiding at the same time selective partiality of evidence. Contradictions, tensions and resistance should be observed.

3. *Derivation*: Interpretation of the narrative should highlight the relationship between the narrative and its immediate context of production and consumption, as well as the network of actors and artefacts that surrounds it. This principle should be observed before the explanation of the significance of the social problem being analysed is attempted.

4. *Validation*: Explanations of the significance of the core narrative in relation to the problem it represents should be endorsed by those involved in producing and consuming all the texts analysed. The use of participant validation and 'thick' ethnographic observations can facilitate this process.

One fundamental consideration that underpins these principles is the importance of the network. Concentrating on a single, isolated text or narrative may produce a 'narrow' analytical perspective that could easily lead to argumentative circularity and explanations based on analyst assumptions. A network of texts that brings together the core narrative and other associated texts offers the possibility of broadening the analytical perspective by considering tensions and contradictions. In considering a work narrative (see Figure 10.1) in which a conflict of power is being narrated, for example, we may also want to consider other stories by the narrator's co-workers and

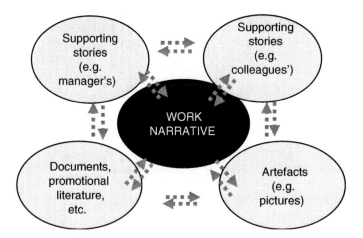

Figure 10.1 A network for work narratives (Gimenez, 2007: 86)

managers as well as other related documents and artefacts produced by his/her community of practice (e.g. documents about the allocation of work, flyers advertising or promoting their activity, or pictures that reveal the history of their profession).

Figure 10.1 shows how the different elements that constitute a network inter-relate with one another despite their different nature. Whereas work narratives are central to the network, stories are supporting elements in the network which prove or disprove the issues that emerge from the analysis of the work narrative. Work narratives are collected using loosely structured prompts, supporting stories are more narrowly elicited. Researcher intervention therefore also varies: work narratives involve very little researcher intervention, but researchers need to purposefully conduct the interviews to elicit supporting data. Documents and artefacts involve no intervention at all as they have not been produced for the purpose of research but rather to document the activity of a community. These theoretical considerations underlie the procedures for constructing and analysing narrative networks, as discussed below.

10.3.2 Designing narrative networks: Putting theory to practice

The process for constructing a network is graphically presented in Figure 10.2 below. There are four major stages in the construction and analysis of narrative

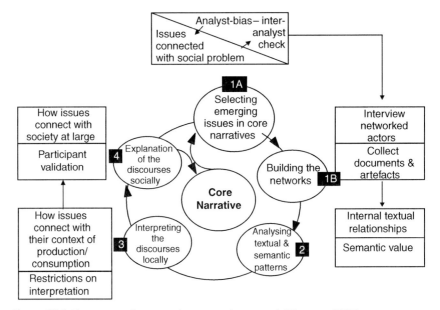

Figure 10.2 The process of constructing a narrative network (Gimenez, 2007)

networks: data collection (stages 1A and 1B), analysis (stage 2), interpretation (stage 3) and explanation (stage 4). This division is obviously artificial. It is sometimes difficult, if not impossible, to draw a clear-cut dividing line between collection and analysis as the act of deciding what data to collect is already an act of analysis.

In the procedures below, each stage starts with a brief theoretical comment before introducing the actual analytical step(s). After each stage, and before the analyst moves on to the next, the procedures include a check that reminds him/her of important considerations at the specific step.

Stage 1: Data collection

This stage focuses on the social problem to be analysed and comprises two substages: 1A – the collection of narratives and the selection of emerging social issues from such narratives (steps 1–3); and 1B – the design of a network (steps 4–8).

Step	Action	Example
Step 1	Select a social issue/problem you want to examine.	Oppression, social exclusion, immigration, gender and inequality, etc.
Step 2	Collect narratives that may illustrate the issue/problem you want to examine.	Narratives of immigrants, narratives in the workplace, narratives of marginalized groups, etc.

| Step 3 | Analyse the narratives in search of emerging issues. You can use AQUAD or NVIVO[3] to help you identify the issues. | How immigrants deal with legal issues, how women bank managers may have to struggle against double standards, etc. |

Check 1: Check for analyst bias by asking a second analyst to do step 3 independently. Also check that the emerging issues are representative of the social problem being examined.

Step 4	Based on the emerging issues, prepare questions to investigate through interviews.	How do immigrants find the legal system? How are opportunities for promotion distributed in banking?
Step 5	Interview other people who are 'networked' with the core narrators.	The narrator's colleagues at work and their line manager, an immigration officer, the female manager's subordinates, etc.
Step 6	Analyse their interview answers in search of supporting as well as contradictory evidence. You can use AQUAD or NVIVO.	Immigrants find it hard to understand legal issues and the language of legal documents. What support is there in place to provide them with the linguistic resources necessary to understand documents, for example?
Step 7	Collect documents and artefacts that may throw new/different light on the issues investigated.	Pictures, historical/organizational documents, organizational charts, etc.
Step 8	Use the issues you identified to build up the narrative networks around them.	Issue: position of women in banking. Network: interviews – what do women think about it? What do men think?, documents that explain promotion policies, pictures of the history of banking, etc.

Check 2: Check for different ways of organizing the support stories, the documents and artefacts. Different organization of the texts may shed new light on the issues being analysed.

Stage 2: Data analysis
This second stage analyses the textual and co-textual features present in the chosen texts. This analysis will consider co-textual relations and internal patterns in the text (collocations, prosody, etc.), the semantic value of these relations and patterns, and any interpretative possibilities and restrictions imposed on readers by the text itself and its analysis.[4]

Step	Action	Example
Step 9	Identify internal textual relations. You can use corpora for this (see Chapter 5).	Collocations (how certain words normally co-occur) and colligations (how certain grammatical choices co-occur) in phrases which trigger the main meanings in the narratives.
Step 10	Identify the semantic value of textual relations. You can use corpora to support your analysis.	The semantic prosody (the connotative value) of main phrases in previous step.
Step 11	Decide how textual and semantic relationships restrict interpretation.	Do the collocations 'female-dominated' and 'male-dominated' have the same semantic prosody?

Check 3: Check for possible alternative interpretations. You can compare the textual and semantic patterns of the main phrases in the narratives with those in a corpus and see how similar or different they are.

Stage 3: Data interpretation

Based on the results from stage 2, this stage focuses on the interpretation of texts as social practices, where other elements such as the participating actors, their beliefs and their social artefacts are located and brought to the analysis.

Step	Action	Example
Step 12	Based on the restrictions identified in the previous step, how do the issues relate to their immediate context?	What do the emerging issues from the analysis tell you about their context of production? For instance, are the difficulties some immigrants face when dealing with legal issues their own individual problem or do they reflect a wider problem in the immigration system?

Check 4: Go back to your fieldnotes to help you interpret the data you are analysing. Make sure your interpretation reflects the context you have observed.

Stage 4: Data explanation

This last stage explains the significance of the narrative networks in broader socio-cultural and political terms. This explanation should incorporate the relationships (problematic, contradictory, other) between the issues in the narrative and the social practices they represent, and a reflective validation of the explanation by incorporating participants' interpretations of the significance of the text, alternative interpretations of its significance and ethnographic observations.

Step	Action	Example
Step 13	Seek participant validation for your interpretations.	How do they see your findings? Do their interpretations support or challenge your findings?
Step 14	Establish a link between the issues you have interpreted and related issues in society at large.	What are the social patterns that these local issues illustrate? What do they represent? What do they challenge? What voices are represented/silenced? For example, does the label 'female-dominated profession' (e.g. nursing) refer to women dominating 'in power' or 'in number'? Does it indicate that women (the majority) dominate in number and men (the minority) dominate in terms of power?

Check 5: Go back to the social issue you wanted to examine in step 1 and check for the connections between explanation, interpretation and analysis.

10.4 Conclusions

As Toolan (2001: viii) advocates 'narratives are everywhere'. They have been and still are a popular data source in a wide variety of disciplines. In this chapter I argue, however, that the analysis of narratives, even when appropriately located in their context of production, has tended to examine narratives as isolated discursive realizations, failing to make a link between the local, sometimes personal, issues and their broader sociolinguistic context. But the local or the personal does not happen in a vacuum. As narrators, we have been socialized to perform in a given way, and it is thus essential to examine the link between the narrator's local performances and the social patterns such performances represent.

To do this, we need a wider network of texts. We need to expand the analytical possibilities offered by local narratives by networking them with the local as well as global social contexts where they are produced and consumed. As an analytical framework, narrative networks can help us achieve this. But we also need to adopt a critical approach to the analysis of narratives more broadly. We need an approach that focuses not only on the text itself but also on the mechanisms, actors and resources involved in its production and consumption. As researchers, we also need a deeper awareness of our influence on the research processes, which starts at the selection rather than the data analysis stage. The act of deciding what issues or problems to research is in itself an act of exercising our power to choose and decide. Distancing ourselves as researchers from the data does not in itself entail a critical analysis of the data, and procedures like participant validation (Ashworth, 1993) can take us a step closer to more balanced interpretations.

Notes

1. The term 'componential analysis' conventionally refers to the decomposition of the whole into its parts, as in structural semantics where the meanings of words are examined by their semantic features. Following Hogan (2006), however, it is used here in its broader sense to refer to the *relationship* between the whole and its parts.
2. For detailed discussions of CDA, see Chouliaraki and Fairclough (1999) and Fairclough (2001).
3. AQUAD (Analysis of QUAlitative Data) is a very useful software package for coding qualitative data. A demo version is available at http://www.aquad.de/. NVIVO is a similar, probably more complex but more powerful, package. You can find information about it at http://www.qsrinternational.com.
4. For a more detailed discussion on this, see Widdowson (2004).

Further reading

Bearman and Stovel (2000) – Although offering a different take on the 'networks', this article provides a good description of how networks can enhance linguistic analysis.

Daiute and Lightfoot (2004) – This edited collection provides a solid introduction to the theory and analysis of narratives from a variety of perspectives. It showcases topics such as school-based violence, generational trends among women and undocumented immigrants in the United States.

Webster and Mertova (2007) – Webster and Mertova describe the theoretical background to the development of narrative inquiry as a research method, illustrating its application through case studies from a wide variety of fields of study.

References

Ashworth, P. D. (1993), 'Participant agreement in the justification of qualitative findings', *Journal of Phenomenological Psychology*, 24, 3–16.

Balfe, M. (2007), 'Diets and discipline: the narratives of practice of university students with type 1 diabetes', *Sociology of Health and Illness*, 29, 136–53.

Baxter, J. (2002), 'Competing discourses in the classroom: a post-structuralist analysis of girls' and boys' speech in public contexts', *Discourse & Society*, 13, 827–42.

Bearman, P. S. and Stovel, K. (2000), 'Becoming a Nazi: a model for narrative networks', *Poetics*, 27, 69–90.

Bearman, P. S., Faris, R. and Moody, J. (1999), 'Blocking the future: new solutions for the old problems in historical social science', *Social Science History*, 23, 501–33.

Brockmeier, J. and Harré, R. (1997), 'Narrative: problems and promises of an alternative paradigm', *Research on Language and Social Interaction*, 30, 263–83.

Cheshire, J. (2000), 'The telling or the tale? Narratives and gender in adolescent friendship networks', *Journal of Sociolinguistics*, 4, 234–62.

Chouliaraki, L. and Fairclough, N. (1999), *Discourse in Late Modernity. Rethinking Critical Discourse Analysis*. Edinburgh: Edinburgh University Press.

Coates, J. (2003), *Men Talk. Stories in the Making of Masculinities*. Oxford: Blackwell Publishing.

Daiute, C. and Lightfoot, C. (2004), *Narrative Analysis. Studying the development of individuals in society*. Thousand Oaks, CA: Sage.

Dyer, J. and Keller-Cohen, D. (2000), 'The discursive construction of professional self through narratives of personal experience', *Discourse Studies*, 2, 283–304.

Fairclough, N. (2001), *Language and Power*. London; New York: Longman.

Gimenez, J. (November, 2005), 'The gender of institutional structure: What text, co-text and context can tell us about systems of inequality'. Paper presented at the BAAL/Cambridge University Press Applied Linguistics Seminar: Theoretical and Methodological Approaches to Gender and Language Study.

Gimenez, J. (2007), 'Gender as a structuring principle in social work and banking: a critical analysis of work stories'. Unpublished Ph.D. thesis, Queen Mary, University of London.

Goodwin, M. H. (2003), 'The relevance of ethnicity, class and gender in children's peer negotiations', in J. Holmes and M. Meyerhoff (eds), *The Handbook of Language and Gender*. Malden, MA: Blackwell Publishing, pp. 229–51.

Herman, D. (1996), 'Review of Charlotte Linde, life stories: the creation of coherence', *Style*, 30, 175–8.

Hogan, P. C. (2006), 'Continuity and change in narrative study. Observations on componential and functional analysis', *Narrative Inquiry*, 16, 66–74.

Labov, W. (1972), *Language in the Inner City*. Philadelphia: University of Pennsylvania Press.

Labov, W. and Waletzky, J. (1967), 'Narrative analysis: oral versions of personal experience', in J. Helms (ed.), *Essays in the Verbal and Visual Arts*. Seattle: University of Washington Press, pp. 12–44.

Langellier, K. M. (1989), 'Personal narratives: perspectives on theory and research', *Text and Performance Quarterly*, 9, 243–76.

Lazar, M. M. (ed). (2005), *Feminist Critical Discourse Analysis: Gender, Power and Ideology in Discourse*. Basingstoke: Palgrave Macmillan.

Lieblich A., Tuval-Mashiach, R. and Zilber, T. (1998), *Narrative Research. Reading, Analysis and Interpretation*. Applied Social research Methods Series, volume 47. Thousand Oaks, CA: Sage.

Linde, C. (1993), *Life Stories: The Creation of Coherence*. Oxford: Oxford University Press.

Ochs, E. and Capps, L. (1996), 'Narrating the self', *Annual Review of Anthropology*, 25, 19–43.

Pentland, B. T. and Feldman, M. S. (2007), 'Narrative networks: patterns of technology and organization', *Organization Science*, 18, 781–95.

Schegloff, E. A. (1997), 'Whose text? Whose context?' *Discourse & Society*, 8, 165–87.

Schiffrin, D. (1996), *Conversational Style: Analyzing talk among friends*. New Jersey: Ablex.

Solis, J. (2004), 'Narrating and counternarrating illegality as an identity', in C. Daiute and C. Lightfoot (eds), *Narrative Analysis*. Thousand Oaks, CA: Sage, pp. 181–99.

Sydserff, R. and Weetman, P. (1999), 'A texture index for evaluating accounting narratives. An alternative to readability formulas', *Accounting, Auditing & Accountability Journal*, 12, 459–88.

Toolan, M. J. (2001), *Narrative: A Critical Linguistic Introduction* (2nd edn). London: Routledge.

Webster, L. and Mertova, P. (2007), *Using Narrative Inquiry as a Research Method*. Oxon: Routledge.

Widdowson, H. G. (2004), *Text, Context, Pretext*. Critical issues in discourse analysis. Oxford: Blackwell.

Wodak, R. (2001), 'What CDA is about – a summary of its history, important concepts and its developments', in R. Wodak and M. Meyer (eds), *Methods of Critical Discourse Analysis*. London: Sage, pp. 1–13.

Index

Note: Page references in *italics* refers to figures.